Antrim And Beyond   Part

" Tales of Distant Lands "

Bobby Cameron

Front cover, top: Cruising at the San Blas Islands off the coast of Panama in a dugout canoe. Author is centre, hand up and holding a camera. The skipper is up for'd, and has a tin can in his left hand – just out of sight of the photographer, and which he used to bale water out of his charge from to time!   Lower sector: A felucca on the river Nile in Egypt.

Antrim And Beyond **Part Three**

"Tales of Distant Lands"

CH:	**Contents**	

The following mostly relates to the San Blas Islands off Panama, Rain Forests in Central America, travel to Islands in the South Pacific Ocean (including Easter Island and Pitcairn Island), East Africa, Oman and the Emirates – as below.

Third Coloured photograph selection: Also included are a few from author's travels elsewhere, while others are of a rare or of general interest.
Colour   Starts P 155

Fourth Coloured photograph selection: Also included are a few from author's travels elsewhere, while others are of a rare or of general interest.
Colour   Starts P203

Antrim And Beyond Part Three

" Tales of Distant Lands "

Copyright © 2018 Bobby Cameron

First Edition printed 2018.

A catalogue record for this book is available from the British Library.

IBSN 0-9539723-3-X

Published by:

Escoumains Publications
14 Ashville Park
Greystone Road
Antrim
Co. Antrim
N Ireland
BT411HH

Every effort has been made to trace current copyright holders. This may not always have been successful, especially where a change of copyright had taken place. If anyone feels an infringement of their copyright has taken place, an appropriate acknowledgement will be made in future editions.

Printed by: Nicholson & Bass Ltd

Acknowledgements:

I wish to record my thanks and acknowledge the help given to me by the following individuals and organisations who were kind enough to give me of their time, and enlighten me on many diverse matters. There are also others around, who simply by their expressions of good will and kindly interest in what I was doing, greatly encouraged me along the way.

The late Captain James Bothwell, Master Mariner, for sharing reminiscence with me of the MacAndrew Shipping Line; also for the photographs of the "Perla," Spain's first submarine and of Mr. Tom Birch, my one time Chief Engineer Officer on the MV "Villegas," MacAndrews Line; My continuing gratitude to Mr. Stephen Downes B.Sc. for noble computer rescues performed at times; I would also like to record my gratitude in respect of the help given to me by the late Sir Philip Foreman CBE DL, former Chairman and Managing Director, Short Brothers PLC for his early and constructive advice in person, and also through his letters to me on pitfalls to avoid in writing, and his continued interest in my efforts; The late Mrs. Joan Horn, for her indefatigable efforts towards the reconstruction of this book following a destructive computer breakdown; Mr. Bruce Johnston of San Francisco, for providing the photograph of the replica Confederate submarine, H.L. "Hunley,"and his photographs of the first atom bomber, the B29 " Enola Gay;" My close friend, the late Mr. John Kerr, former Chief Engineer Officer of the Head Line Shipping Co., Belfast for all his reminiscence with me - especially his account of the loss by torpedo attack of his ship, the ss "Bengore Head," Convoy OB 318, 9[th.] May, 1941 (see Chapter 2 for a reference to this event) ; The late Mr. Georg Högel, Munich, who was the Radio Operator on the German submarine U-110 when it sank the ss "Bengore Head." Through an amazing coincidence, he was another who corresponded with me for many years. Like John Kerr, his information ref. Convoy OB318, and the sinkings of the SS "Athenia" and the ss "Fanad Head,"(when he was on the U-30), has been simply indispensible; Mr. John Mann, former U.S. marine, (and a one time resident in the San Blas Islands, Panama), for the helpful information given to me when I met him on one of these islands; My thanks to "Voyages of Discovery" for the information in their cruise booklets, namely "Mini Guides to Djibouti and the Emirates;" My thanks to Mr. Cecil Millar B.Sc, for his ever present help and advice on computer graphics; Gratitude for early information given me by my old friend, the late Mr. George Harry Plowman DSM, Wellingborough, N'ants, Leading Signalman of the British submarine E11 on his experiences on North Sea patrols and his three transits of the Dardanelles, Turkey, in 1915 ;The late Mr. Jimmy Spiers, Marine Engineer, for reminiscence with me of our time together on the ss "Rathlin Head," the Ulster Steamship Co., Belfast; The late Mr. Jimmy Storie, late of the11th. (Scottish) Commando, founder member of "L" Detachment (later the S A S) at Kabrit, Egypt in 1941. There, with Blair Mayne DSO (and three Bars,) his accounts of their experiences at the battle of the Litani River (Syria) in 1941 and behind the lines in North Africa during 1941- 43 are again, also indispensable; Also thanks to his wife Morag, now, in 2017, still an indefatigable source of information on " where they all are now ;" Mr. Denis Young, a member of the gallant crew of the MV "Clyde Valley,"for his information to me on its voyage of peril on the N. Atlantic.

Photographs which appear in each Chapter

Lest We Forget

The following is an extract from the Preface of "Antrim and Beyond," Part Two: "They Served In Time of War."

Homeward bound and close to the end of August, 1975, the MV "Velarde" was proceeding across the Bay of Biscay. Around twenty minutes to midnight, I asked Jack the greaser to call the watch as I busied myself in preparation for completing the engine room log. When he returned, he appeared to be upset . Presently, I asked him if anything was wrong. After some hesitation he replied: "Ah, you know when you asked me to go up top - I then saw we were just off Ushant Light. Ushant Light has a bad memory for me. It was that time on a steamer during the war – about 1941, I was on watch

The MV "Velarde."

with the [*] Third – a lad just like you, just talked about things the way you do. The Third asked me to call the watch – something, you know, before 4 am.

I was up there when the torpedo struck. We rushed down to see if the Third was alright. At first we couldn't see him – then we found him lying up on the funnel uptakes. He was dead. There wasn't a mark on him – the concussion had killed him. But the boat was sinking fast and had to be abandoned with the Third being left to go down with her. It saddens me badly at times when I remember. It happened just abreast the Island of Ushant off the French coast but well out - convoys were then being routed well away from land."

A little over two days later, I said farewell to Jack, the motor ship "Velarde" and all my recent companions on the deep at Shed 2, Canada 3 Docks, Liverpool. They became " ships that passed in the night " and I was never to see any of them again. With a "fair wind" and some luck, I would make it home in time to attend a Staff meeting in Lisburn Technical College in Co. Antrim where I was teaching there in the Engineering Dept. (I had been sailing on the "Velarde "as a relief engineer at sea for MacAndrews during part of my Summer vacation – and a world away from my life in a classroom).

[*] Third, short for " Third Engineer Officer."

*   *   *   *   *

Some years later, my good friend the late Captain Jim Bothwell, Master Mariner, knowing I had some connections with the MacAndrew Company, sent me a copy of the Company losses in the World Wars. (Jim himself had sailed with MacAndrews some years previously.)

Now, with a strange, nostalgic eagerness, I searched those losses during the Second World War. I was looking for "a steamer sunk off Ushant in 1941."

Suddenly it was there – the MacAndrew steamer "Ciscar II,"of 2,436 tons, and which was torpedoed in convoy off Ushant, on August 19th. 1941, 49°10 N, 17°40 W, with 20 of her crew of 39 being lost.

(Ushant Island, lies about 5° W, just off the coast of France but in 1941 was under the Nazi yoke.)

Thus, Jack's convoy indeed had been keeping well clear of the land at 17° 40 West. [*] See two pages from end of Chapter 10 – for further information.

It is amazing how our memory selects some items for lasting retention while disposing thousands of others to the winds.

I have often wondered who that Third Engineer Officer of the SS "Ciscar II" was - and from what part of the country had he come from?

And Jack had said, "A lad, just like you."   Lest we forget indeed! Author.

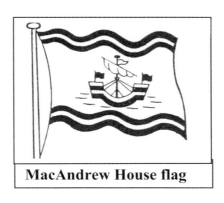

MacAndrew House flag

Chapter 1

Early days:
A first encounter with history.

I started my primary education during the Second World War at a school half a mile from my home and known as Ladyhill Primary School, Antrim. Actually, when I started attending there, it was known as Ladyhill Public Elementary school. This was made clear to all who might pass by, as this grandiose title was proclaimed in four inch high wrought iron letters on the front wall of the school which stood about four miles north of the town of Antrim, in Co. Antrim, Northern Ireland. Then one day – I cannot remember exactly how, but we became aware that our school would in future be known as Ladyhill Primary School. I had started in a class known as "Baby

Mrs. E. McIlwaine

Infants" in the "Junior's" room and my teacher was a Miss Ena Houston, shortly to become Mrs. Ena McIlwaine.

Now it came to pass in those days that I was promoted from this Junior status but not, regrettably may I say, by reason of academic distinction!

No, it was simply because of advancing years that I become a pupil in the Senior room. There, along the path of the knowledge of good and evil, the struggles thus encountered intensified – coping with things called sums, extracting information from Railway Timetables and other mental tortures that for me, caused a profound weariness of the flesh!

It was then that I often longed for a return to the days when our school would once again be a Public Elementary School.

Ladyhill Public Elementary school, as built 1932.
Courtesy of Dr. David and Mrs. A. King.

The elementary bit had appealed to me – I thought that I could have coped with it better than this Primary intruder, but, Ladyhill Primary School it was and here to stay - see photograph on left.

Upon the promotion conferred upon me as above, I met my new teacher, the principal teacher who also taught the Senior classes.

She soon showed some diligence in her attempts to further our knowledge.

Here, to correct the failings of the flesh shown up in our attempts to absorb this knowledge, she used the latest technology of the day known to men. It was a common stick.

She applied this stick at times with gusto and zeal indeed! Verily, at Ladyhill Primary School (now the home of a well known psychiatrist), nothing had changed since the days of Nicholas Nickleby!

Yet it was not just so common a stick, though, because it come from the Willow tree, and it was called a "Sally" rod. Its user command was "Hold out your hand!" It happened, that in due season our new teacher would announce that she required a replacement Sally rod. Being in the countryside, most pupils knew where Willow trees grew in our locality and presently – after a day or two, a number of specimens were offered up at our teacher's desk.

Now in the euphoria of my recent promotion to the educational status now currently being experienced (coupled with a fair degree of naivety), I somehow imagined these offerings to

1

be in some way analogous with the offerings that Cain and Abel had presented. (At this moment in time indeed, it so happened that we were learning about these two gentlemen of the Old Testament in our morning devotions.)

But here a tradition had grown up and laid down different rules. It was that whosoever had presented the offering accepted by the teacher, got the first slap on the hand when the rod was first used in anger, and I do recall, that this in fact was true for several cane providers.

A Hudson Bomber of the type which crashed at Carnearny

But soon our attentions would be drawn to something else more startling – the presense of soldiers –from Britain, USA, possibly Canada and later on from Belguim, all arriving in our quiet, rural Crosskennon, the district where I lived, not far from Ladyhill school. We were at war and if we thought that war was something that happened to folk in those faraway places – well, we would soon be on a fast learning curve. Bombs, prematurely jettisoned from aircraft having difficulty in maintaining height over our pastoral fields, would then have to be blown up. But then a Hudson bomber from 206 Squadron, only having arrived at RAF Aldergrove a few days previous, crashed into nearby Carnearny Forest and some of us children, actually then saw what the aftermath of destruction and death looked like! I can still clearly recall seeing blood stained sheets lying in the wreckage and two crewmen had lost their lives with another dying later in hospital. Children would hear of the German U-Boats sinking our ships. One such sinking my parents talked a lot about was that of the SS "Athenia." Amazingly, forty odd years on ,I would find myself in fairly regular communication with the Radio Operator of the U-30 which sank the "Athenia." His name was Georg Högel, from Munich, Germany, and his, was an interesting story. See Chapter Two.

Amazingly also, was that as time passed, there were times when I thought I was even going to like my Primary School – (alas I never really did). Those times of enlightenment came about when we had short lessons on the past – history, and tales of foreign lands.

A German U-Boat. the U-802.

These spoke of a time when knights rode horses into battle, Robin Hood stalked the green woods of Sherwood Forest, Nottingham, and Sinbad the Sailor set forth to discover new lands and peoples. Little did I know that one day I would find myself in the very place that he had set out from, a port called Salala in the country of Oman on the Arabian Peninsula. But a more sombre note however, sounded in these lessons because there were references made to the losses suffered in the First World War. Then our teacher, gave us a history in which there were references made to the losses suffered in the First World War.

In particular, there was a poem about a young person lost in that earlier war. It started with "He is gone, the beautiful youth, the soul of honour -----" and that is all I can now remember of it.

But even to children, it cast a mantle of solemnity over our class, an awareness we all could feel but not fully understand. We probably would have known of course, that a death was something that brought tears, gloom and sadness into the homes and lives of people – indeed one of our classmates had recently lost her mother, and I was soon to lose both my grandmothers.

The presentation of the poem as delivered by our teacher must have been impelling. It appeared out of character, as she normally seemed to be made of stern stuff and not given to softness and sentiment. With the passing of the years, I have observed that our memories are very selective and only a few incidents from my Primary School days have succeeded in claiming residence there, but this one has done just that – and has done so for the past fifty years. Further, the poem prompted speculation among us that in some way our teacher had a connection with the young man –" the beautiful youth." It was thought by some of those with whom I shared learning the poem, that the connection might might have been a romantic one, and that when she was a young girl, perhaps she was the girl friend of this young man who was lost in the Great War. At least, it would pass nowadays as a successful lesson because we never had any other lesson like it which prompted such discussion and analysis. Strangely also, and many years later, I found myself for some reason being reminded about those Sally rods with my thoughts becoming centred upon finding the reason for their need of replacement. I had never seen any of them having a "roadside breakdown!"

On an early cycling tour in Scotland. Author at the John Cobb Memorial. T. Talbot

However, as more time passed, history, " tales of foreign lands" and "those far away places with their sweet sounding names" would never be far from my waking thoughts. Such thoughts, once firmly rooted in my being, would remain with me for the rest of my life. A successful travel experience does not need to be an expensive one. Some of the most memorable times for me came about by riding a humble bicycle with a bag on my back, the same yellow and blue bag as seen in many of the following photographs. Later on in my life (when reason was giving way to rashness), I had the temerity to start racing a bicycle and I needed such a bag with several zipped pockets to carry extra "liquid fuel," lights, spare tubes, a chain breaker, a piece of wire and pliers, a rainproof, something warm - oh things just short of the kitchen sink went into that bag. I bought the bag at a sale in the Athletic Stores in Belfast for about three pounds. When I finally decided to keep my day job and stop racing the bicycle, I increased my interest in travel where the bag became a constant companion.

And you know what? Nothing of cycle equipment was ever lost from it - either at home, or even later did anything ever go missing from it in deserts, rain forests or from anywhere else I happened to be. Even the original zips are still doing their job. Look out for it, as it travels with me to distant lands.

But in case someone might think that nothing can go wrong with a humble bicycle – please read Part Two of **Chapter 20** first!

Now, in a serious way, changes in my life would have to come about because a big question was, "Where would I go when advancing years again called for change and the end of my labours at Ladyhill School?" One thing that was always was put to me by various people, was that in the absence of more education, the possibility was real enough that I might end up driving a herring cart - and a horse drawn one at that!

"When reason gave way to rashness -" being pushed off by Bill Kerr.

I had never seen one of these but I was determined to avoid such a thing at all costs.

So I sped off to sit the entrance examination required to enter Ballymena Technical College, and amazed everyone (including myself), by being deemed to have passed it. It was an event that seemed to put a smile on everbody's face. Even our stern lady Principal seemed to relax her guard by a jot or two – surely in deference to my walking tall, and even smiled as the small children around her frolicked behind their work books. She even put away the cane for a whole day ! Indeed in my perceived elevation, I might well have had a sort of empathy with "Mad Carew, " thus:

"But for all his foolish pranks, he was worshipped in the ranks, and the Colonel's daughter smiled at him as well."
From "The Green Eye of the Little YellowGod," J. Milton Hayes.

Our Principal even sent me into Mrs. McIlwain's room for that lady to read the letter from Ballymena Technical to make sure that we all had read the contents correctly. She duly complied and proclaimed, "Well done, Davy McClelland." (Mr. David McClelland was Principal of Ballymena Technical in those days. He was not inclined to suffer fools gladly!)
I have always maintained that to acquire a Technical Education was the best Earthly

The rick shifter a common sight to children who often would have "hitched" a lift at the back of the rick. Courtesy Miss Mirium Stevenson

decision that I ever made. Through it, I would be gaining an education, avoiding the herring carts of this world, and leading to an apprenticeship that eventually carried me – almost, to the uttermost ends of it. That apprenticeship was in mechanical engineering, in the great firm known then as Short Bros. and Harland, Ltd, Belfast. It was a firm that became a pioneer in encourageing Further Education for its apprentices by providing day release to assist them in their studies.
At one time during my own years working in Further Education,

it could be said that former apprentices of Short Bros. and Harland Ltd., could be found teaching in every Further Education College in Northern Ireland. For Shorts, this could also be said:

In those days, everything we made there - flew.

* * * * *

Note - previous page: John Cobb from Surrey, England was the first man to reach over 400 MPH on land, and the first to reach over 200 MPH on water.
During an attempt on the world water speed record on Loch Ness on 29th. September, 1952,

his jet propelled boat Crusader achieved a speed of 206.89 MPH on the first run. On the second run in the opposite direction, it hit a number of waves, bounced badly and sank after breaking up to some extent. John's body was quickly recovered from the water but had sustained injuries from which he died. The Crusader sank in the deep waters of Loch Ness but was located some time later sitting upright on the bottom.
The stone cairn was erected by the people of the town of Drumnadrochnt, near Inverness.

Ballymena Technical Days: Author is standing beside an aero engine mounting frame for a Hydrofoil.
Origin Dr. Crawford

The lights were about to go out - all over Europe

But the dark shades of war were about to envelope the lives of everyone through consequences that, for most of us, would last over five years and for some, for the rest of their lives. Now on the first day of the 1939 /45 war, the German U-Boat, the U-30 had sank the Donaldson passenger liner, the "Athenia," and 130 of those on board including some Americans, had lost their lives.

Georg Högel, the Radio Operator on duty in U-30,and with whom I was later in communication for many years, heard the "Athenia's" distress call, recognised it, and told Cmdr. Lemp, "You have sunk an unarmed passenger ship." Many years later he was to tell me that when they returned to Germany, he was instructed (on Hitler's orders), to remove two pages out of his Radio Log. The political implications vis a vis America were obvious to Hitler.

Then came the stopping of the "Fanad Head," after which there was high drama when the U-30 was attacked by two Skua bombers from the British aircraft carrier, HMS "Ark Royal." Then unfolded a disasterous outcome for the British, as the two attacking aircraft were blown up upon the release of their own bombs, and came down in the sea. Both pilots were able to climb on board the "Fanad Head."

They eventually became prisoners of war on the U-30 but their navigators went down with the wreckage and were lost.The complete story of this saga is recalled at length in the author's book, **"Antrim And**

A historic photograph – the old SS "Fanad Head" stopped off Rockall by Cmdr. Lemp(white cap) in the U-30. With the binoculars is Machinist Klobes. Both died later when U-110 was captured by the RN. Origin: Georg Högel, Radio Operator in the U-30 and later in the U-110.

Beyond" Part One, *(Childhood Memories of Antrim in time of War.)*

But a crew member of U30 and one of the attacking pilots woud meet again. Shortly afterwards, the crew of U-30 was transferred to the larger 9C Type, the U-110. After attacking Convoy OB 318 in the North Atlantic on 9. 05. 1941, when they sank Belfast's ss "Bengore Head " the U-110 was blown to the surface and boarded.

On that day, the Chief Engineer was my old friend, John Kerr from Islandmagee . He watched from the deck of the trawler "St. Appolo"- which had rescued him, as the U-110 was fately damaged, and captured.

Some extremely important German Enigma codes were recovered from the captured U-Boat, which documents, some historians arguably claim, shortened the Battle of the Atlantic by two years.

Georg became a POW in Canada but in 1988 he came to Portsmouth to meet Captain Guy Griffiths, one of the two Royal Marine Skua pilots who tried to bomb the U-30!

For many years, Georg carried on a lengthy, helpful correspondance with the author – he had learned his English in a Canadian POW camp. He died in Munich in 2014. Captain Griffiths is now also dead.

Origin and identification of crew: Georg Högel, Radio Operator on U-30 and U-110.

Above: Left, Georg Högel with Capt Guy Griffiths, at their meeting in Portsmouth. Both were artists of considerable ability. For presents, they choose to give each other momentos of the weeks they shared on the U-30 in 1941.Georg is holding a sketch Guy made of the U-Boat's Wardroom, and Guy has a sketch Georg made of a Skua attacking the U-30. When they last met, Guy Griffiths was a prisoner of war on board the U-30.
(I was alerted to this Interesting meeting by Georg)
Courtesy of the "Portsmouth Chronical."

Chapter 2

Beyond Antrim:

My first opportunity to travel outside the U.K. was during a period when, three years after the completion of that mechanical engineering apprenticeship, I went to sea as an engineer in order to gain some experience in heavy engineering. Immediately previous to this, I had

Pastoral scenes like this would now play a minor role in my life.
Origin: Robert Ian Cameron

experienced an unintentional reversal of profits when laid aside in the Royal Victoria Hospital, Belfast, following a motorcycling accident in which a dog had crossed my path. Of the accident I was able to recall little but I do remember the journey to the hospital. As a result of this, I missed sitting for an important final examination which I would now have to resit in a year's time.

In applying to go to sea as an engineer, one had first to be graded by the Board of Trade in an oral interview as to the quality of one's apprenticeship and current experience, and also produce any relevant technical qualifications acquired to date.

Further to this having been done, I was pleased that I had received a Grade 1B and was later informed that I would be exempt from Part A of the examination to award a Second Class Certificate to serve as a Second Engineer at sea. Also, that I was exempt from sitting some parts of the examination for a First Class Certificate. This was the

Author appointed to the ss " Rathlin Head."
Photo from his Discharge Book.

qualification to enable one to become a Chief Engineer at sea. While I was pleased to know this, I had not at that time an intention to pursue these possibilities, being initially only interested in gaining some practical experience in marine engineering. In any case, of course, I had those examinations – interrupted by that dog as referred to earlier, to complete.

I now had to find a suitable position at sea, so armed with my 1B grading certificate, I went to see the local Head Line who had their offices on Victoria Street, Belfast.

The Head Line offered me a job as an engineer which I accepted, and I was appointed thus to stand by an Atlantic freighter, the SS "Rathlin Head." This vessel was powered by Parsons impulse reaction steam turbines, but just now was about to go into the Alexander Dry Dock to undertake her four year survey. At the present time of writing, that dock is the home of the "Caroline,"a First World War light cruiser, a veteran of the Battle of Jutland in 1916, and the only surviving British warship of that battle still afloat.

Therefore, this drydocking which was to facilitate a once in four years survey, gave me a rare chance to see some of a steamer's machinery being dismantled – in particular, its turbines and boilers. However, if a certain motor ship expected soon should appear, priority required that I would sail on it.

In the event, I was, just before we sailed and to my utter amazement, appointed Fourth Engineer on the steamer – watch keeping on my own! More so indeed, as one of the other junior engineers on board had already completed a couple of trips on the ship!

When he heard about this rapid promotion, our Second Engineer, Frank Reeves, was also astonished and told me that I would never be able to do it. " The Log is a yard long and - on both sides!" he said. (However, with a bit of an effort - I managed!)

Then an Assistant Superintendent Engineer told me, in an enthusiastic way, that I was the luckiest man in Belfast, as now my time at sea would count immediately towards my Second's "ticket." I recall his name was Walsh. One other man I remember was the other Assistant Superintendant Engineer - one Percy Duke, a pleasant man to deal with. Many years later, I was to meet his brother, Eric Duke, who was Manager of Felden House Government Training Centre, Newtownabbey. When I last saw Percy, it was when he was appointing me to the SS "Rathlin Head," and his last words to me were:

"When you're down there (in the dry dock) and you see a man called Stewart hovering around, make sure he sees you working. If you happen to have nothing to do – let on you have. He is the Superintendant Engineer! "

I can't say that I ever actually had the pleasure or privilidge of either meeting Mr. Stewart - or even beholding such a man, but from time to time in the future, I would hear tales of his assiduous pre occupation that all who inherited this earth, should be fully and usefully employed! Amazingly, I met his son for the first time, at the last Head Line re union.

I had another insight into Head Line thinking when I at times would inquire into something of my old friend John Kerr, former Chief Engineer of the SS "Fanad Head" and the ill fated "Bengore Head." John had an exhaust turbine on the "Fanad Head," which was connected to the propeller shaft by a chain driven contraption which was said by some to have been last used on Noah's Arc ! If perchance some question related to this method of connection was asked, John would immediately begin, "Oh, that's a sore point with me. On every trip, a link had to be replaced on that chain. I frequently asked Stewart to replace the chain drive with the more modern hydraulic unit but he always said it would be too exensive."

Just now, my Chief Engineer was a man called Andy Shaw, and our skipper was Andy Fee, Master Mariner, from good old Island Magee. There was also one Robert Aiken, a deck apprentice - shortly to become Third Mate. Forty years later, I was to meet three of them at a Head Line Reunion in Belfast – Andy Fee then being deceased (see photographs.)

My first trip would take me across the North Atlantic Ocean, a wild place at times – especially in the Autumn/Winter months.

The route across would be close to that followed by Head Line ships during both world wars and the Company would lose nine out of their ten ships – mostly on this route, during the Second World War. One of these ships was the old SS "Fanad Head," which had left Montreal with a load of grain shortly after Britain had declared war on Germany on 3rd. September 1939. Please now refer to the photograph two pages back

But on the 14th. September, almost two weeks into the war, the German U-Boat, the U-30 spotted a steamer near Rockall off the western approaches to Scotland and fired a shot across her bows.

The steamer stopped and ran out her lifeboats. It was the SS "Fanad Head," and she was eventually sunk by the U-Boat. But high drama was played out over the upwards of six hours after the crew took to the lifeboats.

This remarkable drama has been covered in my book book, **Antrim and Beyond – Part One**, "Childhood Memories of Antrim in Wartime," and here, there will be only space to include one of the most remarkable photos of the battle of the Atlantic, during the Second World War, and some description script.

What is even more remarkable is that two persons who appear in this book are linked to this account. Both were acquainted with the author in different ways. Sadly, both have just died, recently. One was the Radio Operator of the U-30, one Georg Högel who revealed, in much correspondence, details of the sinking of the "Athenia" the "Fanad Head" and the "Bengore

Left: John Kerr. After the"Bengore Head,"loss, he became Chief Eng. of the new "Fanad Head,"until his retirement .

Left: A youthful Georg Högel, a short time before the capture of the U-110 and he became a prisoner of war.

Head" whose Chief Engineer happened to be my old friend, John Kerr, and origionally from Islandmagee ! John watched from the deck of the armed trawler, the "St. Appollo" which rescued him, as Lemp, now commanding the U-110 was forced to the surface. The U-110 was boarded and although she sank the following day, invaluable secrets of the German Signalling Codes were seized and quickly dispatched to Bletchley Park, the Headquarters of the British Code and Cipher Service. Sub Lieut. Balme later to be Lieut. Commander Balme DSO, who led the boarding party, was decorated with the DSO, and until recently, was living outside Southampton, England. King George VI described the action as " the most important single action in the war at sea so far."

Lemp - see photo on P5, lost his life - as did Klobes (also in the photo) in the confusion of abandonment of the U-Boat, and the gunfire directed at them as well. Some reports suggest that Lemp tried to re board the U-110 in order to to reactivate the scuttling charges and was shot when seen doing so during this attempt. It was Georg who sent me the amazing photo, identifying both Lemp and Klobes in the photo. I never understood his feelings on Lemp's end, but he said that Lemp was a gentleman. In the archives of the Belfast

Telegraph,* the testimony provided by the crew when they returned to Belfast, was quite amazingly in agreement with Georg – in particular Lemp's concern for the welfare of the crew (and some passengers). He even sent a message to the British Admiralty informing them as to where the ship's boats were.

More about both John Kerr and Georg Högel will appear later in this script.

*   *   *   *   *

Returning now to what would lie before me during my first trip across the North Atlantic, and when once across that Ocean, the wide expanses of the Gulf of the St. Lawrence River in Canada would beckon. Then it was on to the mighty St. Lawrence River itself. Finally the city port of Montreal would be reached - and a thousand miles from the coast. Further to that, would be to the ports on that river, or ports on its tributaries, such as Port Alfred on the River Saguenay. This latter river flowed through a steep sided gorge which was covered with Maple trees. In Autumn, the Maple trees changed their green coats to ones of a golden hue – a truly wonderful sight.

These Maple trees had not only pretty faces! Their sap provided the raw material for the production of the famous Maple Syrup used in quantity in Canadian kitchens and at dining tables. Nowadays, Maple Tree Syrup in "fancy dress" bottles, is a must for the tourist (and indeed for the Canadian tourist industry) and is to be found in most souvenir shops in

Canada.   ***See full account in "Antrim and Beyond" Part Two.**

Above: Jimmie Spiers, is extreme right, "Buster" McShane is extreme left, here both apprentices in Harland & Wolff's shipyard, Photo: Courtesy Jimmie Spiers.

My first watch at sea: As recalled, we had a couple of young engineers on board, one who had already done a couple of trips as a junior engineer. I was to find him – his name was Houston, very helpful while in dry dock, and quite knowledgeable about the layout of the ship, although he had never taken a watch on his own. I was to meet, however, two others – one the former Fourth Engineer, and the other the former Fifth Engineer. Both had decided to leave the ship. I began to wonder about things ! The final destination was indeed to be the port of Montreal, a city port, then of a population of a quarter of a million people. And thus my first ship, was the ss "Rathlin Head," a steam turbine freighter of about 7,000 tons. gross and built by Messrs Harland and Wolff, Belfast about eight years before. There was accommodation for twelve passengers, and the ship belonged to the Ulster Steamship Co. Ltd., (also known as the "Head Line") whose offices were in Victoria Street, Belfast in. Most of the crew came from Northern Ireland.

The SS "Rathlin Head" on the Saguenay River, Quebec.
Origin: Author

That night for my first watch in charge of a steamer's engine room, I went down to the engine room a few minutes before eight pm. Now the resident Second Engineer, one Frank Reeves, had decided to have a trip out, and a Relief Second Engineer, had taken his place. It was he that I was now relieving. He had just completed the engine room Engine Room Log and was wiping his hands on a piece of cotton waste.

Note: *I was a first year apprentice in Shorts when I first met "Buster" McShane (see photo on previous page) when he arrived to share a bench with me. If my memory is correct, he had become quite a famous weight lifter and again, if my memory is correct, he was Secretary of the Young Communist League of Ireland. "Buster" McShane would, many years later as I discovered, set up his own Health and Fitness Studio and had coached Dame Mary Peters to win Olympic Gold. Sadly, "Buster" was later killed in a car accident.*

            *   *   *   *

But just now I was about to take over the engine room watch on the steamer. The Second was preparing to leave me, saying, "She's settled down well. You shouldn't have any trouble. If you have, just ring the Chief- he's up until twelve."

But just as he was leaving me, our ears were assailed with a horrendous noise, and steam and water cascaded around the front of a boiler. I had never heard such a racket.

The relieving Second had now stepped back - I am sure with great reluctance, into the engine room and looking at me he said, "I think that I had better stay behind for a bit – you may not have done a repair like this before." This was the understatement of the year!

He closed off a couple of valves or so on the offending boiler, and peace reigned once more.

So, with the Second having – in Scriptural parlance, crossed to the other side of the road to help another lying wounded there, we both fell to work and repaired the damage - a blown boiler gauge glass. Then he probably again said "All the best," and thankfully retired to the kingdom above. His name was Jimmy Spiers.

(A few months later when I had left the rolling North Atlantic for warmer climes and was on a steamer called the ss "Grecian," a similar scene was enacted. Again with noise, the water and steam were having a field day. But by then I knew what to do.)

The Atlantic is usually in motion anyway, with a ship that is either pitching or rolling, but now it was at its most violent, and icebergs, earlier released in the Spring time, were still making their way south to the shipping lanes.

Looking blue at a distance, one always felt that the air was colder when they were around. Conditions were not pleasant, as one was thrown about quite a lot as engine room watch keeping had to be carried on again regardless of the comforts of life. As said, the ship would either be pitching or rolling, and in extreme weather when the winds could reach hurricane strength, the crossing took at least two days longer than an average passage – which was usually of about seven days.

But once our ship passed north of Newfoundland and entered the Gulf of the St. Lawrence through the Belle Isle Straits, the ship's motion became steady. Since our ultimate destination was Montreal, we still had about one thousand miles to travel to get there!

Shortly, as Winter tightened its grip on the weather, our route would be south of Newfoundland to avoid thick ice then forming in the north, as in anywhere between 50° N and 55° N the Belle Isle Strait was closed between November and June. By December, the St. Lawrence itself would be frozen over, and other ports further south, like St. John's or Halifax would then have to be used for commerce. (See sketch map of the First Colour Selection). The St. Lawrence would then not be available for shipping until the following late spring. During this first trip, we arrived off the mouth of the St. Lawrence River at about two am one morning and going on " stand by," proceeded to refuel at an Esso Oil distribution station. The boiler fuel was designated (according to some of my old notes) "Esso Grade C, Green."

"Stand by" usually involved engine manoeuvring, and this meant, that in keeping with the traditional Head Line procedure of arrival or departure, all six of us engineers were on engine room duty, from "Stand By" until "Full Away." The Head Line exacted their "pound of flesh," and I don't think we were all needed.

Refuelling was a fairly lengthy procedure during which time I got up top to see my first "foreign" country and spoke to my first Canadian. I remember this as quite a fulfilling moment and I was also to find out shortly, that here in the land of the Maple Leaf, the weather inland was quite mild. While I was attending Ballymena Technical College (after the trials of life at the afore mentioned Ladyhill Primary School with its Sally rods), I remember that at the Christmas Concerts, the girls' choir sang on one occasion, a song entitled **"The Maple Leaf Forever,"** (see nine pages forward for the words) which was the National Anthem of part of Canada for a time.

After we passed the Gulf of the St. Lawrence, and into the river proper, it would be necessary to pick up our first River Pilot, the Escoumains Pilot, and this was accomplished at the mouth of a small tributary of the St. Lawrence called the River Escoumains on the north bank of the St. Lawrence River, and where also stood the small town of Escoumains. The St. Lawrence was a busy commercial water way and dangerous, not least because of the iron ore carriers crossing it. One ore carrier which I remember, sank after a collision at right angles with a Head Line freighter – the ss "Roonagh Head" in the St. Lawrence River. (After Montreal, one could travel about another 1,600 miles and reach Chicago on Lake Michigan via the St. Lawrence Seaway. Then a connection via the Illinois River and the Calumet – Sag Channel could be made to the mighty Mississippi River, on which it was possible to travel all the way to the Gulf of Mexico at New Orleans.)

Peter Bell (whose father had attended Ladyhill School) fronting the ss "Jeremy O'Brien," the last ocean going "Victory" steam ship, seen here at "Fisherman's Wharf," San Francisco, USA.
Courtesy of the Bell family.

The Escoumains pilot earlier referred to, guided our way for the next twelve hours - by which time we had reached Québec (from the native Algonquian word kebec), which means " where the river narrows," which indeed it does. Québec is a place of immense historical interest and indeed is a World Heritage Site. It is mostly predominent in the French style of architecture, and its gabled roofs must have at times reminded homesick French settlers of Paris!

When picking up a pilot in the river, the ship did not always dock or even stop - a hull gangway was in place and the pilot simply stepped off the Pilot boat onto the gangway platform of the ship to be piloted. But it was possible to see some interesting sights from the river - like the cliffs of the "Heights of Abraham" and the nearby Château Frontenac, the latter an expensive hotel dominating the St Lawrence River front.

There was something of interest that caught my eye when first we were inside the Gulf of the St. Lawrence and could see distant shorelines. I don't think it was ever explained to me by any of the old hands in the crew, but what appeared, was a mirage effect that was manifested by the trees there on those shorelines – they appeared to be all standing upside down, sometimes appearing to have no attachment to the ground at all. But no one in the crew appeared to think that the sky was falling - it was just another thing that had always been there, and just like seeing a whale which we had seen earlier in the Belle Isle Straits – it was all in a day's work!

Note: In 1759, Lieut. James Cook had the responsibility to survey the St. Lawrence River, and to assist General Wolfe select a suitable landing site in order that his troops, on their way to the capture of Quebec, could land safely and climb the cliffs which lay below the "Plains of Abraham," named so, after the farmer who owned that land. Afterwards, the cliffs would become known as the "Heights of Abraham." In the preparation for the attack on the French positions, Lieut. Cook suffered serious injuries to his hands when a powder keg he was handling exploded.

His hands were permanently impaired and scarred for life - perhaps the omen of tragic things to come.The landing site chosen was a little cove about three miles upstream from Quebec and below the cliffs referred to above, their estimation of the cliff's height being a hefty 170 feet.There was however a small road which led from the cove to the upper plains, but guarded by a modest number of French soldiers. On the 13th. of September 1759 an advance guard of the British overcome these, and opened the small road for General Wolfe to advance on the "Heights" successfully and eventually capture the French possessions in Canada.

In the initial battles, the two opposing generals, the French General Montcalm, the French General, and the British General, General Wolfe, would both die - just before the final British victory. Sometime in the future, Cook, now Capt.James Cook, and by then a distinguished navigator, would also lose his life. Following a confrontation with some natives after his ship anchored off the North Pacific Island of Hawaii, he was killed and eaten by the natives - who were cannibals.

Retribution by the ship's gun fire on a local village swiftly followed, and resulted with the native chiefs seeking a truce during which time they produced some cooked human remains. These remains contained two hands which were badly scarred and deformed. They had belonged to Captain James Cook.

*　　　　*　　　　*　　　　*　　　　*

During the Second World War (and indeed during the First World War), Britain depended on receiving food supplies – about half the minimum required, from the United States and Canada. Also, much of the means required to wage and maintain the war with Germany also had to cross the North Atlantic as well. Germany used her U-Boat fleet to try and cut off these supplies by sinking the ships bringing those supplies to Brirain. The tonnage of ships sunk reached a staggering figure in the early years of the war - especially in those up to 1943.

It called for extraordinary methods to replace the lost tonnage quicker than the U-Boats could them and a new method of construction was required to harness the mighty production potential of the United States. It was called Sub-Assembly, where components to produce a cargo ship could be made all over the country and then brought to a port where they could be assembled. See earlier photo of Peter Bell with the SS "Jeremy O'Brien" in San Francisco - on previous page.The first designs were of about 7,000 tons nett , powered by triple expansion steam engines which gave a speed of sixteen knots and were known the Liberty ships. Later a larger version – of about 10,000 tons nett with steam turbine or diesel engines giving speeds of up to eighteen knots. These were the "Victory" ships, and after the war, many of these sailed the oceans as part of the merchant fleets of many nations.

Also, with our commencement of the St. Lawrence River transit, where the Gulf of the St. Lawrence was possibly five miles wide (but becoming much narrower as we moved upstream), something else that affected me personally, was my introduction to a "dog" watch.

Firstly, once in the river proper, we were in a busy waterway. Secondly we had a dozen or two passengers on board and certain rules applied.

Whilst in any of the rivers there, we had to be prepared for any emergency, and this called for two engineers to be on watch at all times. I think that the stipulation referred more specifically to "when passengers are on board." All engineering watch keepers therefore had to spend an extra two hours watch keeping with another engineer on his watch. My normal watches ended at 12 noon and 12 midnight. So I joined the Second Engineer, Jimmy Spiers (the Good Samaratin of an earlier watch) from 4pm until 6pm as my dog watch.

Jimmie was known as a Company Relief Second Engineer, who undertook relief duties for Second Engineers going on holidays etc. As a very experienced officer, he would be available to serve as such on any of the Company's steam vessels .

Second Engineers generally had the responsibility of the day to day running of ships' engine rooms. We happily did not have any emergencies to to contend with, and were able to spend some time in easy chat. The ship's usual Second rejoined us upon our return to Belfast, and the relieving Second left us there at the end of the trip in Belfast, and I didn't expect to see see him again. But I was wrong!

As mentioned in the caption to Jimmie's photograph - three pages forward, many years later, while attending the Meeting House one Sunday morning in Antrim, I casually glanced over to the far side of the congregation during the taking up of the collection. Imagine my amazement when I realised that one of those taking up the offering there, was none other than the former Relief Second Engineer of the ss "Rathlin Head," with whom I had shared those "dog" watches on the St. Lawrence River all those years ago! It was Jimmy Spiers of course, and today, he is my close acquaintance of over forty years standing – and living until recently, about half a mile from my own home.

An Interlude :

Forty four years on, a Head Line Reunion was held in 2004. Jimmy Spiers suggested attending and I was pleased to accompany him there. I was to be amazed to find that of those who had survived the intervening forty four years, there were four officers of the crew of which I had been one on the "Rathlin Head." These were Andy Shaw, Chief /Eng, Jimmy Spiers, Second Eng. and myself were from the engineering side and Robert Aiken (now a Master Mariner) was from the" boys on the Bridge." But Captain Andy Fee had passed on.

Note 1: During the Second World War, the Head Line lost nine of their ten ships – and **all but one, in the North Atlantic.**

Note 2 : *The Chateau Frontenac, located in Old Quebec City, is within walking distance of the former battle area on the sprawling Plains of Abraham* (See later photographs of the Frontenac.)

The SS "Rathlin Head" on the River Saguenay. Auther 1960

The Jacques Cartier Bridge, Montreal.
Auther 1960

From left, Brian Kane, Master Mariner; Jimmy Spiers, Second Engineer ; Tom Swann, Office Staff; Robert Cameron, (author); Shaw Heddles, Master Mariner deceased). Origin: Taken at Head Line reunion 2004.

Head Line reunion cake 2004
Origin: Author 2004

The approaches to Montreal

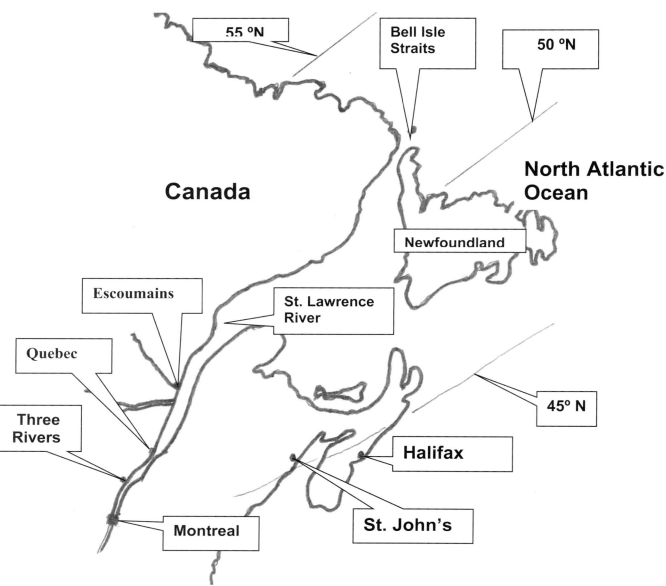

55 °N

Bell Isle Straits

50 °N

North Atlantic Ocean

Canada

Newfoundland

Escoumains

St. Lawrence River

Quebec

45° N

Three Rivers

Halifax

St. John's

Montreal

Jimmy Spiers on the manoeuvring platform of the SS "Carrigan Head." Courtesy: Jim Spiers

Right: from left, Andy Shaw, author's former Chief Engineer (since deceased), SS "Rathlin Head"; John Hanna, Master Mariner; Robert Aiken, Master Mariner; author. Origin: Taken at Head Line reunion 2004.

The Maple Leaf For Ever   by Alex Muir

In days of yore, from Britain's shore
Wolfe the dauntless hero came,
And planted firm Old England's flag,
on Ca-na-da's fair domain!
 Here may it wave our boast , our pride
 And joined in love together,
 the Thistle, Shamrock, Rose entwine
The Maple Leaf forever!

At Queens-ton Heights, and Lundy's
Lane
Our brave Fathers, side by side,
 Freedom, homes, and loved ones dear
Firmly stood, and nobly died;
 And those dear rights which they
 maintained
 We swear to yield them never! Our
 Our Watchword ev – er - more shall be
 The Maple Leaf forever.

**This was once the National Anthem of part of Canada and was often
sung at concerts etc. in British and Irish circles – but hardly in French
ones!**

The Quebec pilot's duties ended at Three (Trois Rivieres) and here another pilot would join us for safe passage to Montreal. Since we travelled at night as well as day, and also stood our watches, there was only a limited time to watch the scene unfolding on the river – mine being to a few hours during each early afternoon. Occasionally, the ship would stop at Three Rivers for a short time.

This would give one an opportunity to witness the scene at this place. Here were literally mountains of log timber piled high, and this timber appeared to be of the spruce variety – and in endless supply.

In many places on the banks of the St. Lawrence River, trees, mostly of the Spruce or Maple family, would be seen to grow thickly. Along the banks of the River Saguenay which flows through a deep gorge, the Maple tree – especially when one was approaching the Autumn/Winter months of endless low temperatures, was now proclaiming its presence by changing into its seasonal coat of gold, a wonderful sight – see photo three pages back (although the lack of colour is disappointing). This was best seen when travelling on the River Saguenay all the way to the river port of Port Alfred, there to load drums of blank paper for, perhaps, the Belfast Telegraph. Maple trees, of course, grew along the St. Lawrence – and indeed all over Canada.

 Needless to say, Maple Syrup is always available as a present, when homeward bound.

Montreal was an amazing introduction to the "New World" of glitter and neon signs, neon not yet in quantity display in the U.K. The length of the streets was literarily breath taking – St. Catharines Boulevard – a main thoroughfare, was fiffhteen miles long and many main streets ran from the docks area to cross it - one well known street was simply known as "China Town" and another popular one was San Laurent. I knew the latter well as I used it to get to St. Catharines Boulevard because on occasion I attended St. James United Church of Canada there if I was not required for any urgent work on the ship on a Sunday morning when it happened we were in port of Montreal, Quebec. I imagined the latter to be by majority, French speaking – and many there, appeared somewhat sallow in complexion. What a change when attending a church with roots in the British Isles!For here, everyone had a ruddy face such as seen in Ireland or Britain, and I found myself most strikingly at home. Referring again to neon signs, a film recently released and currently proclaimed in bright lights as showing in the local cinemas at the time, was "The Fall of the House of Usher" which eventually appeared in the U.K. cinemas and later, on television. I had a standing invitation to visit a home in the Sherbrook area of Montreal – I remember the bus number to get there was number 32! The Flemming sisters lived there and their father had attended the same school as I had done, except - he had attended an older building known as Ladyhill National School in the area. He thus had missed being both at a Public Elementary School and also at a Primary one! Thus, he must have been a happy man!

*   *   *   *   *

Above: The "Heights of Abraham," up river from Quebec. Photo taken by author from the deck of the ss "Rathlin Head" on the St. Lawrence River.
Origin:Author,1960

The Chateau Frontenac, taken in clour in more recent times. See forward, for a comparison with one taken in 1960.

Above: Reunion Invitation / WelcomeCard of 2013.The only person author recognised from the 2004 reunion in attendance in 2013 was Robert Aiken– and no further photographs seem to have been taken. Who will switch off the lights, I wonder?

Left: Author on the deck of the next ship sailed on – the SS "Grecian," of Ellerman Papayanni Lines, Liverpool, (and somewhere down the Mediterranean.)
Origin: Stan Pacer 3rd. Engineer.

Above, about ten years later: Having a brief cruise – a working holiday as a Relief Engineer during School Summer vacation on the MV "Sangro,"of Ellerman Wilson Lines, Liverpool. The "Sangro" was a very modern motor ship, with Bridge control and variable pitch propeller – note the McGregor hatch cover chains.
Origin: Some of my "mates."

Author passing Kilid Bahr Fort in the Dardanelles, Turkey, in 1974.

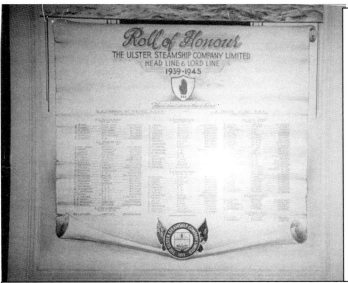

The 1939 –1945 Head Line Memorial for the lost crews.

The Memorial to Quen Victoria on a site close to the Old Port area of Montreal. Origin: Author 2013

Above: The Head Line Memorial to the Company's lost ships and crew members in the Second World War, 1939-1945, placed in all postwar vessels.
In the Second World War, the Head Line of Belfast lost 9 out of its 10 ships – with one exception, all in the North Atlantic. One hundred crew members lost their lives. There is a similar one for the 1914-1918 war.

Below: How does a Belfast Harbour pass chit (Pollock Dock) survive for fifty years?

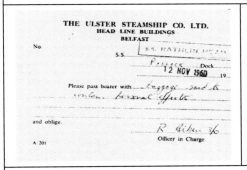

Left: How and where did this chit to get me through the Belfast Harbour gates at Pollock Dock ever survive over fifty years? It had been issued by the Third Mate, Robert Aiken, SS "Rathlin Head," – see his photo two pages back.

Author 2013

Above: The British racing car of the pre Second World War /post Second W.W.2 was the ERA (English Racing Automobile) with a Riley 1.5 litre OHC, short push rod engine and super charged using methanol fuel. Above is the ERA (R14) used by Bob Gerrard, a well known racing driver in post war days .Origin: Jonathon Williamson, one time resident in Muckamore, Co. Antrim, and now resident in England.

19.2.2013

Dear Bob,
Many thanks for your photos and interesting information re the Head Line. The copy of the baggage pass was a real reminder of all those years ago and brought back many memories
I trust we will have another re-union sooner rather than later and I look forward to seeing you there.

Above: Robert Aiken, Master Mariner, but one time Third Mate of the SS "Rathlin Head," writes to thank me for some photographs taken at the 2004 reunion, and also for a copy of the pass which, as Third Mate, he wrote out in 1960! This enabled me to pass out of the Pollock Dock with some bags or other, upon a return to Belfast. We could not believe how much time had away.

Author, 2013

All the senior engineers, and the senior officers on the bridge (where the ship was navigated and steered from) and who had served in the recent wars, wore their campaign ribbons on their uniforms. There were others also entitled to wear the same ribbons – stewards, greasers, firemen, store keepers (sometimes also known as donkeymen), bosuns , general seaman branch AB's (Able Bodied Seamen), E.D.H.'s (Efficient Deck Hands) and anyone else who had sailed in these dreadful waters in wartime. However this latter section of the crew were seldom in a formal uniform, and thus didn't usually have an opportunity to put up their ribbons.

The Head Line had sailed in convoys during the Second World War on the North Atlantic to the very ports we were now going to and had lost eight of their ten ships in so doing along, with about one hundred crew members! Another vessel was bombed in Belfast docks becoming a constructive loss – nine out of the ten that the firm had started the war with were lost. This knowledge now brought home to people like me, the magnitude of the sacrifice that was required to bring to the children of the U.K. and possibly those in the South of Ireland as well, the orange juice concentrate, and cod liver oil, plus sugar and cocoa to make the three quarters of a pound of confectionary for each child - each month and to win the Battle of the Atlantic as well. I was to be appalled to find out just how many of those whom I had met at sea (including my present Head Line colleagues) had been torpedoed, and that 30,000 seamen had lost their lives manning **the ships of the**

Merchant Navy in the Second World war. *   See "Antrim and Beyond" Part Two, Chapter 8, p116.

*   *   *   *   *

I must now take the opportunity to recall two men, one British and one German, who years later were able to tell me - in writing, in word and at first hand, something of what it was like to fight a war in those dreadful waters:My thanks indeed to two men who never met each other but who, at one time, were not far apart – possibly within one mile during an epic event in the North Atlantic in May 1941 and which had far reaching consequences for the outcome of the Battle of the Atlantic then raging.This was during the sinking of the ss "Bengore Head," a small Head Line vessel, on May 9th. 1941.

John Kerr, Chief Eng.,Whitehead.

Georg Högel ,Radio Operater, U-30 and U -110, Munich, Ger.

One of these men was my old friend John Kerr, late of Whitehead, Co. Antrim, but originally from close by Islandmagee, that peninsula off the North East coast of Co. Antrim renowned for producing seamen but in particular, Chief Engineers and Master Mariners. John was sailing as Chief Engineer on the "Bengore Head" on the day she was sunk by the German U-boat, the U-110, south of Iceland - see photo of this "Bengore Head" on p19. Also Georg Högel from Munich who was a Radio Operator on the U-110, which was captured and boarded in the following action in which the British found significant secret monthly codes for the German encoding Enigma machine – giving the British Naval

cryptanalysts at Bletchley Park a major break through in solving the German U-boat Enigma cipher system. Here Georg was picked up and became a POW and spent the rest of the war in a POW camp in Canada. John Kerr became Chief Engineer of the ss "Fanad Head," from 1941 until he retired from the sea in 1967.

Over the years, both men, in recalling their experiences to me of what life was like on the North Atlantic in wartime, contributed mightily to my understanding of that struggle. In particular their Information was invaluable when I came to write an account of Convoy OB 318, the U-110, and the sinking of the ss "Bengore Head," * and to analyse the direct consequences of this for the outcome of the Battle of the

Atlantic – in quite an amazing sequence of events. John passed away in the year 2,000 shortly after his 100th. Birthday. Georg passed away on 27th. March, 2014.

 There is a full account of the sinking of the SS "Bengore Head," in the Author's earlier book,

 Antrim and Beyond, Part Two (They served in   time of War)   Chapter 8, entitled "**John Kerr."** * and see there again, the photo of the original **SS "Bengore Head,"** now lying two miles beneath the surface of the Atlantic Ocean off Iceland.The photo may also be seen in in this book two pages forward.

One day, on a return voyage from Canada to Liverpool in the worst weather I had yet experienced, I had my lunch, and then visited "Sparks," the Radio Officer in his Radio Cabin (sometimes referred to as "the Radio Shack.") I quite often visited him – he always had fresh bits of information from the "outside world." That day our chairs were anchored by chains to the floor and earlier our lunch plates had been placed on wet table cloths in efforts to "glue" them and their contents to the tables. Presently "Sparks" turned to me - after one 30 degree roll had him holding onto his desk, and said, "Would you not be better off down the Med. This run suits me as I live in Newcastle Upon Tyne on the north east coast, and as soon as we dock in Liverpool, I lock up here and I'm home in a couple of hours."

So I asked him what companies traded there. "Oh," he replied, "the Prince Line of London, Moss Hutchinson, Ellerman and Papyanni Lines, Furness   Withy – the lot. Once you get over the Bay and down the coast off Portugal in sheltered water, you'd be laughing." Later that evening with the weather showing no signs of a let up, I considered what he had been saying.

So, upon reaching Liverpool, I decided to give Ellerman's a call where I met Mr. Fergie Brand the Superintendant Engineer. He offered me "a place in the sun," on a steamer. When I had confirmed in writing that I had severed my links with the Head Line, I received a letter naming a ship that he wished me to join on a given date, and the name of the dock she was expected to discharge at in Liverpool.

Subsequently, I was to join the SS "Grecian," two days after Christmas .

But first, just a little incident which took place during my time on the "Rathlin Head" ere I trod her gangway for a last time - a small item from my "Memory Selection Box" and one that has remained fresh fresh through the ages!"

Of those early days when I was with the Head Line Shipping Company of Belfast, I am surprised that my memory is so selective in clearly recalling events which couldn't be described exactly as earth shattering. Yet other serious events - such as the one which involved a collision at sea on my first trip and resulting in loss of life among our crew, are no longer within one's power of complete recall. But one such occasion in events from the **non earth shattering** mode, is memorable perhaps more for recalling the irresponsibility of youth - rather than for content.

Midnight, deep in a Canadian Forest.

It came about, that we arrived late one Saturday evening at a small loading dock literally on the river's bank at a little village on the Saguenay River. After sailing all afternoon and early evening up this wide and deep tributary of the St. Lawrence River, we thus arrived at Port Alfred. The steep banks of the Saguenay were by now thickly covered with the ubiquitous maple trees of Canada, now arrayed in their splendid coats of autumn gold.

 It was the custom for to dock at Port Alfred on the Sagueney River – by literally pulling in to a jetty on one bank of the river in order to pick up cargo. This, as I recall, usually consisted of bulk paper rolls for the Belfast Telegraph (about the size of the plastic covered rolls in which farmers store their hay nowadays) and sheet aluminium. At this point in time, I had discovered that I had forgotten to post some cards etc in Montreal. So I inquired as to if and where the nearest post box at Port Alfred might be - and I got the necessary directions. So, as we had now broken watches and I happened to be off duty for a time while loading was proceeding, I arranged to leave the ship to seek out this post box. Thus, on a fairly pleasant evening shortly before midnight, I set off in the pale light of the moon along a path through the tall trees of a forest which flanked the river in the province of Quebec in Canada. I recall, that I was soon aware that I was not exactly alone became the distant sounds of the creatures that obviously lived there, seemed to be getting closer.

Presently, I realised that I was in uncharted waters but continued to walk deeper into the

Above: A " black and white" photo of the Chateau Frontenac, on the St. Lawrence River at Quebec in Canada taken in 1960 by the author using a 620 Brownie camera, while passing on the Belfast steamer, the ss "Rathlin Head."
    Origin: Author as crew member 1960.

Above: A more recent photograph of the Chateau Frontenac. The sky outline has not changed much.
Origin : Thought to be taken from a travel promotion publication.

forest, until, when about an estimated half a mile from the ship, I came to a railway line which I had been told to expect. I was aware indeed - as twigs cracked under my feet , of the strange animal or bird sounds in the forest, reminding me that I had company not too far off. I later remembered, how that I then had began to have second thoughts about proceeding any further. I wondered what would happen if I stumbled and broke my ankle. What indeed, if, at such a moment, a hungary Bear or some other predator should come along looking for a meal and certainly would investigate a casualty? And a Brown Bear was capable of spurts of 30 MPH!

Proceeding over the railway line with caution, I began looking for that post box and to my intense relief, about one hundred yards further along, there was the Post Box. I posted the cards, and made off in the direction of the River Sagueney and the SS "Rathlin Head" as quickly as I could.

Above: The ss "Rathlin Head," built by Harland & Wolff, Belfast in 1953, as features in this book. She lived to die in her bed in a scrap yard in the 1970's
    Origin :Sam Smyth, 5th./Eng. 1961.

Above: A rare photograph of the 1922 built "Bengore Head," built on the Clyde but now lying two miles deep off Iceland. Photo probably taken on the St. Lawrence or the Baltic, and recently found in the clearing out of a house.

The ss "Bengore Head," was built by Irvines on the Clyde in 1922, and was lost in convoy OB 308 on 9. 05. 1941 when torpedoed by U-110. *

Midnight, deep in a Canadian Forest contd:

Some time afterwards, I reflected upon these things, and the thought came to mind that not such a long time ago, some of those sounds that I heard might have emanated from another source – like a Red Indian intent on removing someone's scalp !
I imagine that I was very glad to get back to the ship! Shortly we would reverse our course on the River Sagueney and then, upon rejoining the mighty St. Lawrence River, we would soon be heading for the North Atlantic Ocean. It was certainly a silly thing to do - although none of my more experienced fellow crew members seemed to think it a big deal!

*Around this time, as I recall, a film had recently been made further up river towards the source of the River Saguenay, and in the area of the rapids there. It was called **"The River of no Return,"** starring Robert Michum and Marilyn Monroe. Eventually, it also became available in the U.K.*

      *   *   *   *   *   *

The SS "Grecian," Ellerman Papyanni Lines, Liverpool.

A different ship - and a change of climate.

Thus I joined the ss "Grecian," a triple expansion steamer of about 5,000 tons nett at the West Bromley Moore dock in Liverpool. By our return, Spring would be in full swing. We were soon ready to sail for Gibraltar and the Mediterranean.Two days later- on a Sunday actually, we left the chilly weather of Liverpool behind, calling in at Cardiff the following day. In three days time the coast of Portugal was in sight as was a promising sun. Before that, however, two things occurred that reminded me that this was not going to be a cruise without problems. Shortly after entering the Bay of Biscay, an oil fuel leak was discovered under the boilers - coinciding with the news that a severe storm was developing in the Bay. A fuel leak close to a heat source like the boilers, was potentially a very dangerous situation should fire break out, and I was given the job of investigating the cause and putting it right! Lowering myself through the engine room deck plating with the ship starting to roll badly , I found myself on a tank top – one of several in the very bottom of the ship that were known as the "double bottoms" which could be carrying liquids like oil fuel, fresh water, or even on occasions, liquid cargo – say vegetable oil - like margarine.

With Stan Pacer, 3ʳᵈ· Engineer, torpedoed twice in the North Atlantic – a street wise guy! Focus not good!
Origin: Some fellow crew member.

Arrival in Gibraltar

The latter oil would usually be carried in what are normally known as "deep" tanks, which can be pumped up above sea level. Just now, fuel was already sloshing over the top of these double bottoms but fortunately I soon found an oil pipe with leaking flanges, and having tightened those up securely, I retired from this very uncomfortable place.
 Next morning, I came out on deck for a breather, and discovered that instead of going dead south, we were heading due west - to America. What was happening?

Now we had been carrying, as part of our deck cargo, a number of huge elm logs, each about three feet in diameter and each about fifty feet in length. They had been positioned, wedged and secured upon the top of the hatch covers over the holds.

I had looked at them on the previous day and had thought them uncomfortable bed fellows. So when the ship started rolling badly during the storm, these monsters broke their securing ropes, and fell off the hatches down between the latter and the side of the ship.

We had thus a cargo shift and a significant list to starboard.

The ship's head had therefore been turned due west into the wind to reduce the rolling, and thus proceeded west at reduced speed. Work to re secure the elm trunks was commenced, and completed sometime around noon the following day. The ship resumed the passage to Gibraltar where we arrived at about 6 o'clock on a Friday morning. It would be my first visit to what I regarded as a foreign country, to a Mediterranean climate and a place with a couple of hundred years of recent history to explore.

Stan Pacer, 3rd. Eng. SS "Grecian."

Note: Gibraltar has been an Overseas Territory of Britain since 1713 under the Treaty of Utrecht and occupies a commanding position at the Western Gateway to the Mediterranean. At one time it was occupied by the Moors from North Africa and indications of that time are still to be found as, for example, in the Moorish Castle. I well remember emerging from the engine room into the early morning light to get my first glimpse of the mighty Rock and was not disappointed. A short distance away, two British warships – destroyers I believed them to be, were tied up and there, at the foot of the Rock and winding itself upwards to it, was the town itself - a place that for me, was, for the first time, surely where East meets West. It was quite a fascinating place, with the shops all well stocked with souvenirs where a "first footer" in Gibraltar would surely find something to bring back - something perhaps bearing the word "Gibraltar."

Below: Breakwater and harbour at Gibraltar, the Western entrance to the Mediterranean. Photo taken from the Old Moorish Castle. Orig: Author 1961

We would also soon also meet those cheeky fellows, the Barbary Apes!
I had become very friendly with Stan Pacer, our Third Engineer.
He was a Pole, had served in the Polish Marine pre Second World war, and had managed to flee Poland when the Germans invaded. He then joined the British Merchant Service and had been torpedoed twice in the North Atlantic during the Second World War. After the war he had a spell with Irish Shipping. He was a street wise guy! I was glad of his company for my first tour of a "foreign"

Above: This is the triple expansion steamer, the ss "Grecian," of Ellerman Papayanni Lines. Origin: Photo taken later in Turkey.

town. Apart from the purchase of the souvenirs, there was so much to see – also strange smells, strange faces - and beautiful, mild weather. Seeing the harbour was very interesting. During the Second World War, Italian Frogmen had emerged from their base in a partially submerged Italian tanker in Spanish waters, to attack Allied shipping with limpet mines in this very place – Gibraltar harbour.
We were in Gibraltar for about three days, unloading supplies - mostly for

the three services then stationed there . Then we set out due East for Malta, the George Cross Island of Malta.

Malta is a small island, half way, approximately, between Gibraltar and Cyprus. It lies directly south of Sicily, and we are told that it has been inhabited since 5,000 BC.

It was once part of the British Empire from 1800 until 1964 and its capital, Valletta, was home to the Royal Navy between the World Wars, only moving in Egypt in1937,for security reasons. During the Second World War, Malta was very much the key as to who would succeed in winning control in the area.If the British in Malta could succeed in holding Malta, then the Axis forces would be frustrated in supplying their forces in North Africa. If Britain lost Malta, they would therefore lose their submarine base from which the Axis convoys supplying their forces in North Africa were harassed. As well, Britain would also lose their airfields in Malta. In the event, Britain narrowly succeeded in keeping Malta supplied and defended, and the Axis were eventually expelled from North Africa.

We were not long deployed at Valletta – I think about two days while the ship was anchored stem to the Quay – thus avoiding possible propeller damage at the dockside, as a normal berth was not available. Cargo was off loaded into barges alongside, and this meant that to get to dry land one had to use the services of the local boatmen who used a high stemmed row boat called a Dghaisas, (singular and plural spelt the same and pronounced "Dy-so") and also known as a "gaily painted Maltese Gondola."

During the time we were in harbour - mostly discharging cargo, I worked at night – partly to keep an eye on the engine room and also to carry out repairs to equipment damaged in daytime working. This latter would mostly be repairs to the steam winches as they were driven during the day without mercy by the Maltese dockers (and eventually by

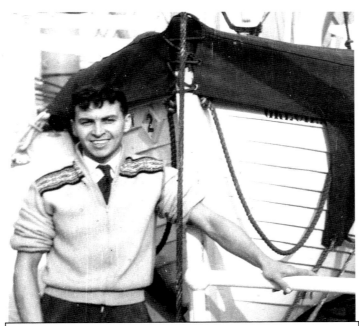

Author beside "Grecian's" Number Two lifeboat, a wooden clinker built lady - on a sunny morning down the Med. As the man said, "- it was enough to make one feel that life wasn't too bad after all!"
Origin: Stan Pacer, 3rd. Engineer.

those of other nations), the damage usually occurring to the plain "big end" brass bearings of the steam engines providing power to the winches. This meant that I was my own boss during these working hours with the ship nearly all to myself. A duty fireman and a duty seaman shared with me the catering duties and the old sea cook always left out a generous quantity of eggs and bacon etc. So we dined in leisure in somewhat balmy conditions, and typical of the Mediterranean, beneath a full moon and stars that hung low in the heavens. It was nearly enough to make one believe indeed, that life wasn't too bad after all!

The dghaisas were kept busy with off duty crew men – liberty men, going ashore and returning. Here I was to witness a most humorous incident : I heard a voice crying somewhere near the gangway and thinking that someone might have fallen into the water. I made my way round to see what the commotion was. I found a man and his dghaisas at the foot of the gangway. He spoke in a language unintelligible to me but beckoned with his finger to the bottom of his boat. There, resembling something between a scarecrow and a sack of potatoes, was a crumpled body. Upon closer examination I realised that it was the body of one of our firemen and the Dghaisas man was anxious to get it off his craft and onto the ship.

22

It was not going to be easy. The gangway was lashed to the side of the ship with but a very small platform at the bottom. Getting him dragged safely onto that platform was the problem – what if he fell from our grasps and into the water?

Well, we managed the first part, and then, half dragging, half carrying this seemingly unconscious being, we progressed up the gangway. At the halfway mark, strength appeared to be returning to his legs and at the top we managed to dump him onto the ship at which stage I managed to depart the scene.

A few minutes later I heard the dghaisas man calling again in the most plaintive tones, and upon investigation, I discovered that our beastly drunk and "unconscious" fireman had

Dghaisas man in the Grand Harbour, Malta.

quickly recovered his health and had disappeared into the inner sanctums of the "Grecian" never to be found again! The point that the dghaisas man was making, was simply was that the fireman had "forgotten" to pay his fare!

I could scarcely believe it – he had acted completely limp and it wasn't without some effort and not a little danger that the beast was hauled up from the dghaisas and onto the gangway platform. I was learning fast - but maybe not fast enough.

However on the plus side, my uncomfortable travelling companions, the elm logs

Above :A dghaisas man – but is it "our" man? In the Grand Harbour, Malta.
Original: Author

which were destined for Baillie's Dockyard in Valletta, were safely laid to rest on the dockside.

The main thoroughfare in Valletta was known as "Kingsway" and the town itself was not unlike the average town at home in the UK or Ireland. In Gibraltar, Malta or Cyprus, nothing brought this home more strikingly than a visit to the l painted red and blue local Post identical with a GPO in the UK and while in Valletta I visited St. John's Cathedral and saw the George Cross awarded by King George V1 " to the Island fortress of Malta - its people and defenders." This was in recognition of its peoples' resistance to the Axis powers in the early days of World War Two!

Here in Valletta was where, in August 1942, the damaged oil tanker, the SS "Ohio" limped into the harbour supported on either side by two British destroyers, HMS "Ledbury" and HMS "Penn," with HMS "Rye" acting as a stabiliser at the stern, and accompanied by four other supply transports. These five were the only survivors of "Operation Pedestal," the operation to relieve Malta. It was here that Malta is said to have been saved from losing " the will to sustain itself " from collapse.

It was also from here, sadly, that some of Britain's most successful submarine commanders left - on their last missions.

Cyprus

We departed Malta for the island of Cyprus, an island which had declared war against the Ottoman Empire in 1914 and was annexed by the United Kingdom unilaterally about this time. Following strife between Greek Nationalists and British forces, independence came in 1960. However, following an invasion by mainland Turkish forces in 1974, the island was divided into Greek Cypriot and Turkish Cypriot sectors. After the invasion and the civil war which followed, thousands of Greek Cypriots fled south – about 130,000 in all, and about 45,000 Turkish Cypriots fled north. These vacated their properties - some in both communities with washing still on the clothes lines. Thus was formed the ghost towns that one can see today.

We were now heading for the commercial port in Famagusta to load potatoes, the port itself lying in the Turkish part of the town, the two parts of the town being about half a mile apart. It was then possible to walk freely in either part and one day I walked into the Greek town – which may have rejoiced in the name, Varosha. There I found the post office, a replica of any one might find in the U.K. The layout and décor inside was just the same as at home!

On another afternoon when I was not otherwise usefully employed, I was having a look around the old Turkish part of the town area which was much smaller than the Greek town (and not so tidy or substantial either) when I saw something that struck me as unusual. I saw a building that either was, or had been, a Roman Catholic Church. However, it had, if I were not mistaken, a minaret mounted on one side. It was truly something of interest. I took a photograph of it with my old 620 Brownie camera (with a set of bellows that wouldn't have been far out of place in a blacksmith's forge) but upon my return to the ship, nobody could enlighten me about the building - see photograph, two pages on.

There the matter rested in the meantime but amazingly, the question as to its history, was not answered for me fully, until almost fifty years had passed. I was to pass this building on one other occasion, and this time, I saw a man coming out of it carrying a double barrelled shotgun - no explanation.

"It proclaimed itself as Othello's Tower." Note white board over door - saying so!   Orig: Author

Also on that same day, and not far away from the latter building, I discovered a tower which proclaimed itself as "Othello's Tower," and took its photograph - see left. Back on the ship, to my inquiries regarding this Church /Mosque and this Tower, none of my companions had been able to offer explanations for either of my discoveries. In due season however - in fact some fifty years later, the explanations tumbled out, thus:

The Tower was actually a medieval tower or fortress of which one Othello was a Venetian Governor around 1506 - see additional note on this two pages forward .

The building with the minaret had indeed been a Roman Catholic Cathedral built in 1298 and which was consecrated in 1328. It became a Mosque when the Ottoman Empire captured Famagusta in1571 and would now be known as the Lala Mustafo Mosque! Oranges were plentiful in Famagusta in 1961 and before we left I bought one dozen very large ones for one halfpenny (old money) each. We left Cyprus to make fairly quick calls at some Turkish ports, first at Mersin, a port on the south coast of Turkey and about 30 miles south of Tarsus, the birthplace of St. Paul and where the photo of the ss "Grecian"was taken. Then at Iskenderun, a Turkish Naval base where one can see the substantial crescent formed in the mountains there, and which is to be seen in tourist publicity information publications. Referring back to Othello's Tower, it is referred to in one of Shakespeare's plays. Here one Othello is described as a Moor. As previously mentioned, when back on the ship and to my inquiries regarding this Church /Mosque and this Tower, none of my companions could offer explanations for either of my discoveries. This amazed me as the ship had been trading to Cyprus for years!

Then we sailed down the Levant coast for the nearby Syrian port of Latakia (which in 2015, become a base for Russian Fighter bombers, in support of the current Syrian President.) Again it was a case of no berth immediately available, so the "Grecian" swung at anchor in the breakwater adjoining the port. **With the engine room on stand by**, unloading cargo was then commenced, the cargo being placed into barges (also referred to as lighters), which were secured to the side of the ship. It was quite amazing how strong were the currents exercising in the area. One time you would look out seaward to see what was going on and you would be facing south, and an hour later if you looked again, you would be facing the East, the barge moving with the ship.

Unloading was supposed to be a half day job – when a ship is in port it is judged not to be making money for its owners so we would be moving again soon, this time to Beirut in Lebanon, just down the coast. But the best laid plans of men and mice are, as Rabbie Burns said, " apt tae gang aglee." A circumstance now came about that someone like myself would never have dreamed likely. The wind rose - as likewise did the seas, and soon there was real concern for the ship.

The problem was not one of the ship actually foundering, but of dragging her anchor and run aground! A few weeks previously, a sister ship, the SS "Anglian" had taken the ground close to where we were and was severely damaged in the after end - probably to the propeller and propeller shaft. She had to be towed back to the U.K. for repairs, thus the state of alert on the "Grecian."

So the barge was quickly unshackled from the ship, and the telegraph soon rang for an engine movement. We up anchored and proceeded rapidly until the ship was in deep water again, and far enough from land to ride out the storm in safety. The idea was to keep the ship's head facing into the oncoming seas as much as possible.

I can still recall my amazement when the bridge actually rang down for 89 revolutions of the propeller, and I never discovered exactly why such precise revolutions were called for!

Thus we paraded up and down on a given stretch of seaway and well out from the coast. The violent storms into which we were thrown were to last for several days before it was considered safe to return to the docking facilities then existing at Latakia. I wondered if such a loss of working time would be recovered from insurance.

Here we were allocated a safe place where it was possible to tie up stem to the dock side as the policy at Valetta in Malta allowed, and to discharge cargo into a barge as previously done there.

Afterwards I expressed my surprise to Mr. Gardner the Mate that such weather should be in the Mediterranean, and was to be further surprised when he, recalling having been at sea all his life – including during the Second World War, said that the highest seas that he had ever seen, had been in the Eastern Mediterranean! Those few days parading up and down off the Levant coast would have been a costly stop over for Ellerman Papyanni Lines, the owners of the ss "Grecian!" A ship makes little money in being at sea - and going nowhere.

Our next port was, but a short distance down the Levant coast to visit Beirut in the land of Lebanon where the Cedars of Lebanon once abounded. This was where the once local King Hiram agreed to provide King Solomon of Israel with, among other building materials, the cedar wood required to hasten the building of King Solomon's Temple as well as the Master Mason, the skilled masons and their craft apprentices to accomplish the work in stone.

Today, a stone sarcophagus – said to be that of Hiram, is in Beiruit but the only part associated with that Temple which is still standing today, is better known as the Wailing Wall in Jerusalem.

In Beirut I visited the Square of Martyr's, a famous place of buying and   selling – also eating and drinking wine. During the time when under the yoke of the Ottomans (Turkey), fifteen local men were executed here, being accused of terrorist activities, and the Square was later built as a Memorial to them.

I regret that I seemed to have taken no photographs of the Square on this visit. But when visiting Beiruit forty years later, I sought out the site of the Square of Martyrs and discovered that in the various battles fought across Beirut over the years, the Square had been flattened beyond recognition. But here some cargo was loaded – an animal feed product called husks, as far as I recall. At this time, Britain was engaged in helping suppress an insurgency in Borneo brought about by some invaders from Indonesia. Ellermans were contracted to carry supplies to Borneo and there was a possibility that the "Grecian" might be re routed and loaded with urgently required materials already in Alexandria in Egypt. From there she would be sent out East to Borneo via the Suez Canal. However, another ship was found to do the job and that castle tumbled in the air ie the possibility of getting a run through the Suez Canal.

St. Nichola's Cathedral, now the Lala Mustafo Mosque. Note minaret top left. Origin: Author 1961.

Author sitting on the wall on the road linking the Turkish town port of Famagusta with the Greek town of Famagusta, the latter now in Turkish Cyprus and deserted since Cyprus became divided. Note Turkish lady attending to some shopping.

Origin: Stan Pacer 1961.

Above: Close to the Port of Iskenderun, Turkey, it appears sunny, but it was still Winter atop the mountains. Note the snow – and centre right, the crescent, the latter appearing frequently in travel brochures etc. Origin: Author 1961

Further note - see photo two pages back: Othello's Tower, Famagusta, Cyprus, is thus proclaimed on the white notice board above entrance. In one of Shakespeare's plays, one Othello is described as a Moor. The Tower is associated with a Venetian who was Governor here at one time. Author's photo shows a badge above the distance gateway and it appears that this was the badge of Venice – a winged lion! Apparently Shakespeare himself would have known little of Cyprus, and had never visited the place. Origin: Author 1961

Arrival on Juan Fernando Island (now officially known as Robinson Crusoe Island). Home of the Scottish Seaman, Alexander Selkirk who was marooned here in 1704-09.

Actually we were eventually routed back to Famagusta with an almost light ship to load up with potatoes for Glasgow and finally then to Alexandria in Egypt.
When en route Alexandria, we actually crossed the mouth of the Suez Canal – why we were so far south I never knew, and I could only look on wistfully as we passed the Canal mouth with all its perceived mysteries. Reference is made to this again in chapter 19 of this book – see **"Travels in the East".**

Alexandria

The "Grecian" arrived in Alexandria with high hopes for some interesting sights to see in the Land of the Pharaohs – the Land of Gosham. From Alexandria it would have been possible to travel due south by bus – and visit the three great pyramids of Giza,namely Cheops, Chephren and Mycerinus built for father (Cheops), son and grandson. (Their Egyptian names are Khufu, Khafre and Menkaure.) But it was not to be – the main condenser of the engine needed urgent maintenance as it appeared that several tubes were holed thus allowing salt cooling water to enter the feed water to the boilers and had to be repaired. All hands were needed including the Chief Engineer. Even so it was a temporary repair. The leaking tubes were located and their ends were sealed using wooden plugs.These damaged tubes would be replaced when the "Grecian" reached the U.K. where discharging cargo and loading up usually took five days or more – adequate time for maintenance of that sort.
But it would be over forty years, before I saw those Pyramids!

Egypt and Syria were at that time known as the United Arab Republic - the U.A.R. and it was a rigid place as far as visitors were concerned. Photography was strictly forbidden and in reality it may not have been then possible for a foreigner to travel inland. Tourism as we know it today, did not exist. So, eventually with the condenser boxed up again and with little evidence of salt now in the boiler feed water, we sailed for the U.K.
 It was now Springtime and a leisurely ten days or so of steaming, brought us to United Kingdom waters, stopping once at Ceuta in what was then Spanish Morocco (opposite Gibraltar), for fuel. Then, rounding the corner at Gibraltar, it was on to a rather pleasant crossing of the Bay of Biscay, then entering the Irish Sea, past the Tuscar Rock off the south east coast of Eire and close to the ferry port of Rosslare, past Belfast (Belfast Lough being easily recognised on the Bridge radar screen), and past Ailsa Craig to Glasgow on the Clyde in Scotland.

After working by in Glasgow and Liverpool while the old "Grecian" was discharging cargo and loading up, I left the "Grecian" to return home to study and eventually sit for those examinations which I had missed the previous year due to injuries. She was going to only three ports, namely Lisbon in Portugal, Famagusta and Istanbul up the Dardanelles and I was to get cards from all these places.Those examinations as recalled earlier, had been missed following a motor cycle collision with a dog which had crossed my path as I was returning home from work one evening, a short time before I was due to undertake same.
   Following the resulting collision, I had been a "guest" in the Royal Victoria Hospital, Belfast for a time. It was during this "layup" that I decided to get some engineering experience at sea – as described. I was now doing exactly that!.
I was successful in passing these examinations, and following this I did one more trip to sea - in a motor ship, a 1,500 ton, 16 knot ship of Coast Lines - with British Polar twin diesel engines. She was called the "Hibernian Coast." The trips here were of short visits to ports in the U.K., and Dublin in Eire.
(Reference and re acquaintance with this ship is made further on - **see the end of next chapter.**

Engineering work ashore in various capacities followed for several years until appointed to the world of Further Education as a Lecturer in Mechanical Engineering in a very good college - Lisburn Technical College in Co. Antrim. But I was also to meet the old ss "Grecian" again and also the ss " Sicilian," and

Below: The MV "European Gateway."

their crews - and in particular, a few of my former shipmates on the "Grecian," when they docked at times in Belfast over the years - nostalgia indeed. In time, there would also be an interesting development in educational thinking in technical catch up!
Some time during the late 1970's, a scheme was introduced to enable teachers who had no industrial experience to enter industry or commerce for short periods and also to enable technical teachers who had been away from industry for some time, up date progress in technology –

Below: Author in the engine room of the "European Gateway."Orig: 3rd. Eng. Conway.

especially new methods in the "hands on" side of maintenance and manufacture. Some catching up was called for indeed! We had by then moved into an age of electronic controls in manufacturing and automation in ship's engine rooms – even to the extent of unmanned engine rooms in some ships. I had requested that I might have a placement where I might observe something of the latter. So in June 1981, it was arranged for me to observe engine room watch keeping on a very modern cross channel ship, with bridge control of the main engines, variable pitch propellers and an engine room console in which to monitor pressures, temperatures and log any variations that could result in eg excess fuel consumption or other readings that might cause concern – and with technology light years away from that of the old fire tube boilered, triple expansion engined ss "Grecian."
This modern ship was the MV "European Gateway," a Townsend Thoresen ferry with two Stork Werkspoor diesels of 11,000 HP total, and using heavy oil fuel, purified and heated (the latter reducing the Sec number of 900 to 90 Sec.)
 I joined the ship each morning at Larne for the 8 am sailing to Cairnryan and usually I returned to Larne on the 4pm sailing. For reasons of insurance I would not be assuming a watch keeping role but was free to understudy the duties of those who did. There was a lot to study. The console was an insulated sound proof room **inside** the engine room – and virtually every temperature, pressure and condition on board was easily recorded although the five senses of man would still have a significant role to play when one was outside the console. Here the engineers wore ear plugs or ear muffs when an occasion called for them to be outside in the engine room. Electronics in full, was just around the corner. It was a most worthwhile experience. **But the sea was still a dangerous place.**
 Shortly after I returned to my classrooms, the MV **"European Gateway"** was lying on a sand bank at the bottom of the North Sea after being in collision with a freighter there off Felixstowe. Six crew members were lost. Some years later, I was in attendance at a dinner in Islandmagee, Co. Antrim, an area once renowned for producing Marine Captains and Chief Engineers. A stranger, who was sitting beside me, remarked in the midst of a general conversation, that the next day was the seventh anniversary of his father's loss at sea. I casually asked what was the name of his father's ship.
 He told me that the ship was called, the **MV "European Gateway."**

But later in life, I was, in more life like terms, able to sample for myself being a watch keeper again at sea as a summer relief engineer for short voyages with the MacAndrew Company of Liverpool during some of my long summer school vacations.This experience would be on motor ships, as steam had become a very much endangered species and fast disappearing into the history books as a means of moving people and freight. I suppose there was an underlying thought that I might one day have enough sea time to apply to sit for my ticket in either steam or motor. I had a bit of sea time on each, but it would have to be in either one or the other. It was now most unlikely that this could be achieved without resigning my teaching post – which, as a man now with a family, would be considered unrealistic and unwise for me to do.   So "watch this space" for Chapter 10.

Right: Third Engineer Conway - of the **MV "European Gateway."** He appears to be working on what is maybe a fuel filter/ transfer pump. Origin: Author, June 1981		**Note: The mv "European Gateway"** was sunk on December 19th. 1982, but was raised, salvaged and after serving a number of ferry companies, was finally known as the mv "Penelope," and scrapped in 2013. The ship that was in collision with the mv "European Gateway," was the MV "Speedlink Vanguard."

Below: An extract from the author's book, **"Before That Generation Passes,"** where a quotation has been made, as below, from the **"Chart and Compass International."**

Extract:

considered such experience a desirable thing and approval was granted. Further, my satisfaction was total when the Board introduced the "teacher return to industry" scheme, and my last such trip to sea was made in 1981 when I sailed on the ill-fated MV "European Gateway" on the Larne Cairnryan run for a period - and was given leave during term time to do so. The "European Gateway" was lost through a collision in the North Sea afterwards. (All this was in the future.)

Six die as ferries collide off Felixstowe

"The European Gateway ferry disaster Illustrated the breadth and importance of the work of the Felixstowe Sea-farers' Centre. On the day before the fatal collision, Rev Malcolm Pears had held a service on board "European Gateway". They sang hymns, read verses of Scripture and said prayers. A few hours later tragedy claimed the lives of six seafarers and the same Chaplain spent many hours comforting bereaved relatives."

('From the Chart and Compass International' - British Sailors Society, Summer 1983).

The loss of life affecting British Merchant Navy members in the Second World War is often given as 30,000 – and mostly in the North Atlantic Ocean. A loss like this is barely comprehensible. Even today in peacetime, a ship larger than a fishing trawler, is lost somewhere on average, in the world each week. Below, the seafarer's hymn:

Eternal Father,strong to save ,
Whose arn doth bind the restless wave,
Who bidd'st the mighty ocean deep
Its own appointed limits keep;
Oh hear us when we cry to Thee
For those in peril on the sea

Oh Trinity of love and power,
Our brethren shield in danger's hour ;
From rock and tempest, fire and foe,
Protect them wheresoe'er they go:
Thus evermore shall rise to thee
Glad hyms of praise from land and sea.

William Whiting 1825 – 1878.

Chapter 3

Humour – even on a visit to the USSR:

I had become interested with the changes in social, political and industrial life which must have followed the advent of technological advance in mid nineteenth century Britain. It had all come about because of the Industrial Revoluton which some see as beginning in the mid eighteenth century. It had therefore taken quite a time to develop.

This advance had of course followed in the wake of the Industrial Revolution, and some of this in turn, had accelerated and expanded greatly in time of, for example, the 1914-18 war.

I was some years into my teaching career in Mechanical Engineering before I began to look at where we –the "men of the hammer and file brigade" had come from and crawled out into the open! Arguably, there had been more progress and advance in technology between the time – mid nineteenth century when Bessemer had first used his converter for the industrial manufacture of steel, to the present era - than in the previous two thousand years.

At the start of this period in time,Britain had launched the S.S. "Great Britain" in Bristol. It was the first steamer of its size (albeit with sail retention), to have a propeller. It was probably also the first time such a vessel had been used as a troopship, when, shortly, the "Great Britain" was so used in the Crimean War (1854 –1856).

Britain was here in the middle of her industrial revolution.

H.Q. Communist Party, Kremlin, Moscow.
Author 1987

I had undertaken some studies at the Open University which would cover the history of science and technology from about the time referred to above, and which would also take on board the inevitable historical change in politics that had been emerging - with a so called industrial 'middle class' arriving on the scene. It was to be with considerable reluctance that the cash strapped aristocracy of Britain, rubbed shoulders with these wealthy newcomers to the social scene!

Shortly, even another class would make its voice heard – the " working class " – or *proletariat.*

Part of my study included a fairly large section on "Politics of the Soviet Union." When I started upon this latter, it never entered my mind, that all this would soon be history itself indeed, and that the blue and white flag of Imperial Russia would soon replace the Red Flag. But first, I decided that I had better have a look at something of this very large country.

My first visit to the U.S.S.R.

I first visited the U.S.S.R. during 1974, and seeing Odessa and Yalta, (both in the Ukraine).This was during the "bad" old days of Leonid Brezhnev.

This huge land mass is said to occupy one sixth of the surface of the Earth. In fact, Dr. Hewlett Johnston, at one time Archbishop of Canterbury and whose left wing politics earned for him the title of the "The Red Dean of Canterbury," wrote a book after the Russian Revolution which he called "The Socialist Sixth of the World." In the realm of politics, he had Socialist views on things. But with the benefits revealed by the passing years, many now see how the Red Dean, George Bernard Shaw and others who visited the Soviet Union in deference to Stalin, had the wool well and truly pulled over their eyes! Stalin, eventually First Secretary of the Communist Party of the USSR, only showed them the things he wanted them to see! They saw well fed children – but none of the thousands of those being deliberately starved to death by the Bolshoviks. These were the children of those deemed "well to do"and named Kuluks. If a Kuluk owned a horse or a plough, he was considered a capitalist and most likely a candidate for a ticket for Siberia.

By contrast, Georg Orwell had given us a different perspective on the things he saw there - eg in his book, "Animal Farm." Another book which brought him considerable fame was, namely, "The Road to Wigan Pier."

Travels in Odessa and Yalta, cities in the Ukraine.
Arrival in Odessa

The only Russian Orthodox Church in Yalta still open – note faded yellow onion domes. left. mid centre. Author: 1974

Above: The children's guard of honour at entrance to the Sailor's War Memorial (with everlasting flame), Odessa, U S.S.R on the Black Sea.
Flanking the avenue, are the graves of well known resistance leaders who fell during the struggle against the Nazis in the Second World War. Note the *solemn bearing of* these *young people* .

Source: Author 1974

Left: Lenin: Such a photo was once a common sight in the U.S.S.R. He is not wearing his cap here !

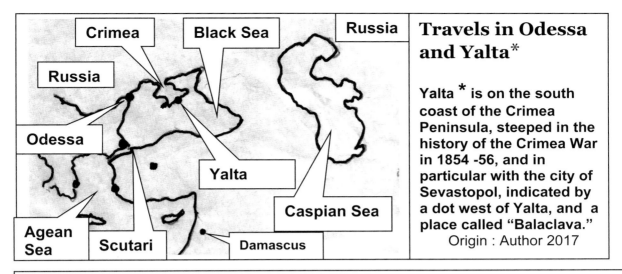

Travels in Odessa and Yalta*

Yalta * is on the south coast of the Crimea Peninsula, steeped in the history of the Crimea War in 1854 -56, and in particular with the city of Sevastopol, indicated by a dot west of Yalta, and a place called "Balaclava."
Origin : Author 2017

(Map labels: Crimea, Black Sea, Russia, Russia, Odessa, Yalta, Caspian Sea, Agean Sea, Scutari, Damascus)

My visit referred to above, was made by ship, passing through the Dardanelles Straits in Turkey, thence into the Sea of Marmora, where one could see the former hospital of Florence Nightingale at Scutari (which is approximately opposite Istanbul - see sketch) as one enters the Bosporus Straits to join the Black Sea, then due north, eventually to make a landfall at the port of Odessa in that part of the then U.S.S.R. known as the Ukraine.

The Crimea was later reached at Yalta in the extreme southeast of the Crimea Peninsula, an area steeped in the history of the Crimea War in 1854 – 56, and in particular with the city of Sevastopol. Early travels here were indeed in the "bad" old days of Leonid Brezhnev. Both these places - Odessa and especially Yalta, lay close to the former battlefields of the Crimean War, but visits to places like Balaclava, the scene of " – into the valley of death, rode the gallant six hundred," was out of the question at this time. Today, of course, there is no such problem – you just need American dollars as I discovered when Perestroika, (restructuring) was in vogue as I was to discover later around 1987. The Russians were now – in 1987, very glad indeed to see anyone coming in with dollars to spend . (Actually it was always so, but they did not openly broadcast the fact.)

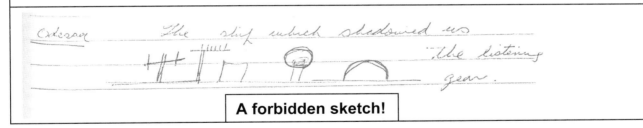

A forbidden sketch!

Extract: "The approaches to Soviet ports during the'cold war ' was occasioned by our being 'escorted' into Yalta, by a destroyer bristling with all kinds of surveillance and listening hardware on its deck. Photography of such a vessel was strictly forbidden, although I'm sure someone took a snap from behind a port hole! I couldn't resist sketching something of what I had seen – see insert above. It was 8.30 a.m. when we made fast at Yalta, and already crowds of Soviet citizens were lining the port barriers. Few would ever be allowed any closer to the West than this barrier.   Yalta was known as a sanatorium town, and these folk were probably enjoying a holiday – possibly for a month, and only available to privileged active Party (Communist) card carrying members. For such a large land mass, the U.S.S.R. has a very short length of warm water coast line, much of this on the *Black Sea" coast.*"Thus a break in the sun would be seen as a priviledge – for the relative few.

* *From " Before that Generation Passes."*
Origin: Author, written in 2001.

The Winter Palace in Leningrad, (now again St. Petersburg) – and stormed by the Bolsheviks in 1917. Origin: Author 1985.

The Magnificant blue and white Cathedral of the Smolny Convent, Leningrad, now of course, St. Petersburg. Source: Author 1985.

Author at the well known piece of sculpture known as "The Worker and Peasant," Yalta, 1974.

Author at the Chekov Memorial, Yalta, 1985.

Above: The HQ of the Communist Party, Moscow. Source: Author:

Left : Author outside the Lividia Palace, Yalta. *Origin: Author 1974*

Palace of Peter the Great, Gulf of Finland. Source: Author: 1985

(2) Scots at the court of Peter the Great - but nobody appeared to find them out of place! *Source: Author 1985.*

(3) The Tsar's Bell in disaster mode ! 1735. Excess water, used following a fire in the foundary after casting caused the bell to crack.
Source: Author 1985.

This is the "back up" rocket, for the original one that put the first Sputnik into space. Moscow Science Space Museum. *Origin: Author 1985*

This is a "back up" Soviet moon buggy, but it was never required. As seen in the Moscow Science Space Museum.
Author 1985

Return to the land of the Tsars ,1987.

Following my 1974 visit to the USSR in Leonid Brezhnev's time, I was in the "new country of Russia," thirteen years later. The countries that formerly made up the U.S.S.R had largely broken away when Perestroika, (restructuring) was beginning under Mikhail Gorbachov, the then Soviet President. I first visited Leningrad – so named after the revolution in 1917 to honour Lenin, the Bolshevik leader.
It had also been known at other times as St. Petersburg (after Peter the Great), then Petrograd – as it was at the time of the revolution. Following the collapse of communism after 70 years, it was again St Petersburg. Travel was also made to Rostov on the river Don, Yalta in the Ukraine, and finally, Moscow. Perestroika notwithstanding, Russia was still not a place to look for smiles on people's faces, and humour was difficult to find. I was advised to take a bar of Cadbury's fruit and nut - as a gift for our guide. It was good advice!

My early memories during that visit to Leningrad, are to do with water – not surprising perhaps, as this great city was built on marshy ground, and there are many canals to be seen. Originally named, as mentioned above, St. Petersburg, after Peter the Great, it was the premier city of Russia (and the adjoining nations which had found themselves under Russian jurisdiction) for hundreds of years. When the communists came to power in 1917, they moved the capital to Moscow, presumably to separate the new government more completely from the seat of power once sat in by the Tsars. Russia is, and has been, an amazing place. Covering six time zones, it was not until the late nineteenth century that the peasantry were, officially at least, released from serfdom (in the emancipation pronouncement of 1861). Indeed, the privileged, ruling classes had themselves been under an obligation to support and serve the Tsar, an obligation that seems only to have been removed or at least become conditional, in the previous century. The Tsar's rule was absolute, an autocratic monarch who, according to a dictate inherited from Peter the Great, "was to give account of his ruling to no one on earth"------- and that ruling, was to be according to his "own will and judgement !"

There is much to see in Leningrad, now St. Petersburg. Probably all visitors will want to see the Winter Palace, stormed by the Bolsheviks in 1917, or visit the " Aurora," the Russian cruiser moored nearby - see photograph on next page, which it is believed, fired the shot (some say it was a blank), which signalled that storming the palace was about to begin. The Hermitage Museum is a vast collection of artefacts and priceless art, and often a must on the tourist itinerary. One may travel from here on the Gulf of Finland by hydrofoil, to visit the Palace of Peter the Great – as I did, now fully restored after being virtually razed to the ground by the retreating Nazis. It must not be forgotten, that Leningrad itself withstood a siege by the Nazis, lasting two and a half years.

The Russian battleship "Aurora" anchored in the River Neva, St. Petersburg (formerly Leningrad) as seen in 2008. Unfortunately the ship was in dry dock at the time of my visit and I did not see the " Aurora." To the "Aurora" goes the distinction of having fired the opening shot of the October Revolution in 1917 (according to some reports it was a blank). Blank or live, the shot signalled the storming of the Winter Palace in the city. This photograph shows an interesting flag up forward!

Photograph: Mr. Martin Sloan, Newtownards, Co. Down, N. Ireland.

Moscow

The day that I arrived in Moscow was not a good one for the Ministry of Defence in the old U.S.S.R., but this had nothing to do with me! Because a mere twenty-four hours before, the defences of the Soviet Union had been breached and an East German had flown a light aircraft under the Soviet radar, and had landed the aircraft at the bottom of Red Square,near the Lenin Museum. It didn't take long before the pilot was bundled off to prison, but the authorities in the Kremlin were now advanced to high alert. One felt under personal surveillance out on the streets of Moscow that day, and if you had to stop to tie a shoe lace, why - you felt that some guy wearing a cap with a large high peak, would soon be over to see what you were doing!

Inside the Kremlin.

The next day I was on a conducted tour of the Kremlin, which lies behind that wall in Red Square. At the top of Red Square, it was through the entrance there under the clock tower, that past generations of the communist party elite, proceeding at great speed in their Zil cars to the government offices in the Kremlin, had often been filmed by TV crews.

The Headquarters of the former communist party was there, as were a number of important church buildings, the latter always almost compulsory on the guided tours hit lists. At the time of communist rule, they had been turned into museums, but by now, may well have been restored as places of worship. (I was in a church – a Russian Orthodox one, in Moscow on one occasion, when worship was actually taking place). The Kremlin is a city within a city, a kind of Russian Vatican.

During the Cold War, in Britain a significant number of Russian spies or even possibly British citizens spying for the Russians, were apprehended and ended up being given lengthy prison sentences. For their part, the Russians apprehended a relatively small number of Britons, mostly guilty only of some minor infringements of regulations – train spotting near a sensitive area of aero test flying, or photographing of facilities at some minor port etc. This offence could be judged worthy of a prison sentence and could end up with a train spotter being exchanged for an atom spy. In the next two pages will be seen photographs of the docks in Odessa. The photo of the steps looking outwards - showing the docks and shipping etc. contravened Russian regulations. The photo of the Potemkin Steps looking inwards, is permissible.

Author in Red Square, Moscow in the area where the light aircraft landed the previous day!
See notes (1) and (2).

The monument to a Russian World World Two Machine Gun Company, near Rostock on the River Don, South Russia.
Origin: Author 1987

Fountains at Peter the Great's Palace on the Gulf of Finland. Origin: Author

A typical Cossack house near Rostock, on the River Don.
Origin: Author 1987

Notes *(1) Previous page: **Red Square Moscow**. Author is standing on the spot at the bottom of Red Square, where the light aircraft, flown by an East German landed, after flying*

in below the Russian radar the previous day. At the top of the photo, can be seen St. Basil's Cathedral. To the right is the Spasskaya clock tower, under which past U.S.S.R. rulers sped in their Zil cars into the Kremlin, behind the wall on right. They really were driven in at very high speed indeed – the road had to be cleared!

(2) The man who took this photograph of me was on vacation in Moscow. He came.
from the Russian island of Sakhalin, off the Pacific coast of the U.S.S.R., and near Japan.

The Potemkin Steps: When taken, this photograph – showing the docks, contravened Soviet laws. Origin: A friend in London.

When taken, this photograph –looking away from the docks (sensitive area) was within Soviet law. Orig:The London friend.

Referring to a previous comment relating to taking liberties in foreign countries, no matter how small such things might seem to us, yet, when in regimes - like what the Iron Curtain countries were like, it could be a serious business indeed. Suspicion was everywhere.

It is indeed quite true that in the past, Westerners, apprehended on a trivial matter, could find themselves a pawn in some exchange, relating to a genuine Eastern spy. Even within the European community, countries have reacted quite viciously recently, where train or plane spotters were judged to have contravened some - perhaps local regulation.

And the U.S.S.R. really was not the place for light hearted pranks of any description, full stop!

Now the photographs above, taken in 1975, show the "Potemkin Steps" in Odessa. Being a port, it was sensitive photography wise, and it is not difficult to see why. In England, during the build up to D day in 1944, for example, anyone who had holiday snaps taken during holidays pre 1939 in France – in particular of beach areas, was asked to let the planners for the invasion examine them. Five hundred were forwarded. For the same reason, the U.S.S.R. authorities would only permit photographs of the "Potemkin Steps" in Odessa, to be taken looking towards the land, as in the one on right, with author standing on the steps – safe from apprehension!

Now on the other hand, the one which my friend Owen took, showing the port layout - ah now, that is one that I'm sure would have called for some censure indeed! (Needless to say, I'm very glad that Owen did the decent thing and got me this excellent photograph!)

Note: The Potemkin Steps in Odessa, take their name from the pre – revolution battleship "Potemkin," which was seized by Russian sailors in a revolutionary demonstration in 1905. Later, however, these steps were the scene of a massacre of men, women, and children, when the Tsar's army and police fired on them, during a demonstration there in1905. Subsequently the Soviet film producer, Eisenstien, made the famous film, "Battleship Potemkin," in 1925.

*   *   *   *

During that visit to Moscow in 1987, I, and the other members of the group I was with, were told by the management of our hotel that two Russian academics – professors of economics or something akin, would like to meet with us, and in particular, to share in an exchange of views and values on any subject we choose.

Most in the party agreed to do so, and we met across a large oval table, where the Russians, speaking good English, initially engaged at a fairly low level of cultural exchange – did we own a car, how many square metres of living accommodation did we have, the size of the average family in the U.K. etc. Then up a stage to inquire our views on an integrated Europe, etc.

Here some of our people with elevated notions about economics engaged them at some length, while all the while I pondered the possibility of being able to make some intelligent contribution to the proceedings. So I suggested to our Russian companions that it seemed harsh justice to many of us, that only one man was deemed responsible for the Chernobyl disaster and sentenced to twenty five years in gaol, when there must have been many more who were guilty.

 One of the Russians elected to answer my comment.

"You know," he said, "you Western people have a strange sense of justice. Around the same time as we were having our problems at Chernobyl, a ferry, having just left Harbour, capsized after a crew member had left the bow doors open – and this was not noticed either by the ship's Captain or his officers! One hundred and sixty five passengers and crew lost their lives. To date, not one person has been charged with their deaths."

We could only agree that he had a point there! No one was ever subsequently convicted or deemed responsible for the sinking, on March 6th 1987 of this ship, which was called the "Herald of Free Enterprise." As these lines were being written today, the 6th March, 2017, people in Dover, England, and in Zeebrugge, Belguim, were holding services of commemoration on the 30th Anniversary of the tragedy.

The Russians seemed pleased with having met us.

As we retired from our meeting, I shared the lift with one of the Russian professors, and got a brief insight into what they knew of my country! He inquired as to where I came from, and upon hearing that I came from Northern Ireland, he immediately asked the question: "Are you a prod?"

I must say that I was taken aback – mildly!

It is likely, that such expressions are now taught there as idioms of our speech. Years before, I once heard a Russian lady say, "There are more ways of skinning a cat than one!" Later, I was enlightened that such was probably taught in a foreign language class which even might have given priority to teach another country's sayings, euphemisms etc.

I never thought that the communist regime in the U.S.S.R., the history of which I had partly studied, would ever have come to an end during my lifetime. However, it collapsed like a pack of cards.

Today, in 2017, I often wonder if it could have regrouped!

 But viewers of television at Christmas 2003, watched in amazement as the former Beetle, Paul McCartney, rocked Red Square, Moscow, with Beetles' music and his own solo compositions. When all this was being filmed in May 2003, thousands gathered, and it was then claimed by prominent Russian artists, that Beetles' music, secretly enjoyed for years by as many as could lay their hands on a record, had played a prominent part in bringing about such a change – through a perceived message of freedom, in the style and words. Prominent members of the Russian Government, including president Putin and his Minister of Foreign Affairs appeared in what seemed an approving role, and Paul McCartney, the former Beetle in greeting former President Gorbachov, was heard to say to him, " You are a great man."

It had been an amazing transition in the affairs of the former U.S.S.R. and its satellite states. Church bells were again calling the people to worship, but it is hard to know what the ordinary Russian people are thinking. Moderate and friendly voices seem, in 2017, to be some way off in the distance.

Chapter 4

Egypt – land of the pharaohs.

On the trail of the children of Israel.

Alexandria:

I have been in my lifetime, in some part of Egypt on six separate visits. The first was, as recorded earlier, when I was an engineer on a steamer, the S.S. "Grecian," in Jan. 1961, that time on the "Grecian" being described in Chapter Two. On the other occasions, I arrived as a tourist.
First, a recap on that first visit as described in, *"Before That Generation Passes," Author 2001.*

Extract: *" We were arriving at Alexandria in Egypt where I had hoped to set off in search of the Pyramids of Giza - if free time was available. Earlier that morning, I had washed some of my clothes –shirts etc, and all were hung up to dry on a line above the engine room deck head. But it was not going to be possible to visit the Pyramids as all hands had to turn to - including the Chief engineer, in order to carry out vital maintenance, especially on the leaking main condenser. When I returned to the "laundry" later to collect my washing, the cupboard was bare. I soon discovered that the thieving locusts had carried all before them – nobody had warned me about them. It was well known by all but utter greenhorns, that you had to have everything under lock and key while in the port of Alexandria. "*
From: **"Before That Generation Passes**," Author 2001.

Sinai, Mount Sinai, and St. Catharine's Monastery

I was now in 1977 to make a modest acquaintance with part of the Biblical Land of Egypt namely the peninsula known as Sinai – and in furtherance to that visit of 1961as a crew member of a ship. Other visits would soon cross paths which at times were used by the Children of Israel on their Exodus, and would eventually take me to a place, which would be as far as one particular Israelite would go. This Israelite was Aaron, the brother of Moses, and the place – the Biblical city of Sela or Seir, which today is known as Petra. Aaron is buried near Petra, on the top of the mountain named after him – at least locally so. It is called Jabal Harun, and can be easily seen by passing travellers in that region.

A Step Back In Time. Sinai had been captured from the Egyptians in the 1967 war, so I had travelled to Tel Aviv, in Israel, arriving very late at night where I slept on the floor of the airport until morning. My travel to Jerusalem by bus was along that road which, for Israelis, immortalises the Israeli struggle in the 1948 war. It commerates battles fought along this road, through the relics of their wrecked vehicles. These vehicles, now painted black, have become monuments, and left for posterity at the scenes of ambushes of Israeli relief convoys travelling to Jerusalem. When available, steel plates were fitted to these vehicles making them the nearest thing they had to an Israeli armoured car.
Some are now, I believe, in a museum – under cover.

Thus, when I visited South Sinai in 1977, it was by travelling onto the peninsula from Eliat in Israel to do so.

I had stopped over in accommodation at St. Andrews Church of Scotland Hostel in Jerusalem, where rooms are mostly always readily available for anyone. It was a short distance south of the Jaffa gate.

The church in itself, is a memorial to the Scottish soldiers who, under General Allenby, died during the capture of Jerusalem from the Turks in 1917.

After an overnight stay at Eliat - in the extreme south of Israel, I joined an organised group of people all intent on climbing Mt. Sinai and visiting St. Catherin's Monastery, close to the mountain. We would be in the hands of Israeli guides.

Using vehicles – something like Land Rovers, we set off for Sinai via a small resort described nowadays in holiday brochures as the "Coral Island," and popular with coral seekers and other sun worshipers.

Sadly, in 2004, this little resort, now of course back under Egyptian control, received the attention of the bombers, and sadly, there were casualties.

The terrain of the Sinai Peninsula - and we were heading to South Sinai, is not likely to be thought of as another Wimbledon tennis court. North Sinai, while relatively flat and considered good tank country, has its share of sand, shale and rocks, but South Sinai, where we were headed, consists of rocky hills and wadi, around which the traveller has to wind first this way, and then that way, in a seemingly endless series of loops. There were Germans, Americans and at least one Danish traveller that I recall in our party, and we travelled in three vehicles. With the temperature in the afternoon said to be 140 ° F, we were instructed by our Israeli guides to drink, drink, drink. The water was being carried in a number of four gallon plastic cans, due to be replenished at the St Catherin's Monastery.

We had to sleep out of doors on the warm desert sand that first night. The spot chosen where we could partake of an evening meal, was near the dwelling of one Raschid – see later photographs, a Bedouin of Sinai, complete, he informed us, with three wives. I only saw one of them – at a distance, and they lived, apparently, at separate accommodations. Then, the Israeli guides showed us his "garden" – a number of twig like trees, but referred to as pear, plum etc.

Author on Mount Sinai, where Moses received the Ten Commandments. This photo was taken shortly before the sun appeared over the mountain – when cameras started to roll. 1977

But then they also showed us something else – really something else. This was his swimming pool! Imagine a land "wherein no water is" – yet standing there on the desert floor, was a rectangular wall structure, perhaps of 10m x 5m dimensions and over 1m high – and filled with cool, fresh, water! It was not long before we were all in, happily splashing about (see the photograph!). I think we all knew that it had little to do with Rachid. Tourism, promoted by the Israelis, was making inroads into Sinai in a big way. And I could never imagine Rachid ever using ithe pool!

After supper – a very good chicken and rice creation cooked by the guides, Raschid produced his fiddle – a one stringed instrument made from an empty one gallon petrol can, with a wooden shaft protruding out of the cap! He then proceeded to entertain!

I do not seem to have put on record , what it was like! Looking back afterwards, I concluded that we had indeed been at a staging post for the blossoming tourist industry. The Israelis Authorities I'm sure, had set Rachid up, had built the "swimming pool," and piped in the fresh water – but from where?

They must have had an artesian source available and it goes without saying that it was indeed a most convenient place to stop overnight.

(Some years later, when watching a BBC television documentary, I saw to my complete astonishment, our very own Raschid being interviewed, complete with that one gallon petrol can fiddle - with its single string !)

Some lands, where it is hot during the daytime, experience a sharp drop in temperature as night approaches - with no clouds about to help retain the heat. But here the night was, as earlier mentioned, warm, and we went to sleep on the desert floor, slept well, and set off the next morning at about four am to drive to Mount Sinai – and climb the mountain!

During the completion of the rocky climb to the top - albeit in a leisurely manner, we saw the sun rise in the East. Mount Sinai (or Mount Horeb) is 7,500 feet above sea level and during the climb, we passed a plaque which stated that here -

"The Lord our God made a covenant with us in Sinai and the Lord handed down to Moses the Ten Commandments." (see photograph on previous page.)

The climb, winding upwards along a gravel path (with deposits of coarser rubble to get over at times), had been planned to coincide with the sunrise – a favourite photo opportunity for the many who climb Mount Sinai. **The moment the sun rose over Sinai, the cameras would start whirring.**

Then the descent (using a different route), was made down a series of steps – three thousand, seven hundred and fifty of them!

St. Catherine's Monastery from Mount Sinai, with rocks in every direction.   Author 1977.

Below us, with another wonderful photo opportunity, was the Monastery of St. Catherine, complete in the form one sees today but built during the period, 542 – 551 A.D. The wooden doors at the church entrance are, according to the authorities at St. Catherine's, 1,400 years old. Surprisingly, there is also a mosque in the complex. This was probably built during a period of Arab conquest in thein the area - perhaps to placate less benevolent rulers!

During the turbulent years of the past, visitors seeking admission were hauled up thirty feet in a basket using a winding mechanism in order to be allowed to enter. If the monks did not like what they saw in the basket, they let it down very quickly indeed!

We would, however, be allowed to enter at ground level, the walls of St. Catherine's being between 30 and 60 feet high! The two arms for the winding structure used and referred to above, are still there to be seen today – right in front of the building, above a now unused door. But no one I know who has been there, has ever thought of photographing them –including myself !

Later we had a tour of the Monastery – a Greek Orthodox Monastical Centre with a continuous life since the 6th century. There was a small garden, and in it, was a single grave.

No ordinary grave indeed, but one, that reputedly had received the remains of all the deceased monks who, in turn, had lived there over the years. Here a body remained, until eventually, in a state of decay, the skull was removed and placed in the house of skulls -

the charnel house, an external underground repository, reached by a short flight of steps, but usually out of bounds to visitors.

It is not unknown of course, for someone at times to sneak down and take a photograph! What happened to the rest of such a body, we were not told and this remains something of a mystery or – just left to one's imagination!

However, if one happened to be a Bishop, the complete skeleton, clothed in a Bishop's regalia, would be placed upright in the church within the Monastery, as we were to see presently. This church was in beautiful condition.

The reason for such a procedure with the grave, lies in the fact that there was and still is simply no other suitable ground available – pure rock all around, and the rest of the small garden was required for vegetables.

The Monastery or, more correctly, that part known as the "Chapel of the Burning Bush," stands on the traditional site of the "Burning Bush." Now a bush was found there, and described by a woman pilgrim, one Etheria from Spain, in the 4th century. She gave it the name "Burning Bush," and it flourishes until this day – just to the East outside the chapel, but inside the walls of the Monastery. It was transplanted there, so that the holy altar of the chapel could be built upon its roots. It has, apparently, never been possible to transplant it to any where outside of Sinai, and it is the only bush of its kind growing in the entire Sinai Peninsula. From memory, it was about the size of a large black currant bush. As the symbol of the Presbyterian Church in Ireland, it held a special interest for me and the Americans.

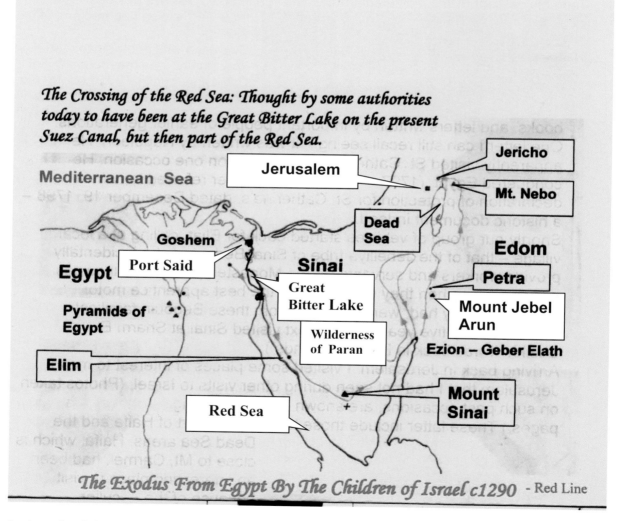

The Crossing of the Red Sea: Thought by some authorities today to have been at the Great Bitter Lake on the present Suez Canal, but then part of the Red Sea.

The Exodus From Egypt By The Children of Israel c1290 - Red Line

Just north of the Monastery Church but inside the ancient walls, one is shown the well where Moses helped the seven daughters of Jethro, the priest of Midian, to water their

flocks – after his escape from Egypt. He then worked for the priest of Midian – and in return was given a wife! Her name was Zipporah. (see Exodus Ch. 2., v 16 – 21.)
In Exodus Ch. 3, v 2, is found how God later made himself known unto Moses:
"And the angel of the Lord appeared onto him in a flame of fire out of the midst of a bush: and he looked, and, behold, the bush burned with fire, and the bush was not consumed."
Thus, many centuries later, the "Burning Bush" became the symbol of the Presbyterian Church in Ireland.
The children of Israel are thought to have crossed into South Sinai in the 13th century B.C. and moved down to Elim. This is believed to be the present El-Tur, with its 12 wells and 70 date palms, on the Gulf of Suez, (Red Sea), and West across from Mt. Sinai (see Exodus 15:27).

       *   *   *   *

Fifty days after their departure from Egypt, they reached the sacred Mount Horeb (or Mount Sinai), and received God's Law. Another prophet, Elijah, came to this area, 600 years later, fleeing from the rage of one Queen Jezebel, and lodged in a cave on Mount Horeb, also called Mount Sinai – see 1st. Kings19: verse 8. Referring to St. Catherine's again, one can say that for such an isolated outpost of civilisation (apart from the associations referred to in the past), it has important contributions for today. For example , the library of the Monastery is second in importance only to that of the Vatican, in both the number and the value of the number and the value of the manuscripts

Masada fortress : Here the Jews committed mass suicide as preferable to compromise with their Roman rulers - see later script.   Courtesy of Wikipedia.

it contains. Of the 3,000 items, two-thirds are in Greek, while the rest are in Arabic, Syriac, Georgian, Armenian, Coptic, Ethiopian, and Slavonic. The library also contains some 5,000 books, and letters written by important people of earlier generations. One letter I can still recall seeing – it was written by Napoleon! He apparently visited St. Catherine's Monastery on one occasion. He conquered Egypt (1797 – 1804) and the letter referred to, was a declaration of protection for St. Catherine's, dated December 19, 1798 – a historic document indeed.
Shortly our group of vehicles started back for Eliat, calling at a local village – that of the Jebelliya tribe of Sinai Bedouin (who incidentally provide workers and servants for the Monastery). Our Israeli guides surprised us, when they revealed that the best apprentice motor mechanics they had, were recruited from these Bedouin families! (When, twenty-five years later, I next visited Sinai at Sharm El Sheikh, it was in Egyptian hands.)
But now, arriving back in Jerusalem, I visited some places that I had not seen before – as for example, a visit to the Dead Sea.
Photos taken on other occasions eg on other visits to Israel made later, are also on the following pages and these latter also include those taken, for example, in the port of Haifa.
To get to old Jerusalem from St. Andrew's – where I stayed for a few days after returning from Sinai, one passed a number of places where accommodation was also available – one Franciscan, one at the Y.M.C.A.,and one affiliated to the Church of England. This route also

led to the Jaffa Gate (through which General Allenby and Lawrence of Arabia - Col. T.E. Lawrence passed following the capture of Jerusalem in 1917.)

The port of Haifa, which is close to Mt.Carmel, was an interesting place to visit because of the peculiar structure of the city – built on three separate elevations. It is 20 miles from Muhraka on the Carmel mountain range and within sight of the traditional site where Elijah the Prophet had his famous and successful contest against the false prophets of Baal.There the Bible relates how he slew the four hundred and fifty false prophets of Baal (see 1ST. Kings Ch. 18, v 40). Also, note in the same book, Ch. 19 v 8, where he later fled into Sinai, to Mt. Horeb, to escape wrath of one Jezebel, wife of Ahab, King of Israel – both of whom worshipped Baal. Again in reference to Jerusalem, close to the Jaffa Gate one could also see the King David Hotel. This had been blown up by the Jewish Stern Gang just before the 1948 war, which latter event confirmed the parameters of the State of Israel.

(These were in a somewhat different form, to the arrangements proposed for them following the ending of the British Mandate in 1948!

One could spend a long time looking at the ancient Biblical sites in the land of Israel, and they are interesting in different ways. One, at Qumran, near the northern coast of the Dead Sea, is where, as pointed out in the following photographs, the Dead Sea scrolls were found. Then, about half way down the Dead Sea coast, is Ein Gedi, where David hid in a cave to escape King Saul's wrath. Just south of Ein Gedi, is Masada, where Herod's magnificent palace and fortress stood. It was to be the site of the last heroic Jewish stand against the Romans in 73 AD, and the mass suicide of its 960 defenders. It can be plainly seen by anyone passing in a bus, a Jewish fortress perched on a rock pinnacle. Inaccessible, but the Romans overcome this by an approach ramp – it is still there today!

But just now I wish to return to that hope in 1961 when at Alexandria. From there, I had hoped to see the Pyramids - but I was to wait a long time before I saw Pyramids – in fact, not until 1993! This is how that came about. This is what happened when that hope – turned to realisation!

★   ★   ★   ★   ★   ★

The Pyramids of Giza.

In 1993, I travelled to Alexandria again – this time by taking brief passage on a cruise ship, the MV "Agean Spirit " whose itinerary would enable me to strike inland at Alexandria, visit the Great Pyramids and Cairo and then rejoin my 'carriage' at Port Said.

Upon sailing from the Greek port of Piraeus (the port of Athens), the "Agean Spirit" passed a well known Italian liner, the "Achilles Lauro" (with its all black hull and white upperworks),and which was docked there. Some time before, this ship had featured in a high jacking, during which an American invalid man was pushed overboard by the highjackers.

But a few weeks after leaving Piraeus, the "Achilles Lauro" was at the bottom of the Indian Ocean, following a fire at sea that had raged out of control.

Presently, I got into conversation with a man who earlier had asked if he could have some of my sun lotion, to save him a trip back to his cabin. An interesting man he turned out to be indeed, not least his being a veteran of the Second World War, in fact a veteran of the Eighth Army. He would soon be in familiar territory – in the Sahara desert!

I had met Bill Kinnock, the uncle of Neil Kinnock, the former leader of the British Labour party. Shortly we would travel in the same bus to the Great Pyramids of Giza, a journey of about one hundred miles from Alexandria.

Upon arrival in Alexandria, we boarded a bus and travelled south to Giza, through what our guide called the "Sahara Desert " - which I suppose was technically correct , albeit being through the extreme Eastern Sahara. The area of Giza is home to the three Great Pyramids – built as resting places for, in descending order of size with the Egyptian name in brackets - the Pharaohs Cheops (Khufu), Chephren (Khafre), and Mycerinus (Menkaure) – father, son, and grandson. The largest, Cheops, was about 150 metres in height when constructed, but over the years, has become a few metres shorter, now being 146.5 metres in height. That of Chephren is about 3 metres shorter than the Cheops Pyramid, and is the only one to retain some of the original limestone (or marble) cladding on its apex – all the rest having been removed from the Pyramids for the buildings in nearby Cairo (about 3 miles away) many years ago. The Sphinx, thought to have a facial likeness to Chephren (on what basis for this I know not), has extremely large paws, and is close to the Pyramid of Chephren.

Note: **Thought to have been built between 2600 B.C. and 2500 B.C., the Great Pyramid is 150 metres in height, contains 9 million tons of rock, and the Cathedrals of Florence, Milan, St. Peter's (Rome), and Westminster Abbey would fit into its base area.**

During the bus journey to Giza, our guide drew attention to the possibility of claustrophobia for some who might have wished to visit the inside of the Great Pyramid or that of the others. It was explained that it was quite a long distance in the tunnel leading to the stone sarcophagus on which a Pharaoh would have been laid. In the event, the Great Pyramid of Cheops was closed that day, but that of Chephren was open for tourists. I decided to enter and found that the passages in the Pyramid of Chephren were big enough to stand up in, and wide enough to permit people to pass one another with electric light to show the way. All traces of the bodies, along with the wealth buried with them, has long since disappeared of course – probably the main reason for the decision for later burials to be underground. This is what happened in the Valley of the Kings near Luxor, five hundred miles away to the south, where the tombs were hidden underground - for example, that of Tutankhamun. There was a lot of security presence around the Pyramids that day, terrorist activity being evident in the country. In fact, an English tourist was shot dead at Luxor – 500 miles south, on that very day, and in the near future, some Germans tourists were to die when attacked by gunmen at the Memorium Temple of Hatshepsut, (one of only two woman ever to come a Pharaoh), in the Valley of the Queens.

Right above: The face of the Sphnix showing the deliberate damage caused to it.He needs a face lift!
Yet the Sphinx seems to be smiling through it all!
Source: From a photograph taken by J. Marshall, London, 1993.

Left: The camel drivers await the tourists, at the Great Pyramid of Giza. There was an Egyptian security presence at the Pyramids, to control the terrorist threats – and, at times, those of the camel drivers, persistent at times to sell their wares!
Source:.J. Marshall,London 1993.

I would have thought that few would have suffered from claustrophobia during our visit to the Pyramid of Chephren. The interior of the pyramid was indeed quite well lighted but lengthy, sometimes flat, then a short incline and so forth until one reached the room where the stone sarcophagus upon which the deceased Pharaoh would have rested was seen. It was an interesting experience. It was at this point that my camera started to " come away at the seams." Later, after arrival in Cairo we had lunch in the Mena Hotel in Cairo, a visit to the local papyrus paper factory, and then on to Cairo Museum. There on display was Tutankhamun's treasure, buried with him in the Valley of the Kings and whose tomb was discovered by Howard Carter in1922.

This treasure, with its collection of artefacts, is immense - hundreds of items. Some exhibits remain in one's memory longer than others – like my favourite, the two wheeled chariot, each wheel having six spokes, then the large chests, one enclosing each of the four coffins of Tutankhamun, and each chest getting progressively larger. When first discovered, his body was in the innermost coffin. Presumably, it is in this coffin, that the remains of Tutankhamun now lie in the Valley of the Kings, Luxor, five hundred miles south of Cairo. Some years in the future - as revealed later, I would see this coffin.

(See later description in "Valley of the Kings" Chapter 6)

As referred to, there was an ongoing security problem, as fundamentalists sought to disrupt the Egyptian tourist economy by directly attacking the tourists themselves. As above, my camera had decided to "come apart at the seams" and I was grateful to one of Bill Kinnock's friends who kindly undertook to take the photographs for me seen here.

Below: The Great Pyramids of Giza

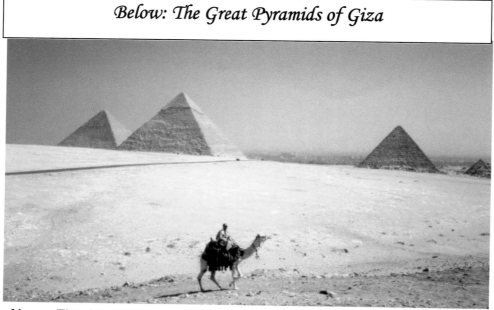

Above: The three Great Pyramids with the Great Pyramid of Cheops extreme left, at Giza, (also known by the Egyptian name of Khufu), with Cairo in the distance. Note the speeding car close to the centre pyramid – and the camel! The middle pyramid of Chephren is the only one to have some remaining cladding – seen at apex. Source: J. Marshall, London 1993.

The Journey to Port Said.

Therefore, with deference to the security situation, it was with the local police chief leading in a car with flashing blue lights, and with the tourist buses in convoy - two abreast across the road - the road being closed to any other traffic, we commenced our "homeward" journey to Port Said, where the M.V. "Agean Spirit" should be waiting for us. So it was East for Ishmalia on the Suez Canal, where hopefully, a left turn on a road parallel to the Suez Canal would bring us north to Port Said.

Above: Author right, with Bill Kinnock, uncle of Neil Kinnock, former leader of the British Labour Party, outside the Great Pyramid at Giza.
Courtesy: J. Marshall

Left: The Sphnix himself, photographed outside the Pyramid of Chephren.
Courtesy: J. Marshall

Now this route would shortly also take us through an immence and astonishing collection of strange structures – each built like a tomb, some small but others very large and miles of them. It was something difficult to describe later - after only fleeting glances as we sped past. To mystify things still further, clothes lines and what appeared to be television aerials were on display in places. Could people be living here?
We were about to see something we had neither heard about - or read about. We were about to enter the **Cities of the Dead** outside Cairo!

"Cities of the Dead!"
These amazing sights, which we were now about to see as we passed through this "City of the Dead," actually consisted of numerous tombs and mausalea, centuries old and appeared to stretch for miles on both sides of the road actually as one found out later.

We eventually discovered that these were mostly created by the Mamaluk Overlords and Sultans in Egypt of the 17th., 18th. and indeed early 19th. centuries. Originally these structures were their tombs, and some were built in the most advanced styles of their era. The Mamaluks (the word means slaves) were a peculiar people originally purchased as children from impoverished families in the countries of and adjoining Russia. Taken to Egypt by their owners, they were brought up as excellent horsemen and warriors and trained in the skills of being rulers in Egypt. These peculiar rulers spent lavishly on the construction of these final resting places.

The tombs, above the ground and the size of small houses, are adorned with the best of Islamic culture and design, most topped with domes in keeping with typical Eastern architecture, and, as already noted, there were miles of these structures! In his excellent book, "Blue Nile," Alan Moorhead has described these tombs thus: *"The huge domed and minaretted tombs of the Mameluk beys, standing in the desert outside the walls of Cairo, are also an architectural triumph of their kind, and not even the dust and squalor that now surround them, or the hordes of ragged children who haunt this city of the dead can quite obscure the revelation that there was a vision here that rose above a barbarous and material life."*

How did these structures come to fill another role around the end of the nineteenth century?

The Cemeteries that became Cities – an explanation.

I was once a high class tomb – now I am a home.

Above: Former poor family tomb - now adapted as home!

Above, left: The density of the tomb homes in the "City of the Dead" is staggering!

In Egypt, around the early twentieth century, serious housing shortages brought about a remarkable happening:The homeless simply went into the tombs of the Mamaluks, cleaned them out (one supposes), and took up residence. As recalled, the Mamaluks were of foreign origin, a ruling / part warrior cast, brought to Egypt from Russia, Armenia etc. and trained for the role of rulers. As we now drove past these structures, evidence of domestic activity was evident as washing lines and TV aerials eventually sprawled in abundance, and it was seen that extensions, (and not up to the original style and elegance!) were being added.These rows of tombs now have street numbers, indeed stretch for mile after mile - four miles to be precise, and truly present an incredible sight to the beholder! Presently we turned North, and travelling parallel to the Suez Canal, we eventually arrived at Port Said. I was in for a surprise !

Now generations of servicemen and seafarers generally but in particular those stationed during the World Wars in the Port Said area of Egypt - brought home strange tales of an Arab boat vendor at Port Said.

He was one of the countless bum boat vendors who in the past pester travellers with all manner of trinkets for sale but who spoke with a strong Glasgow accent and called himself McTavish! I was sure that the McTavish heard by those in past years would have long gone.

But, when I was eventually passing through the Dock gates and about to step on the pontoon to which the "Agean Spirit" was attached, I was dumbstruck to find a young Arab vendor offering his wares - intermittent with telling the world who he was in a strong Glasgow accent - McTavish! Was he a son of Old McTavish (or more correctly, perhaps one of the many sons of old McTavish!)

First Coloured Selection

The routes of the Children of Israel following the Exodus from Egypt.

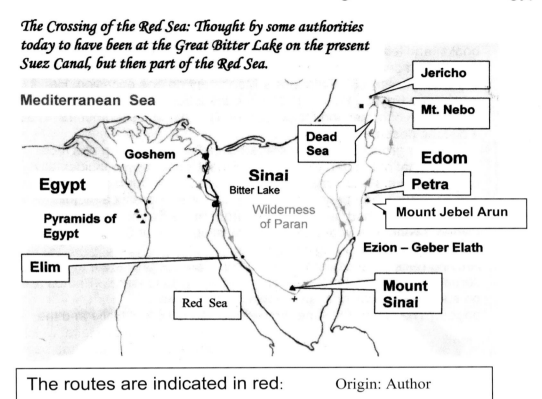

The Crossing of the Red Sea: Thought by some authorities today to have been at the Great Bitter Lake on the present Suez Canal, but then part of the Red Sea.

Mediterranean Sea

Goshem

Egypt

Pyramids of Egypt

Elim

Red Sea

Sinai
Bitter Lake

Wilderness of Paran

Dead Sea

Jericho

Mt. Nebo

Edom

Petra

Mount Jebel Arun

Ezion – Geber Elath

Mount Sinai

The routes are indicated in red:	Origin: Author

Bethlehem – the Star

Shrine of the Book where Dead Sea Scrolls are kept.

In the church of the Holy Sepulchre, Jerusalem.

The Way of the Silversmiths Ephesus –See Acts Ch. 19 v24 – v 29.

The theatre in Ephesus where the riot took place see Acts 19

Temple of Diana, Ephesus - see Acts Ch. V 19 v28 "Great is Diana of the Ephesians."

The statue of Queen Victoria in Montreal, situated close to the old port area and San Laurent.Orig: Author 2011.

The ss "Rathlin Head," on the Sagueney River in Canada, 1961 Origin: Author 1961

Above: Photo of the Chateau Frontenac, Quebec, Canada, taken by Author from the deck of the ss "Rathlin Head," 1961. Compare with that below, taken in the 1990's.

Above: The charnel house at St. Catherine's Monastery,Sinai, where all the skulls of the deceased monks are collected and stored. It is situated some distance – a few hundred metres outside the monastery walls. Underground, it is usually out of bounds for photographers but sometimes people go down there.   Source uncertain

A photo of the Chateau Frontenac, Quebec taken in the 1990's showing little change in outline. Origin: Thought to have initially appeared in a tourist magazine.

This is the Torpedo Firing Head in its operational days, offshore Antrim.

Left: TheTorpedo Firing Head, on the foreshore on Lough Neagh at Antrim. Here British Naval Mark 8 torpedos were tested along firing ranges for such things as depth keeping, direction stability, speed etc.The structure had an heavy electrical power cable on board, emergency accommodation, food- and a boat. Its remains is now a bird sanctuary. Author once worked on the Mark 8 torpedo refurbishing at RNAD Antrim.

Above: Rachid is here showing that he was more than a violinist. He now attempted to sweep the audience off their feet with a vocal contribution - oh, in Arabic! Source: Author 1977.

An Israeli guide entertains – hand across Rachid's good fiddle. Perhaps approval is on the right, but on the left?
Rachid appears to be veiling his ears - with his arms! Note that fiddle against the wall!
Source: Author 1977.

Above: Author at the Cheknov Memorial Yalta, in 1985.

Photographs of Jerusalem and Haifa. Author 1975

Above: A famous landmark in Antrim, the "Chimney Corner," birth place of Dr. Alexander Irvine, author, minister and social reformer. Origin: Author

Top left: The Wailing Wall in Jerusalem, all that remains of King Solomom's temple – destroyed by Nebuchadnezzar. Top right, author at cracks in the Wall where Jewish people come to remember, carry out devotions, and leave messages between the stones. Bottom left: The Jaffa Gate through through which passed General Allenby accompanied by Col. T.E.Lawrence (Lawrence of Arabia) and others thus completing the capture of Jerusaem. Bottom right, author standing on Haifa beach with Mount Carmel the distant mountain
Author 1975.

Stretching the legs in a very hot Sinai.
Author is centre, arm raised, white hat.
Plants in Sinai, eg yellow, beyond group,
sometimes have no rain for two years,
becoming very toxic. Photo source: The
traveller from Denmark,1977.

With one Rachid, Sheik of Sinai, found in
possession of three wives, one single
stringed violin made from a one gallon
petrol can (reclining against the wall), and
a swimming pool – deep in Sinai.
                    Source: Author 1977.

An astonishing discovery ! About to take
the plunge. Rachid's swimming pool in
South Sinai – it was * difficult to believe
one's eyes, until you dived in – what a
shock to the skin. It was made of four stone
walls and a floor, and it apparently, was
water tight. As sometimes it does not rain
for two years in Sinai, one assumes that
the water came from an artesian source.
But: Note surveillance aerials etc against
sky, one white and one just seen as a black
dot. Not likely put up by Rachid!
Source: Author 1977.

" in a land wherein no water is ! *

A wayside café deep in Sinai, where Coco
Cola or Seven Up is the order of the day –
unless one prefers goat's milk! The
proprietors were likely to have been
members of the Jebeliya tribe of Sinai
Bedouin. The yellow object at right, is a door
of our vehicle.   Source: Author 1977.

53

The Dardanelles, Sea of Marmora and the Black Sea

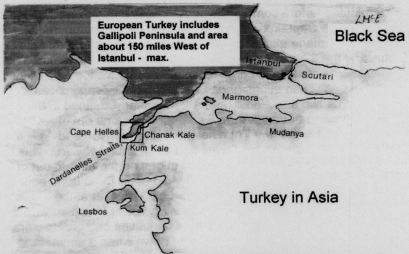

European Turkey includes Gallipoli Peninsula and area about 150 miles West of Istanbul - max.

Black Sea

Istanbul

Scutari

Marmora

Cape Helles

Chanak Kale

Kum Kale

Mudanya

Dardanelles Straits

Turkey in Asia

Lesbos

The Black Sea, fed by the great Russian rivers, flows through the Bosphorus, Sea of Marmora and the Dardanelles to the Agean Sea.

Nagara Point

Peninsula

Agean Sea

Kilid Bahr Fort

Chanak Kale

Gallipoli

Fort Dardanus

Sedd El Bahr Fort

Dardanelles Straits

Minefields

Major Turkish Batteries

Mobile Howitzers

Search Lights

Cape Helles

Kum Kale

The Dardanelles, 1915

The Dardanelles, as it would have been in 1915.

Graphic Enhancement: Courtesy of Miss Lisa McErlean, Randalstown, Co. Antrim, 1997.

Left: Jerusalem. On left, Mark , (Owen's cousin), Jean, author's wife, centre, and Owen Shepherd (London). This is Owen, who took that forbidden photo from the Potemkin Steps of the port area in Odessa, the previous year !
See "Potemkin Steps.".

Origin: Author 1975

Above: St. Andrew's (Church of Scotland) Church, Jerusalem. It is a Memorial built after the 1914-18 war in memory of the Scottish soldiers who died in the battle to capture Jerusalem in 1917. Situated close to the British Embassy, it lies a short distance from the King David Hotel and a little further from the Jaffa Gate.
It also has an excellent 30 room guest hostel close by, where people from across the world (including the author), stay when in Jerusalem.

Origin: From a Church postcard.

The "Belfast,"a heavy lift freighter by Shorts, Airport Rd., Belfast.

At the River Jordan, Front : Jean, Owen, then Mark (hiding)
Origin: Author 1975.

The Wailing Wall, or Western Wall, Jerusalem. (Enlarged version of previous photo of same.)This is all that remains of King Solomon's Temple, destroyed by Nebuchadnezzar – but never forgotten. Origin: Author 1975

Author outside the Livadia Palace beside the famous sculpture of the Worker and Peasant.
This is where the Yalta Conference was held during W. W. Two between Churchill, Stalin and Roseveldt to decide the fate of post war Germany. Orig: 1974

Israel : Author (with paper) in the Dead Sea where the River Jordan flows into. The Dead Sea, is the lowest place on Earth, 1,300 feet below sea level. With no outlet, its high density is due to high salt and mineral deposits, and it is possible to float in it and read a newspaper. Origin: By an unknown hand in 1977.

Author at the caves at Qumran, at the Northern tip of the Dead Sea. In 1947, a shepherd boy threw a stone into a cave. The breaking of pottery was heard, and looking in, he found the Dead Sea Scrolls, rare historical documents written on animal parchments.
Source: A passing local, 1977.

From left, Brian Kane, Master Mariner; Jimmy Spiers, Second Engineer ; Tom Swann, Office Staff; Robert Cameron, (author); Shaw Heddles, Master Mariner deceased). Origin: Taken at Head Line reunion 2004.

A local man poses at Qumran. Here two of the Caves can be seen.
Origin : Author 1977.

Below: Propeller from "Lusitania,"in Albert Dock, Liverpool.

Head Line re union of 2004, and the cake was of such ample proportions, that everyone got a portion!
Origin: Author 2004.

MEDITRRANEAN SEA.
Mediterranean Sea

PETRA

EL ALAMEIN
EGYPT
ALEXANDRIA
CAIRO

WADI RUM (REF: LAURENCE OF ARABIA)
Wadi Rum – Ref: Lawrence of Arabia

EGYPT

SHARM E . SHEIKH

NILE

LUXOR

RED SEA

VALLEY OF THE KINGS

ASWAN
1ST CATARACT

2ND CATARACT

RED SEA

SUDAN

CATARACT
OMDURMAN
5TH CATARACT

CARACT
OMDURMAN

SAUDIA ARABIA

Khartoum
KHARTOUM

WHITE NILE

ATBARA

BLUE NILE

LAKE TANA

ETHIOPIA

White Nile

THE SUDD

Blue Nile

Djibouti

LAKE TANA

Lake Albert
EQUATOR

JINGA

Lake Victoria

Dark and mysterious are the Colums in the Temple of Karnak, near Luxor on the River Nile, and about 500 miles south of Cairo. The Avenue of the Columns, is reminiscent of Agatha Christi's "Death on the Nile."
Source: Author 2002

The course of the River Nile is a rather complicated geographical feature to delineate upon because there are two Niles – the White Nile and the Blue Nile. To add to this difficulty, there is an area of disagreement as to where the White Nile starts off on its 4,000 mile journey to the Mediterranean Sea.So is the start at Jinga, or lake Albert or from any number of tributaries - certainly there are some candidates might be considered in countries south west of Lake Victoria? See following, Chapter 5, "The Nile."

Chapter 5

The Nile

Travelling on the Nile, March 2000.

The River Nile, (as the White Nile), is understood by many to start at Jinja, on the northern coast of Lake Victoria, in Central Africa, and flows for about 4,000 miles before reaching the Mediterranean Sea, but some maintain that its real origin is a lake that feeds into Lake Victoria. See map on pevious page indicating the course of the River Nile from just north of equator to the Mediterranean. Slow flowing, and the longest river in the world, the White Nile is joined at Khartoum, Sudan, by the Blue Nile, a fast flowing river which starts at Lake Fana in Ethiopia. **See previous page for sketch map of the course of the two Niles in the First Coloured Selection**.

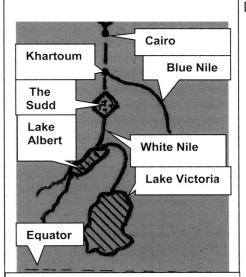

Above: The origin and course of the River Nile

The Blue Nile is much shorter in length than the White Nile, but travels so fast, that the sand and clay it picks up does not settle on the bottom of the river but is carried along in the water. Thus the river appears to have a brownish, blue colour, and that is why it is called the Blue Nile - see later comment.

While in flood, it provides much more water than the White Nile, which picks up no sand or clay and its water is clearer - in fact it is thus the White Nile. This does not mean that it is cleaner – it is not and is infested with the worm like creature known as Bilharzias which, if ingested by humans, invades the liver and causes endemic sickness. Thus the White Nile is generally not the place to take the family out for an afternoon swim! Unfortunately the children of the Nile, while in general all being good swimmers, have few other places to swim.

I had never seen the Blue Nile, because it is a place of mystery – generally, even today because of its many rapids and deep gorges, it is impossible to travel completely along it at river level from Lake Fana to Khartoum, although there are currently reports that such travel has just been accomplished.The steep gorges – hundreds of feet deep and overgrown with trees and undergrowth, make it a dangerous place for the average traveller – and wild animals, crocodiles etc add to the danger. At times, there is little water in the Blue Nile, but when in tremendous flood, it pours into the placid White Nile at Khartoum, and such is the impetus of the Blue Nile, that its waters do not mingle with those of the White Nile, but for miles, are seen to maintain a separate stream of water of a blue brown appearance alongside the waters of the White Nile. Eventually each loses their separate identities to simply become the River Nile. Before the present Aswan Dam was built – and there were several other dams of that name built in past times, the Nile waters flowing through Egypt brought the prosperity that Egypt desperately needed, as 97% of Egypt is desert. The River Nile, eventually loses its identity, as it becomes the Nile Delta, home to the magnificent Pyramids of Giza and the Biblical Land of Goshem, from which the Israelites left for the Promised Land around 1300 B.C.

  The Nile now loses most of its rich mud at the Aswan Dam, and it remains to be seen how this retention will affect not only agriculture, but the performance of the water turbines (generating over fifty per cent of Egypt's electricity), which are located on the down side of the Aswan Dam wall. Already, it is necessary to use artificial fertiliser to maintain the crop production.

I decided to see the River Nile, more especially as an opportunity came my way to spend three days cruising there on a Nile river cruiser – free of charge, yes, a special promotional offer by a company I had previously travelled with and with whom I was about to do further business.

So I started this journey at Luxor (ancient Thebes) which is about 500 miles south of Cairo, and I proceeded up the Nile in a very comfortable river boat. Due to the lack of tourists following the disaster of what is now known as Sept. 11th. in New York, or simply Nine Eleven, most of these boats were tied up here and there, four abreast on the banks of the Nile. I heard that there were normally about 400 such boats on the Nile in Egypt, plying their trade. They are literally floating hotels, with a top sun deck stretching the entire length of the boat, just something like an aircraft carrier, but with a swimming pool included. Our journey, on what is the normal run from Luxor to the Aswan Dam, first took us to the single lock at Esna, (apparently, it is hoped to make it a twin lock, soon). The following day we arrived at Edfu, in order to visit its temple. Our conveyance there was in that typical, four seat, Egyptian horse drawn buggy - the gharry, the impossible design of which makes for great difficulty in finding anywhere to put one's feet – except on top of those belonging to the person opposite you! The concentration of large numbers of these vehicles, converging at the river's side in apparent chaos – the like of which had not been witnessed since before creation, appeared as a scene from another century.

But with the drivers employing a liberal use of their whips on the unfortunate horses, and the skills of local "traffic" police, who applied their long sticks without distinction upon horses and drivers alike, darkness soon became light, and soon we were off to the temple. It is known as the Temple of Horus. This temple complex seem to cover acres – there were acres alone of inscription bearing hieroglyphics whose decipherment had such a profound effect upon European history books and on the monuments of Egypt, following the discovery of the hieroglyphics written on the Rosetta Stone. The Rosetta Stone, now in the British Museum in London, was an irregular block of granite 44 inches (112 cm) high and 30 inches (76 cms) wide dug up by Napoleon's armies in 1799 near the town of Rosetta in the Nile Delta, but was later handed over to the British at Alexandria in 1801. Napoleon Bonaparte, however, had ordered impressions of it to be made before this happened, these copies being used by the Frenchman Champollion in early elucidations of the hieroglyphics written on it. What was written on it, held the key to the understanding of the ancient Egyptian inscriptions etc.

The granite block was about two thirds intact, but this was sufficient to "crack" the code for its script.

The script on it was repeated in three languages, one of which was in Ancient Greek, a language understood. This enabled the mysterious hieroglyphs to be matched to the readable script, and thereafter the meaning of other inscriptions made clear. The actual script on the stone was in the form of a Royal Egyptian decree, a copy of which was supposed to be placed in all major temples and apparently a few other copies have been found.

But I must confess that I grew tired of the good Horus, long before our guide had finished his eulogy of him, and was glad as we galloped back to the ageless Nile. We were soon making a leisurely journey on to Komombo on the good ship "Royal Viking Three,"– again to visit a temple complex. Travellers on the Nile will be familiar with the felucca, the typical sailing boat on the river and those travellers in the past would have included many who left their mark in making history in the region that we are so familiar with today. As we progressed along the Nile, my thoughts were of adventurers like Burton and Speke, or General Gordon on his last journey to the Upper Nile. I then tried to visualise the men who had set off along these waters to attempt (unsuccessfully) the rescue of Gordon – away in Khartoum in the Sudan. Finally, came the army of Kitchener (which included the young Winston Churchill), who man handled their gunboats around the cataracts - it being necessary to dismantle and then reassemble them to achieve victory over Gordon's enemies, the Dervishes, at the battle of Omdurman, near the close of the nineteenth century.

On a Nile River boat. Typically, it would have a flat upper sun deck– not unlike an aircraft carrier, but with some awning and a swimming pool at the bows end of the boat. Smaller ones would suffice with a plunge pool. Origin: Author

Above: A Felucca on the River Nile. Origin: Author

Showing the good Ahhmed a trick or two on the wheel - how to go about things - on the Nile etc! Origin: Some kind unknown.

The River Nile downstream from Aswan.

Today's boatmen of the Nile who crew the craft known as feluccas, are extremely skilful, and are mostly attired in those long dresses worn by some Egyptian men.
They are happy to sail against the wind if required to do so, tacking from one bank to the other, one leg crooked around the tiller, leaving the hands free to operate the sails – all in bare feet! I saw one such craft passing under our bows with a load of stones. Others carry maybe up to thirty passengers, and I became one of these later, on a visit to Kitchener's Island, an island planted with trees plants and flowers from all over the world - by Lord Kitchener, who became Governor of Egypt after his victories in the Sudan in the late nineteenth century. The Nile scenery was constantly changing – here date palms, then grasses the height of a man, bulrushes, then sand, sand, sand, greenery again. Cows indeed, lying almost completely submerged in the waters, appeared as submarines in the Nile with their horns as periscopes.

A typical Egyptian painting

Something of a puzzle, was the presence of white bags of some commodity, which were seen lying in the fields adjacent to the river. One explanation – which now appears to be the correct one, was that these bags contained artificial fertiliser, as there is now no silt being carried down stream, since the advent of the Aswan High Dam. With the Dam Wall across the Nile waters, there are no crocodiles now in lower Egypt, and according to reports, there is currently a build up of between 80 and 100 feet of silt at the Sudan end of Lake Nasser. If so there must be quite a build up at Aswan - and this will be causing problems for the water turbines. Thes mighty turbines currently in situ – they were made in Russia but shortly to be replaced by American ones, are driven by the waters of the Dam, and supply about 50% of Egypt's need for electricity nowadays. In the building of Lake Nasser, 75 Nubian villages were lost beneath the waters of the Lake but, (apart from power generation), the Dam with its store of water has proved its worth in being beneficial in years of drought – as in 1979 and 1988.

The third day brought us to the Aswan High Dam, which has created Lake Nasser and this is vast as far as the eye can see – in fact for about 300 miles long (480 Km.) and backing up into the Sudan. The average depth is 400 feet (150 metres), but can reach 600 feet in places, and is host to the largest fishery in Africa where the yearly harvest is 80,000tons! Close to Aswan is the island of Philae, which was once home to a vast complex of temples. In 1902, an earlier Lower Nile Dam, British built and three and a half miles downstream of Aswan was completed, which meant that Philae Island was intermittently and increasingly submerged by this Lake's waters. It was evident that combining the old and new Aswan dams would likely completely submerge these temples. A decision was made to construct a coffer dam around the temples, cut them into blocks and reassemble the blocks on higher ground on Agilkia island on the Nile.

"The Nile:" continued:

A coffer dam might be described as a water tight cylinder constructed around some object now submerged in water and on which some work has to be done in dry conditions ie after the water has been pumped out of this surround. This was done, and it is now possible to look at these temples and see the water line on some, the indication of being partially submerged in 1902. As well, the steel remains of the coffer dam can still be seen today - in 2002, rising out of the water. The temples of the Nile have been described as "intricately detailed, vast and stunning" and the Temple of Isis on Philae was described as "the Pearl of Egypt." Few would disagree, and it is as well to record, that on the other side of the Aswan Dam in Upper Nubia, the famous monuments of Abu Simbel had been rescued by cutting

Also there, is the Collosi of Memnon, twin stone figures of monstrous size, which are said to be the statues of the Pharaoh Amenhotep III. (Another authority suggests a Greek ancestry.) And, as mentioned in the previous chapter, there is also the shattered, giant remains of the statue of Ramesses II whose user name was Ozymandias. It would have been a massive 97 feet tall - the statue of Ramesses II, thought to be the unnamed Pharoah of the Exodus.

" My name is Ozymandias, king of kings:"

The latter two sites were visited as we returned to Luxor, as was the magnificent temple complex of Karnak, just north, with shades of "Death on the Nile" by Agatha Christie. An important part of the film of that book, appears to have been made there.

A visit had indeed been also arranged to the spectacular Temple of Karnak. This truly amazing complex of the most ancient of ancient temple constructions – the description of which alone could fill a book, was but a short distance away. As one walked along the "Avenue of Columns," captured so magnificently in the film of Agatha Christie's "Death on the Nile," it was done so with a mixture of awe at their sheer size – and fear that something might drop from on high! But the "wicked uncle" wasn't there that day and so we did not have any "accidents!" These columns, which are sometimes written of as the Hypostyle Columns, are 134 in number, stand 60 feet high with a few 79 feet high. Close by is the Avenue of the Rams – 120 Sphinxes, each sporting a ram's head with flowing, curved horns! They get a mention in " Death on the Nile."

That evening, having got rid of all the sand stolen from the "Valley of the Kings" and Karnak etc., dinner preceded a presentation laid on by our Hotel Mercure Coralia people displaying originals and reproductions of Egyptian art – all for sale of course.
This consisted mostly in paintings of Egyptian figures from the past, and all in typical Egyptian style - first angle projection (but showing two dimensions) ie say the figure of a lady showing a side view of her face only; then with shoulders and arms rotated through 90° showing a full front view of same; finally back to a side view of a leg and all appearing in the same vertical plane - see later page for "typical Egyptian Painting." It is indeed strange that the ancient Egyptians never used a more pictorial or three dimensional style of representation. Still, it usually ended with the inevitable purchase. We all need something to take home!
And so to bed for a second night at the Hotel Mercure Coralia. One was hoping for not too early a start the next day for the journey over the Red Sea Mountains to Safaga on the coast of the Gulf of Suez.

*   *   *   *   *

Crossing the Red Sea mountains

For some reason, transport did not arrive for the journey until the afternoon next day. It would probably mean that I would arrive at Safaga in darkness.
Eventually I found myself setting off across the Red Sea Mountains by bus for the Red Sea port of Safaga (technically on the Egypt mainland side of the Gulf of Suez.), where I hoped to join a ship, the "Ocean Monarch " which would take me to the other places I wanted to visit. In taking me across the Gulf of Suez, I would be in that part of Egypt known as Sinai. As mentioned earlier, I was, if not in their footsteps, at least going in the same direction as did the Children of Israel (but hopefully not to dwell or wander there as much as they did!)

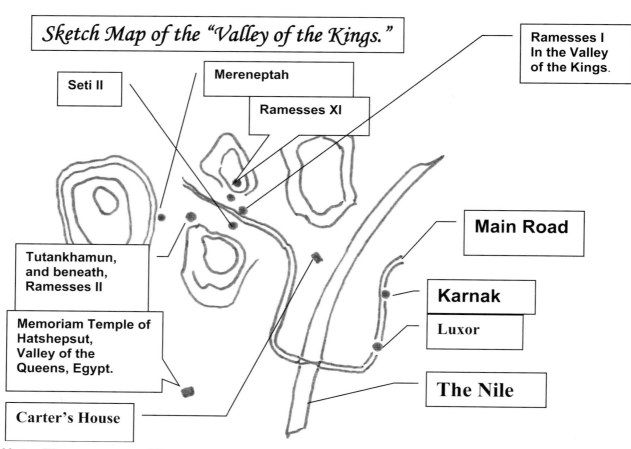

Sketch Map of the "Valley of the Kings."

Seti II

Mereneptah

Ramesses XI

Ramesses I
In the Valley
of the Kings.

Tutankhamun,
and beneath,
Ramesses II

Main Road

Karnak

Luxor

Memoriam Temple of
Hatshepsut,
Valley of the
Queens, Egypt.

The Nile

Carter's House

Note: The mummy of Ramesses II was re discovered in1881, among a cache of the mummies of Pharaohs, placed obviously for safe keeping in the family tomb of a High Priest, one Pinodjem. All these latter, are now in the Cairo Museum. His original tomb was earlier uncovered beneath that of Tutankhamun.

This is the shattered remains of a statue of Ramesses II.
Origin: Thought possibly to be from an old National Geographical source or similar periodical.

Crossing the Red Sea mountains (contd)

Crossing the magnificent Red Sea mountains between the Nile and the Gulf of Suez, (Red Sea) is a journey well worth taking in itself – a vast bulk of granite and desert sand in a lunar setting. It was quite some hours, after driving along this route – some of it in darkness, that the bus arrived at the Red Sea Egyptian port of Safaga – primarily a commercial port for shipping phosphates and importing grain but now also an important holiday resort. But the M.V. "Ocean Monarch" had found a berth to which I repaired, and upon finding my cabin, I fell asleep only to awaken when approaching Sharm El Sheikh at the southern tip of the Sinai Peninsula. I had crossed the Red Sea – at least that part of it known as the Gulf of Suez, a little further south than where the Children of Israel had, it is thought, crossed over. This is held by some historians, as being in that part of the Suez Canal of today, which is known as the Great Bitter Lakes, then apparently part of the Red Sea.

Dark and mysterious: The Colums in the Temple of Karnak, near Luxor on the River Nile, and about 500 miles south of Cairo. This is the Avenue of the Columns, of restricted sunlight, and reminiscent of Agatha Christi's "Death on the Nile."   Source: Author 2002

Sharm El Sheikh was captured by Israel in the 1967 War, developed by them as a tourist centre but now it was back in Egyptian hands. Sharm El Sheikh was a point of departure for those wishing to visit Mount Sinai and St. Catherine's Monastery, but having visited these places before, I spent a relaxing day at nearby upmarket Naama Bay * where I had a trip on a glass bottomed boat to see the fantastic coral reefs just offshore. By the next day, I should be in Aqaba, Jordan.

   *(It was during the writing of these lines in july 2005, that news broke of the devastating bombs that destroyed part of that beautiful place, Naama Bay.

On to Petra – the History.

It is but a short distance from Sharm El Sheikl to the Jordanian port of Aqaba and early next morning, I found myself there, the only port in the land locked country of Jordan. Aqaba is found at the head of the Gulf of Aqaba which is also known as the Gulf of Eliat by Israel, because both ports are close enough to be observed clearly, one by the other, and but a few miles apart. I was here, in order to visit Petra, the modern or Greek name for the Biblical city of Seir (or Sela.) It may also be correct, for certain periods of time in the history of Israel, to read for Petra, the words Edom and Kenite. At any rate, when Moses tried to pass the city or even obtain water, his way was barred by the local king of Edom, something the Israelites didn't easily forget.

Also of considerable interest, was that in Aqaba, I was close to a legend, and walking in the the footsteps of Col. Lawrence DSO – T.E. Lawrence, "Lawrence of Arabia." (Such walking would again take place when I visited in the nearby Wadi known as Wadi Rum, and also in the Fort at Aqaba some years later.)
Lawrence was with the Arab forces led by Prince Faisal, who occupied Aqaba in the 1914-18 War. It was one of the early successful operations conducted in this area against the Turks, who, at that time were allied to the German cause. That campaign eventually resulted in the capture, as earlier noted, of Jerusalem itself in 1917 by the forces of General Allenby. Later, Damascus was liberated - mostly by Arab forces, and where Lawrence was actually Governor for a couple of days!

I and others set off by bus for Petra early in the morning to travel through the Jordanian desert along an excellent road, northward, in the direction of, but passing, the Dead Sea. One Victorian traveller, Dean Burgon, once spoke of Petra thus:

"Match me a marvel save in Eastern clime,
a rose red city half as old as time"

At this time, Iraq, under Saddam Hussein's rule, was subject to certain United Nations sanctions and as the bus made its way along the highway, one couldn't help but notice the unending stream of oil tankers seemingly all going in the one direction – to Aqaba. They each had a blue number plate, were coming from Iraq, and were carrying Saddam Hussein's crude oil to the Aqaba refinery and perhaps other outlets. One assumed that this was part of the "oil to pay for the food/medicine programme," approved by the United Nations.
After an hour or so we came to a road junction sign. It read "Wadi Rum."
Wadi Rum, as I would discover some years later, is a spectacular desert landscape – a dried up river bed, surrounded by high cliffs, and possibly an hour's journey from this road junction. It was described by T. E. Lawrence - (Lawrence of Arabia) using words like, "vast, echoing," or "where a squadron of aeroplanes could manoeuvre unseen." Shortly after, a railway line could be seen to the East, and speculation began, as perhaps this was part of the railway system used by the Ottoman Turkish forces in the First World War, and frequently put out of action by Lawrence and his Arab associates. However, we found out later that the railway line attacked by Lawrence, was further to the East. The Arab campaign was mostly led by Prince Faisal, of the then Hashamite Kingdom of Arabia, later to be king of post war Iraq. Today, the sole surviving branch of that family, is that of the present King of Jordan.
Another hour brought us to Petra, the "– rose red city, half as old as time."
The Petra basin was a nomadic city from the earliest biblical times. It is indeed, a basin-like valley – no green meadows though – just rocks and sand. The early people here with their tents etc, would have been secure in such a place, surrounded as it was, by high cliffs and mountains.One wonders what sheep or goats found to eat in such a place of little greenery. When Moses came this way seeking water and passage north on his way to the Promised Land, he met opposition. They were likely to have been the Ishmaelites – but who were they ?

*   *   *   *   *

In the Old Testament, one reads of Abraham, who had two sons – Ishmael and Isaac. Isaac the younger son, had twin sons, Esau the elder, and Jacob – whose name was later to be changed by God to Israel (Gen. 35, v10). Feeling that Isaac favoured Esau, Jacob plotted against Esau, who incidentally had married Uncle Ishmael's daughter Basemath (Gen. 36: v1 - 5). Isaac's mother Rebekah was unhappy that tribal inheritance might pass into Ishmael's family, since Ishmael's mother was an Egyptian, one Hagar. Following a plot hatched by Rebekah, Jacob tricked his brother Esau out of his birthright.

In the plot, Jacob's hands had been covered with hair, so that his hands would feel like those of his brother Esau, who, it appears, had very hairy skin, which was also very deep red in colour. Esau was, however, the first born, and rightful heir. (See Genesis Ch.25 v 26 - 34, and Genesis Ch. 27).

Jacob so disguised, presented himself to old Isaac as Esau and received the tribal blessing from his now blind old father Isaac who, while blessing Jacob, was sorely puzzled: "The voice is the voice of Jacob," he said, "but the hands are the hands of Esau." As some of us might say today, Isaac had the wool pulled over his eyes!

Finally we read in Genesis Ch. 36, v 6-9, that Esau, (probably in disgust), went "into a far off land … and dwelt in the hill country of Seir," the place we now call Petra.

It therefore follows, most likely, that the descendants of Esau became the inhabitants of Seir. The name Petra, a Greek word, was only first used when the site was rediscovered in the nineteenth century, and means stone.

They became part of the Ishmaelite people. Esau's wife was, remember, a daughter of Ishmael, and later we can read that the jealous brothers of Joseph, Jacob's youngest son, sold him "to a caravan of Ishmaelites, coming down to Seir (Petra) from Gilead, for twenty pieces of silver." There must have been a wry smile on somebody's face, at this turn of events! Joseph was then sold into slavery in Egypt, but was eventually able to welcome all his brothers (and his old father, now called Israel) down into Egypt during the hard times of a famine.

One can read that Jacob had his name changed for him - to Israel (see Genesis Ch. 35, v 10), – thus the "Children of Israel."

Their descendants were later to make "bricks without straw," as the "Children of Israel."
What an amazing historical account that is, and preserved for us in the pages of the Bible.

*　　　*　　　*　　　*　　　*

As earlier referred to, when Moses came this way to the Biblical City of Seir or Sela seeking water and passage north on his way to the Promised Land, he met opposition from the local king. But the city was then a tent city and the tomb city we see today was created by people who came later. They were the Natabeans, and they were the folk who dug the tombs out of solid rock.

To reach the "rose red city" of Petra (to give it its modern name) the approach is made by descending a long narrow gorge - known, as one closes the city, as the Siq, and cut out, it is said, by water action. During the walk, fairly steep at times, one might be passed by those who preferred to travel in the two-wheeled horse drawn carriages available – and they galloped down at a fair old rate of knots! Shortly, rectangular openings in the gorge side appeared – these were the tombs. Evidence of water channels cut alongside one's path appeared from time to time. Suddenly, after a narrowing of the gorge, the Siq opened into a large space, and there in front, was probably the most photographed "building" in Petra – the Al – Khazneh or Treasury.

It has indeed a most impressive facade, its shape suggesting that its convex areas might contain something. The local Bedouin, thinking along the same lines, are said to have fired bullets at these areas in the hope that money might flow out. Marks in the building's fabric, show that something like this had indeed happened. The "Treasury" is said to change colour. For example, in the morning it appears as peach, and in the afternoon, a deep red. One was now in an amazing desert landscape – a valley floor and surrounding walls of red sandstone – it would stretch for maybe five miles, although I didn't go so far. Petra was only "discovered" in 1812 by the Swiss explorer Johann Burkhardt – the word Petra is, as previously mentioned, the Greek word for stone, and thus, the new 'discovery' was so named. There had been little awareness of its existence for perhaps thousands of years although it was really, of course, being rediscovered. The dwellings and tombs are very shallow – the one room in the "Treasury" would be about the size of the living room of an average home in the UK.

Left: The Siq

Left: This is in the deep gorge known as the Siq. It turns to the left where the two figures are standing in the small centre white distance area,one third way (in front of a man's white hat) and opens into Petra, " The Red Rock City, twice as old as time."

Right: The Al-Khazneh,referred to as the "Treasury." Behind the pillars is an average size room cut out of solid rock. Orig: Author

Everyone who visits Petra today, and looks upon the phenomenal excavations there, will surely ask the same question: "How did they do it, and what tools were available for them to do so?" What did they use for scaffolding?

As mentioned, to reach the basin like tomb city of Petra, it is necessary to descend for about one and a half miles, down through that narrow gorge. It is important to note that when Moses and the Israelites passed this way, it was then called Edom, and the King of Edom here refused Moses the right of passage as in the account given in Numbers Ch. 20 – (see v 1 to v 21).

Author outside the door of the porch of the Al-Khazneh, Petra. Orig: Some nice chap!

The occasion was not only marked by such strife as in the account given in Numbers Ch. 20 – (see v 20 and v 21),then from (v23 to the end of Ch.20.) There was a denouncement of the worship of idols – the latter takng place, one presumes, when Moses was absent on Mount Sinai. Then the account of the death of Aaron, the brother of Moses, on Mount Hor has drawn spectulation from some quarters, that the reading of this portion of scripture suggests, that as a consequence of idol worship, Aaron was condemned to death. It is more likely, that here one is reading of a ritual whereby the priesthood of Aaron was being symbolically transferred to his son ie the transfer of his clothes to his son but it is short in detail. Aaron was buried up on Mount Hor which can be easily seen from the nearby main road.

Again, everyone who visits Petra today, and looks upon the phenomenal excavations there, will surely ask the same question: "How did they do it, and what tools were available for them to do so?"What scaffolding was available?

By now of course, the clock had moved on about four hundred years since the day Joseph was sold into slavery.

If one wants to read what happened when the Israelites

came along at this time, many references are available in the Bible, especially when Joshua was the leader: Num: 20: v14 – v29 - (read Seir for Edom);   Deut: 2: v1 – v 9: The death of Moses: Deut 34: v1 – 7.*

During the return journey to Akaba, attention again focused on the railway line referred to earlier. An engine was seen coming from a siding and then proceeding to help a heavily loaded goods train up an incline. The guide explained that this was normal practice on inclines and that this was not the Ottoman Turkish line, so often attacked by Lawrence. It was some distance to the East – disappointment! Another interesting feature, was when we came to a part of the road where it increased enormously in width – as wide as an airfield runway. It was just that – an emergency runway in the desert!

That evening, the "Ocean Monarch" sailed for the Suez Canal.

Moses saw the Promised Land across the Jordan, but was not permitted to pass over the Jordan to see it. He died in this area, the land of Moab (now Jordan). The Bible disclaims knowledge of exactly where he was buried, but some commentators place it at Mount Nebo at the northern end of the Dead Sea - in Jordan. See earlier sketch map showing the routes travelled by the Children of Israel at the start of " First Selection of Coloured Photographs."

☆   ☆   ☆   ☆   ☆

THE SUEZ CANAL.

I started to travel away from my home when I was about twenty-four years old and as an engineer at sea. But I had never planned it that way.

*   *   *   *   *

How an incident of short input - has life long outcomes :
(a short pause, to consider possible outcomes in life)

Following a serious road accident when I was eighteen years of age (and a second year engineering apprentice in the aircraft factory of Short Bros. and Harland Ltd.,Belfast,) I had managed, after a lay-off of two and a half years, to make a very shaky resumption of my apprenticeship in the Queen's Island Works of Shorts.

But my recovery and rehabilitaion was not without setbacks, as after a short period of time I suffered a re fracture of a leg which suddenly cracked at a weak spot where a bone graft had been implanted and initially held in place by two steel six mm screws – (they are still there!)

When18 years old: In the Waveney Hospital, Ballymena, the surgeon had said: " Content yourself. You are going to be here a long time." I was.
With cousin David Cameron. Origin ?

The new bone growth had been too soft. It cracked, and I was back in a full length leg plaster cast for another three months. But about five months later I reported back to work one morning at 7.45 am at Shorts in the Queen's Island , Belfast and the struggle was on again to reintegrate myself back into industry – and as well, into Further Education studies at the College of Technology, Belfast. Eventually, my apprenticeship was completed when I was working in Shorts Precision Engineering Division on Guided Weapons etc in Castlereagh. I had also almost caught up on my Further Education goal and for which I was now preparing for the final examinations. *But one night, homeward bound when I was but a few weeks away from these*

examinations in the College of Technology, Belfast, a dog crossed the path of my motorcycle, causing me to crash heavily onto the road. Of that I have no precise memory, but I do remember something of the journey by ambulance to yet another hospital. This time, it was to the good old Royal Victoria Hospital, in Belfast !

Happily, my injuries proved to be relatively superficial and a few weeks later I was beginning to get around. But it would be another year before I could sit the missed examinations. The castle in the air had tumbled for me - again.

So in the immediate time ahead, I decided to do something a little different from my life up till then. I decided that for a short period of my life – until it was time or there abouts, to sit for those missed examinations, I would go to sea in order to gain some experience in heavy engineering – the science end of which I was studying, but without ever having seen much of it ! This was unlike some of my fellow students eg those who worked in the shipyard and who were seeing many of these things on most days of their lives.

In other words I wanted to experience the practical side of the engineering subjects I was currently studying – steam turbines, triple expansion steam engines, the characteristics of superheated steam systems, handling electrical plant, power generators, learn the lingo -
   " a hand for the ship and one for yourself " and so on.
What happened there and beyond has already been described in Chapter Two and later in Ch. 10.

The serious accident referred to earlier, happened outside Ballymena in Co. Antrim, and involved seven other people. It led to a busy night for the nursing staff of the Waveney Hospital there and I was seriously injuried enough to cause the surgeon there to consider removing my left leg. I would be confined to bed for six long months.

Eventually, when I was in a sufficiently stabilised condition, I had a visit from the surgeon who was an ex Royal Navy Surgeon Commander and had been in the Royal Navy in the Second World war. He was was of a somewhat terse nature, and of few words. He simply said, "You content yourself – you are going to be here a long time."

During that " long time," X-rays of my leg injuries showed every reluctance for the bones to reunite. Things were dismal. Sometimes at night when the lights were dimmed, the night nurse out of the ward, and law abiding patients in repose, I used to drag myself to the side of the bed and lower my good foot to the floor to sense what it was like to feel the earth below me again. But healing takes its own time to complete its process.

*   *   *   *   *

For me, the difficult business of the subsequent rehabilitation referred to, was to be so deeply ingrained in my mind, that many years later, I found it my imperative duty to write a book in 2001 on my experiences of over forty years before, in dealing with the aftermath of serious injuries (from which I never really fully recovered from) – and also with getting on with life as well.

Following the publication of this book, I was subsequently to receive some very interesting correspondence and phone calls - mostly from people I did not know. I was then to discover the amazing empathy that exists among those who have had to walk the road of rehabilitation either through having had a serious illness or a serious accident and - get on with life. But that is only, alas, for those who have managed to recover sufficiently to show that they have again possessed the potential to merit a place in the march of everyman - the march of everyone in the ranks of industry, business or commerce from which their illness had expelled them for a season..

I was eighteen when I was admitted to the Waveney Hospital in Ballymena, Co. Antrim with serious injuries . Each morning the duty nurses there checked my foot for feeling – using a needle applied to my toes.Eventually I was able to respond positively – a hurdle passed. In that brief period, the thought of invalidity in the future, leaving me qualified for nothing but one in the local supermarket filling its shelves with tins of cat food or other, was not far away. It was closer at one point , than I realised.

So what about those who do not make it over the line, and whose illness or affliction assumes a permanence which rings down the curtain on the possibility of a return to their previous calling?

Indeed in his **"Deserted Village,"** Oliver Goldsmith seems to strikes a chord there, as we read where, in one verse, the village schoolmaster welcomes an old soldier to share his hearth - thus:

" The ruined soldier kindly bade to stay,
 sat by the fire and talked the night away.
 Wept ower his wounds and tales of sorrow done,
 shouldered his crutch and showed how fields were won. "

Thus our old soldier tells others of a time when he could do things – but it was now no longer possible for him to do so.

That book which I referred to, was published in 2001, and was called *"Before That Generation Passes, "*-the story of a Short's Apprentice, and quotes from it appear in this book. Since then, I still get requests for a copies and I often wonder, if among some of the recipients, are those who know the full meaning of this word rehabilitation.

        *   *   *   *   *   *

Now, some of my contemporaries – especially my fellow classmates whom I had met at the Belfast College of Technology, had also gone to sea as engineers and some had taken their "tickets"- the qualifications required to sail as a Second Engineer or as a Chief Engineer. I was also somewhat envious of some of their other achievements.

Such were, for example, of my good friend Billy Grills from Kilkeel, sailing with Elders and Fyffe. This was a firm engaged in carrying fruit from the Caribbean to the Pacific side of the USA and also to the UK, and was sometimes passing through the Panama Canal. Another close associate, the late Clive Hughes, was going through both the Suez and Panama Canals on his circumnavigations of the globe with the Blue Funnel Line! He also became the second youngest Second Engineer to serve as such in the history of the Blue Funnel Line. Both were steam men with Billy achieving a double ticket – qualified in steam and motor (diesel).

By contrast, I had only managed to experience the cold North Atlantic, the Mediterranean and at times, the coasting trade around the British Isles in the worst weather ever imagined.

I had then to scurry back to sit for those examinations - missed courtesy of a dog! When colleagues of mine at the College of Technology, Belfast, they shared with me the austerity of the perhaps infamous overflow provisions at a disued textile mill on North Howard Street, off the Falls Road in Belfast. Here floors had been cleared, eight foot high hoardings placed so as to simulate walls of a room – and a door installed. A scenario could arise when one might be in one of these "class rooms," where, say, a lesson in thermodynamics was being meted out, and one might happen to be sitting at the back of the class.

Three feet away - but on the other side of a plywood wall, a maths class could be heard in full swing, transmission being loud and reasonably clear, and coming over the top of the plywood hoarding to you. Result: One perhaps stood a better chance of learning more about Differential Equations than the Entropy of steam!

Later, both my two friends - like myself, had entered the teaching arena - in Further Education.

So, I had therefore waited a long time for this moment – to pass through the Suez Canal, northbound.

The Suez Canal is a man made waterway connecting the Mediterranean Sea with the Gulf of Suez – and leading to the Red Sea. It was built by the Frenchman, Ferdinand De

74

Lessops, who started the work at the Mediterranean end in 1859 and the canal was finished in 1869. De Lessops was not an engineer however - he was a French diplomat. The Suez Canal is 180 km (about 100 miles) long, and the present maximum depth is 15 metres (about 50 feet). From waterline to waterline its width varies along the length but on average it would be 100 –150 metres. Since it was cut largely in sand, its sides tend to slope sharply inwards, the narrow navigable channel lying along a precise route, ships following in convoy at about half a mile distance apart, each ship with a pilot aboard. The average time for a transit is about twelve hours – at a leisurely 8 knots or so, although since the southbound convoy has to wait in the Great Bitter Lakes until the northbound one passed, it probably takes longer for those convoys. (Our convoy actually passed through northbound in about twelve hours.)

We had arrived at Suez in the afternoon, actually coming to a berth in Port Tewfik, (sometimes spelled Port Tawfik), and there are about five ports in all at the Suez end of the canal. Berthed nearby, were a number of white ships which were in use as transport for those on the pilgrimage to Mecca in Saudi Arabia. A floating dry-dock was nearby on which a ship, of about 8,000 tons gross was sitting. Here, undoubtedly, a ritual usually enacted during dry-dockings would be taking place – the removal and overhaul of the sea water valves , where sea water is admitted in quantity to the internals of a ship, for cooling purposes, and ballast, fire fighting, washing the deck, etc. When writers talk of ships being scuttled by "opening the sea-cocks," it's likely they mean the sea water valves. If these valves were removed when the ship was in the water – as at sea, immediate flooding would take place – especially in the engine room where they are usually fitted. Some local inputs of small volume are fitted eg for things like sanitary needs. However, a friend of mine once recalled being on a ship specialising in dangerous cargo shipments, and alluded to flooding valves being fitted to certain holds.

Below: Here the gap in the Bar Lev Line is still maintained, and huge monuments, the most striking of which is this huge bayonet, are to be seen. Below the Bayonet is a flat type Memorial resembling an open book. It says, "Welcome to Egypt."   Origin: Tom Blair

We were due to leave Port Tewfik at 6 am the next morning, but it was 9 am before all the pilots were on board their respective ships and the convoy formed up. We were number four, just behind a very large container vessel reputed to be carrying cars, and the name on the stern was in fact, "Daewoo."

Below: To the Fallen (A broken column.)

Little mechanisation was available for the building the Suez Canal, so it's a good job that a number of dry lakes lay in the proposed path of the canal – like the Great Bitter Lakes, Lake Timsah, and Lake Ballah. It seems that the Suez Canal was too early for its construction to be recorded by cameras or cine, as had happened during the construction of the Panama Canal. At Suez, sketches were used however, to good effect.

When we arrived at the Great Bitter Lakes, the South bound convoy was at anchor, and we proceeded without let or hinder.

The Bar Lev Line : On the Sinai side of the Canal, Egyptian forces in the initial assault on the Israeli defences here, had used high pressure water hoses to clear away this sand and create the gap which remains there. Today, huge Memorials may be seen there, the most striking of which is probably the huge bayonet – as seen on previous page. It is possibly thirty metres in height, in a vertical position on the Sinai bank. As stated, the huge gap there is still maintained through the sand bank as a Memorial in itself. As also mentioned, at another Memorial which is flat, a sign reads: **"Welcome to Egypt"** the huge bayonet being to the right of this and first photo previous page..

Probably for most, the Canal Transit was the highlight of their travel. There was always something of interest along the canal at places, and dredgers were much in evidence.

By the time we reached Ismailia, the sun was beginning to set, and it was quite dark as we approached Port Said. But tomorrow we would wake up in Alexandria and later travel to El Alamein.

Second Coloured Selection

The Ellerman Papyanni cargo liner, the SS "Grecian," as seen at Mersin, Turkey. A sister ship is tied up close by - see in background.
Origin: Author 1961.

This contains photographs of subject matter dealt with in current past script, and, a few outside this area that may be of interest to some.

Left: The Soviet Moon buggy (unused but as proposed for use). Origin: Author 1985, Moscow Space Museum

Above: Author in "Grecian" going for the sun tan – just off Gibraltar. Origin: Stan, 3rd. Eng.

Lenin, the first leader of the Bolshevik Govt., in 1917 no cap!

The back up for the rocket that put the first Soviet Sputnik into space. Origin: Author 1985, Moscow Space Museum

Above ; HQ, USSR Communist Party, Kremlin, Moscow.
Origin: Author 1985

76

Leningrad, now St. Petersburg and the Bolshevik cruiser, "Aurora," said to have fired the first shot – possibly a blank, to start the Revolution of 1917. Courtesy of Martin Sloan, Newtownards, Co. Down.

Sherman tank in the open air museum at El Alamein, near the El Alamein Hotel, Egypt. Origin: Author 2002

The Crescent, above port of Iskendrun, Turkey. Origin; Author

Author outside the Turkish sector, Famagusta, Cyprus. Origin: Stan Pacer 3/ Eng.

The Winter Palace in Leningrad (now again St. Petersburg) and stormed by the Bolsheviks in 1917. Origin: Author 1985.

Above:The Magnificant Cathedral of the Smolny Convent, in Leningrad, now of course, St. Petersburg. Origin: Author 1985.

Above: Odessa, USSR 1974: Passing the graves of executed W. W. Two Resistance leaders, is a Youthful Guard of Honour. Note the solemnity on their faces. Origin: Author 1974

The Al-Khazneh in Petra. Origin: Author2002

Author with Bill Kinnock in front of the largest of the Great Pyramids of Giza - that of Cheops, also known by the Egyptian name of Khufu Origin: J. Marshall, London.

A family grows older– and moves on.

Early Years

Mrs. Jean Cameron who has over the years, looked after all these folk and animals - except when she is away walking! Orig: A professional studio!

Above: This is our daughter Moyna with our most intelligent dog, Jessie. Nearly forty years on, the Victorian plum tree is now 25 feet plus in height.   Origin: Author 1975

Forty years on: Moyna, now living in Canada, has got another dog –a Canadian guy. Orig: Canada source.

Author with Rusty, my aunt's very disobedient dog. He lived at Carnaughts, near Ballymena.
Origin: Walter Cameron, Ballymena, 1956.

Above:This is our son Ian with Jessie. Jessie, sadly, was only 9 years old when she departed this world - and we never thought of having another dog.
Origin: Author 1975

Above:This is now Ian on left, with his son James. Moyna is on right with her son Sam. Someone is having difficulty with the sun.
Origin: Author probably 2001.

Later Years

From left: Sam, Moyna's oldest son, husband Adrian, Moyna, daughter Natasha, and Ben, her youngest son.   A Canadian source.

Sam's High School Graduation, Canadian style.

Grandsons : More of James and Sam

James, here in 2017.

78

The Connaught Cemetery, Thiepval Ref: The "Somme."

A sad reminder of the men of the 36[th.] Ulster Division who emerged from Thiepval Wood (in background) on 1. 07. 1916, and crossed this ground on which now stands the Connaught Cemetery. Note the blue and yellow bag which appears in photos of many of the places described in this book.   Origin: Sam McMurray 1993

Author, as sun rises on Mount Sinai. Plaque ref: The Ten Commandments.

Note on Dr. N Graham MC, below: Later he transferred to the RAF and certified Rifthofen "The Red Baron"dead, after he was shot down.

The rick shifter a common sight to children who often would have "hitched" a lift at the back of the rick.   Courtesy Miss Mirium Stevenson.

The Ulster Tower, Thiepval, France.

Dr. Norman Graham MC, Medical Officer of the 11[th.])Batt., 36[th.] Ulster Division(South Antrim) Family archive

Author with Peter Taylor who was second pilot on the Vulcan which delivered the bombs onto the runway on Stanley Airfield in the Falklands, during Operation "Black Buck,"
Origin: The late Mrs. Denise Blair.

Above: Author with the Rev. Dr. Frazer McClosky MC, former Padre with Col. Blair Mayne's S.A.S. group behind the lines in France 1944/45. Photo taken 1997 by sometime attending the unveiling of the Blair Mayne Memorial etc.

Dr. Norman survived the 1914-18 War, became a lecturer at Queen's University, Belfast and was known to the author as the Clerk of Session in High St. Pres. Church, Antrim, above, right.The title above photo says "Second Antrim Pres, Church"! It later became known as High Street Pres. Church, Antrim, now at the Steeple Antrim. Photo probably made from an old post card.

St. Catherine's Monastery, deep in the south Sinai peninsula, Egypt, is under the shadow of Mount Sinai/Horeb and is an Orthodox monastical center of continuous life since the 6[th.] century. Grateful thanks to the booklet "The Monastery of St. Catherine," from Sinai HQ.

Above: A devout Jew at the Wailing Wall in Jerusalem. They come here to leave messages and prayers, pushed into the spaces between the blocks of the wall
Origin: Author.

Above: A felucca plying its trade on the Nile near Luxor, Egypt – a boat design - little changed in a thousand years. Origin: Author 2002

The cottage of T.E. Lawrence, Col. T.E. Lawrence DSO, "Lawrence of Arabia." This is where Lawrence met with his friends – academics, parliamentarians and certainly some of them, men of high influence.They never cooked meals – "Just opened a tin when hungary"and the famous lady Arabist and archaeologist Gertrude Bell, held him in high regard (she died shortly after the First World War). He was an achiever but appeared to have had a complicated life.
Photo origin: Cecil Millar, Templepatrick, Co. Antrim.

The Czar's newly cast bell "drops a clanger " when, in 1735, fire and excess water caused it to crack. Origin:Auther 1985

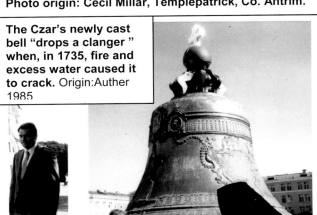

Ian Harvey from Doagh, Co. Antrim, and a former student of Cambridge House Gram. Ballymena, seen leaving the Falklands Islands escorted by a Tornado when flying with Globe Span. Now, he is Captain Ian Harvey, flying the "Dream Liner " for Etihid Airlines. Courtesy: Captain Ian Harvey.

Head Line / Ulster Steamship Company Memorial , Belfast.
Left: The 1939 – 1945 Memorial to over 100 Head Line crew members who lost their lives - and nine out of ten Headline ships lost, eight in the Atlantic and one destroyed in an air raid, at Belfast Docks. Origin: Author /Courtesy J. Corry Ltd.

Above: Large jars, man height and dating from the 16th. century BC, found at Knossos, Crete.Visited by author in 1976.
Photos: Courtesy of Stephen Downes, Antrim.

The Goddess Diana of Ephesus: When the apostle Paul preached against the silversmiths there making false idols, they shouted "Great is Diana of the Ephesions."   See Acts Ch. V28.
Origin: Author 1974

Above: These ornate jars date from the Minoan Civilisation – Bronze Age (16th. BC) in Crete and were used for the storage of wine, oil and grain. Sir Arthur Evans began archaeological work here in 1900 and continued this for 35 years.
Courtesy of Stephen Downes, Antrim.

Left : The famous Tea Clipper "Cutty Sark," now in permanent dock at Greenwich, London.
Origin uncertain

Above: *An historic meeting, after the Belfast steamer, the old ss "Fanad Head" had just safely crossed the Atlantic. She was just off Rockall when stopped on the 14th. of September 1939 by the German U-boat, the U-30, Cmdr. Julius Lemp. Lemp is here seen wearing the white cap. With the binoculars, is Machinist Klobes. Both died later when the U-110 was captured by British destroyers in mid Atlantic on 9. 05. 1941.* Origin: Georg Högel, Radio Operator in the U-30 and U 110.
On the first day of the Second World War, the U-30 sank the Donaldson passenger liner, the "Athenia." Georg Högel the radio operator in U-30 heard the "Athenia's" distress call, and told Cmdr. Lemp, "You have sunk an unarmed passenger ship." After the "Fanad Head" sinking, the same crew in U-110 sank Belfast's "Bengore Head," but, as above, was fately damaged,captured, and important Inigma codes recovered from the sinking U-Boat.Georg became a POW but for many years, he carried on a lengthy, helpful correspondance with author. He died in Munich in 2014.

Above: The Memorial on the water front at Liverpool to the Engineers of the "Titanic" who were all lost following the sinking of the ship in the North Atlantic after hitting the Iceberg, April 12th. 1912. Origin: Author
Note: *At the front of the Memorial, are two figures representing the engineers. One carries a large spanner and the other carries a hammer.*

The SS "Fanad Head, sunk by U-30, 14th. Sept. 1939. Origin: Denis Martin, Historian Dublin.

The rudders and propellers of U-534 after fifty years on the sea bed off Denmark. Courtesy of "Historic Ships" Birkenhead.

Off the Caribbean coast: The only still photograph of the sea bed to come out - we were advised not to use a flash. However, the camcorder results were quite good. Does one see a skull?
Origin:Author 2013.

The attack on the German battleship, Tirpitz, in 1943: Kaa Fjord, where Tirpitz was lying, is seen to the right and where the British midget submarines, X-5, X6 and X7 made their approach. X-6 and X7 were credited with mining Tirpitz but were disabled. X-5 was seen surfaced close to Tirpitz, but disappeared . No wreckage ever found. Origin: Photos taken by a British Missionary, en route Russia.

Author with the Superintendent Engineer of "Operation Mobilisation" when engaged on some voluntary work on the MV "Logos Two" in Belfast Drydock, Belfast in 1995. See the earlier "Logos," on the rocks in the Beagle Channel on page 202.
Origin: A kind man!

The Commemoration Service in 2008 for Allied Prisoners of War who died in captivity in the First World War. Author piping at their Memorial in Köln (Cologne) South Cemetery, Germany on Armistice Day, 11. 11. 2008. Organised by the Ballymena, Co. Antrim branch of the "Friends of the Somme Association."

Left:Remember him?R. L. Graham DFC.   Former bomber pilot, Les Graham with his 500 cc AJS "Porcupine" at the start of the 1949 T.T. He didn't finish that day, but later that season, became World Champion.

Far left, behind Les Graham: Another real character and former wartime Army serviceman from those post wartime days of road races - George Brockerton from Belaghy, Co. Londonderry with his "Dick Chamberlain Bitsa!"This was likely to have been a 500 cc long stroke Sunbean.

Chapter 7

El –Alamein, the Dardanelles, and Istanbul for Scutari.

El-Alamein and Field Marshall Bernard Montgomery are names which are etched into the memories of people of my generation – like few others.

Of the battle of El-Alamein, Churchill said, "Before El Alamein Britain never had a victory. After El-Alamein she never had a defeat."

El-Alamein was somewhere I had always wanted to see, and it would always be associated with the song, "Lily Marlene."

It lies about 50 km west of Alexandria, the route being along the coast which today is amid an unbelievable explosion of housing construction, and I eventually made the journey there with other tourists by bus.

The British War Cemetery is the final resting place for over 7,000 servicemen, a great many of them from the Commonwealth - especially New Zealand. About 1,000 of these graves bear the inscription, "Known only onto God".

In contrast with the cemeteries in say, France, the British and Commonwealth Cemetery at is laid out on the desert sand. It is indeed a beautiful place, with the symmetrical lines of headstones – many appearing to have a single flower, stretching across a landscape, peaceful now, but at one time a place of great violence and death. As I wandered along the neat rows, I would read the inscriptions – many personalised. I came across a Talbot, aged 22 years, from New Zealand – that was my mother's maiden name. I noted also, that certain of my companions had, upon arrival, set off in a purposeful direction – they appeared to know the direction in which to go to see a particular grave.

A few kilometres away westwards, I found the German Memorial – a building containing bronze wall plates on which were inscribed the names of the German fallen. Two Arabs, in long, flowing white dresses, were in attendance.

A short distance away from the German Memorial, is the Italian Memorial and it is an unusual one. It is a large building in the form of a multiple tomb – the bodies appear to be interred horizontally in the walls, in a manner after the style of a large filing cabinet.

Apparently the German Memorial is situated on the line of the most eastward advance by Rommel, the German commander in 1942.

One striking feature of the El Alamein coast, is the almost white sands of the beach, and El-Alamein railway halt lies a short distance south of the coast. There is a good hotel not far away – the "El Alamein," and a museum.The latter tells the story of the battles, with some good artefacts – see photographs.

Surprisingly, there was a substantial account of the part the Egyptian Air Force played in the defeat of the Germans! Soon it was time to return to Alexandria. The final leg of my journey would take me to Piraeus (the port of Athens) in Greece.

The Dardanelles.

It would be by way of Istanbul in Turkey, and this meant another trip up the Dardanelles. This waterway is a place that has been steeped in history and indeed in the more recent history of the First World War. There the battles of the Dardanelles Straits (losses in submarines and battleships) and on the Gallipoli Peninsula, became synonymous with unending bloodshed.

Yet because of family connections and others known to me who fought there, these places continue to hold immense interest for me. In ancient times in the wars between Greece and Persia, Xerxes the Persian king tried to cross the Dardanelles (also known as the

Hellespoint). He built a bridge of boats but the current swept it away and he is said to have punished the waters by giving them three hundred lashes and calling them salt and treacherous!

Byron once swam the Dardanelles, and Florence Nightingale had her main hospital close to these waters at Scutari (not far from Istanbul – then called Constantinople) during the Crimean war. The more recent history of the First World War battles for the Peninsula

El Alamein 2002 – the cost: The British and Commonwealth Graves Cemetery, looking south across the former battlefield. Many of those buried here are from New Zealand. This cemetery on sandy desert, contrasts with below, the green sward of the Connaught Cemetery at Thiepval Wood, France, forever associated with the 36th, Ulster Division, at the Battle of the Somme. (See below.)

Origin: Author, 2002.

A sad reminder of the men of the 36th, Ulster Division who emerged from Thiepval Wood (in background) on 1. 07. 1916, and crossed this ground on which now stands the Connaught Cemetery. Note the blue and yellow bag which appears in photos of many of the places described in this book.

Origin: Sam McMurray 1993

El Alamein, Museum 2002, North Africa: A Sherman tank of World War Two rests in the museum there – one would like to know its history – was it in action, or just put together from parts? It is a small museum, but has some interesting exhibits – like a German 88 millimetre gun, used initially as an anti aircraft weapon, but later effective in an anti tank role.
Source: Author 2002.

Author: The sands on the coast at El Alamein, North Africa, are almost white.
Source: Author 2002

has until lately been within living memory for many of those who were there, and of course it was here that H.M. Submarine E11 with my old friend George Plowman DSM as her Leading Signalman, made a contribution to that history. For the story of George and the E 11, see Chapter One of "Antrim And Beyond," Part Two,
("They served in Time of War.")

An opportunity became available for anyone wishing to visit Ephesus, when the ship stopped at the Turkish Asian port of Kusadasi. Ephesus is an amazing place with a well excavated historic past - and excellent preservation. I had already visited Ephesus in 1974, and the photographs shown a few pages back, date from that time.

As just recalled, the passage of the Dardanelles and the city of Istanbul have always been places of major interest to me. But just now when I arrived in Istanbul, my main purpose was to cross the Bosphorus to Scutari opposite Istanbul, and visit once again, the Siliwiye Army Barracks at Scutari. A small section of the Barracks contains some physical remnants of Florence Nightingale's Hospital which was there during the Crimean War (1854 – 1856). There was a very modest representation of a typical ward of that period when I first visited Siliwiye in 1975 - one museum ward, inside the Barracks.

The passage of the Dardanelles – see the description of the Dardanelles later on, was made during the hours of darkness, and next morning the ship came to a stop outside Istanbul, just in fact off the legendary Leander Tower. This is where George Plowman and the British submarine E11 grounded in 1915. The E11 was the first enemy to arrive off Constantinople (now Istanbul) in five hundred years, and she torpedoed a ship there and also photographed the Blue Mosque through the periscope when submerged! This latter was another first for Lieut. Cmdr.Martin Nasmith, her commander. See below and also in **"Antrim and Beyond " Part Two, Ch. One,** for the experiences of George Plowman DSM, photos on the following page.

Left: The SS "River Clyde,"at Cape Helles. Difficult to know when this photograph was taken - and by whom.
The wire was described in an Anzac source as being "Turkish." The ship was grounded to allow troops to storm the Turkish beach but unfortunately she grounded too far out. Losses were heavy.
Origin: From an Anzac source.

Left: Part of Siliwiye Turkish Army Barracks which became Florence Nightingale's Hospital at Scutari.
Origin: Photo taken by author on an earlier visit there in 1975.
Photography was actually not permitted here – it was still a Turkish Military Base as it was when Florence Nightingale had her sleeping quarters and her day room in this turret wing! Note this building in adjoining sketch.

Sketch of the British Cemetery at Scutari - taken from a book by W J Winton and Florence Witts probably written around 1900 . Where did all the headstones go?Note the solitary one below – and one could count the total there now on one hand! The Hospital is top, right.

British Cemetary at Scutari – a neglected, dog polluted two acres, just a few headstones and strands of wire protecting them. Origin: Author 2002, photo attempt from a cam corder still.

Left: Another image of the British Cemetery at Scutari- a still from a cam corder. It actually shows a piece of Queen Victoria's soaring Obelisk Memorial to the British dead at Scutari Cemetery – a much neglected place to honour the dead.
Author 2002.

Left: George Plowman DSM in his favourite watering hole, the Royal British Legion, Wellingborough.
Origin: Mrs. Lily Plowman

Left: : Author with George Plowman DSM, former Leading Signalman on the British submarine E11, 1915. Upon return from the E 11's first Dardanelles' venture, his Commander, Martin Nasmith, got the VC and each crew member was decorated. George and his wife lived in Wellingborough, North'ants. Origin: Mrs. Lily Plowman, 1976.

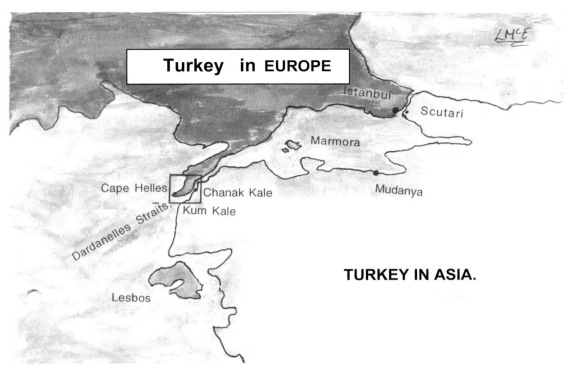

The Sea of Marmora (above) **and the Dardanelles** (below).

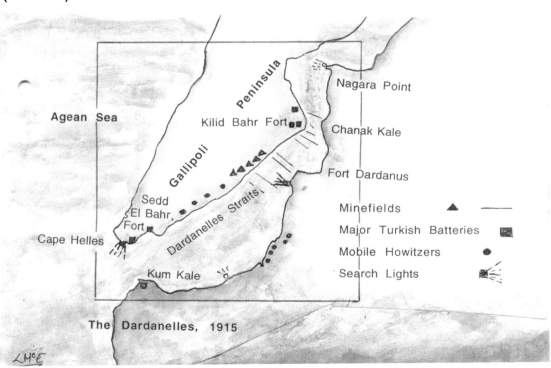

THE DARDANELLES 1915.

Above graphics: Courtesy of Miss Lisa McErlain, Randalstown, Co. Antrim.

88

The Hospital of Florence Nightingale:

This was located in a building earlier built by Sultan Selim III (1789 –1807) and was called the Seliwiye Barracks. It is still known by that name. Any traveller on the approaches to Istanbul or the Bosphorus – that water dividing Western Turkey and Eastern Turkey at Istanbul and joining the Black Sea in the North with the Sea of Marmora in the South, can easily see the building on the Asian side, with its four square turrets, one at each corner. It was in one of these turrets overlooking the Bosporus, that Florence Nightingale had her living and sleeping accommodation. As referred to, I had paid a visit here in 1975, when, through a stroke of

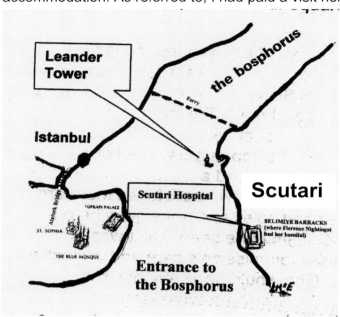

good fortune I was an unofficial visitor – few people were welcome then. Now I was curious as to what it would be like – it had now become part of the official tour itinerary in the area. Dollars had become good! I was not, however, prepared for the change that confronted my eyes and putting it simply, Mr. Market Economy was now the manager! I now found that instead of the large ward I was shown on that earlier visit, with its neat black rectangles on the floor indicating where the wounded soldiers lay on straw mattresses, I now found an area very much set up for tourism. Two Turkish Army officers, in smart suits, had been detailed to welcome visitors, discuss and lecture on various aspects of the Crimean war, and answer questions, etc. About half of the exhibits on display, had a distinct Turkish flavour about them.

The presentation was indeed most professionally delivered, but heavily dosed with an aura showing the predominant involvement of Turkey in virtually everything round. Half the items on display now – including photographs, depicted Turkish involvement – including a *heavy machine gun from the First World War*! Florence was down the queue - the large ward did not seem to be open for visitors that day!

I thought back to that other museum at El Alamein and the account there of how the Egyptian Air Force had played a major role in the outcome Montgomery's victory in 1942!

However, her day room was probably the same one which I saw twenty-five years earlier, as was the spiral iron staircase (but now fitted with fancy wooden steps), leading up to her bedroom. The very large sofa was gone, but I should say, that a number of primitive, medical instruments were still on display. These included scissors, tongs, very crude siphons, pliers etc. and all made out of – probably wrought black iron. No oil lamps were in evidence – such as there was displayed on my previous visit.

Still on display, is much correspondence between Florence Nightingale and important people in England – including a Mr Herbert, who was a Government minister during the Crimea War. The Cemetery, in which about ten thousand people were buried (including a number of nurses from the hospital), lies but a short distance from the hospital. On my earlier visit to Seliwiye Barrack, I was refused permission to visit the cemetery, but now I made the journey without hindrance. Indeed, no one took any interest at all in the bus loads of visitors who arrived to see what is an untidy open grass area of about two acres, and as far as memory goes, is fenced around with a strand or two of wire. The local dogs roam at will. The few headstones there are not of a uniform pattern – all shapes and sizes and trees grow here and there in a haphazard manner. It was plain to be seen that it was not receiving the Commonwealth Graves Commission's care and protection, and I have wondered at times as to who would have responsibility for looking after this – surely it deserves a very important place in our history. I saw one headstone bearing the name of a nurse, and another the name of an Irish soldier, whose father was a Church of Ireland minister in Waterford. The memorial that Queen Victoria caused to be erected there is a large obelisk type – and very tall. Disappointingly, (although I had used my camcorder a lot), I had forgotten to take a few still photographs there, and later had to resort to using very low technology. I tried, with limited success, to photograph a "still" or two from my non digital cam recordings - off the television screen! Not a great success - see earlier photographs of the **Crimean Cemetery** and Queen Victoria's obelisk Memorial.

On the subject of the awful state in which I found the British Cemetery at Scutari, I will now dwell upon it further - for a short season and a reason.

*   *   *   *   *

I grew up in a home where, as earlier recalled, childhood days were spent largely amidst the days of war time austerity, and where indeed in the immediate post war years, things were not much different as rationing was largely still in force until the early 1950's. But although many things were in short supply in our home, one commodity was not, and that commodity was books. The older members of my family had made a significate contributon to this through being annual recipients of Sunday School prizes over the years, but an even larger contribution had come by way of my father who was an avid reader and book collector.
Eventually, in the absence of anyone else wanting to inherit many of these books, they found a home in the attic of my own house. And one day- only a short time ago, I discovered among those books a very old book about the life and works of Florence Nightingale. It contained interesting references and sketches about the British cemetery at Scutari! This book was wiitten by W. J.Winton and Florence Witts and was a very great help researching an important chapter of British history.It was very revealing as to what the British Cemetery was like during the two years of the Crimea War or what somebody wrote about it - without perhaps ever seeing it!
Firstly, an extract concerning what relaxation was available for Florence Nightingale ? Was it a walk in the British Cemetery ? And how indeed the cemetery I described in 2002 appeared in 1854-56. Was it the same cemetery being described?

Extract 1 (References to the British Cemetery at Scutari)

"Miss Nightingale once more settled down to her unending labours at Scutari Hospital, but it was with a heart deeply pained by the loss of so many of her friends and helpers.
Not unaturally , her brief outdoor exercise often took the form of a stroll beneath the trees that often overshadow the beautiful cemetery, where now lie so many of England's bravest sons. No less than four thousand of them are sleeping there. Of all the cemeteries in the Ottoman Empire, that of Scutari is the largest and most beautiful, as well as the most ancient and celebrated. There are said to be enough tombstones in it to rebuild the whole city of Stambul.
From " Florence Nightingale and and Frances Willard"
 – the story of their lives and written by W. J.Winton and Florence Witts.

Extract 2 : (The British Cemetery at Scutari contd:) **But the portion in which the English lie had most attraction for Florence Nightingale as indeed it must have for all of us. It is very beautifully situated on a promontory , high above the sea with Chalcedon beneath, the town of Scutari behind,and the Bosphorous to the right. Here lie the nameless graves of British Soldiers who were mostly buried in great pits. Through all generations the cemetery at Scutari will be a sacred spot to English hearts.   Author's Note: No one seemed to be caring very much for the cemetery I saw !**

When Miss nightingale returned from Balaclava, she started a scheme for erecting a suitable Memorial to the brave men who there await the last great muster. The work was not completed until after the close of the war, but now there stands in the midst of those forgotten graves a great monument of gleaming marble. On a huge square base stand four angels with drooping wings who support a tall, tapering shaft which rises skywards, and with silent finger points to the source of eternal hope and rest. On each side of the base is an inscription, graven in four different languages :

"This monument was erected by

Queen Victoria
and her people."

From " Florence Nightingale and and Frances Willard"
– the story of their lives and written by W. J.Winton and Florence Witts.

My observations were made about one hundred and forty years after the above sentiments were approvingly expressed and indeed one might have walked safely amongst British graves and headstones. But one might ask today who exactly had such a priviledge of a separate grave and who then were the 4,000 referred to as nameless British soldiers who were cast "into great pits?" The two acres or so of cemetery is there, presided over by the great obelisk Memorial on which is claimed that it was erected by Queen Victoria and her people. I wonder what they would think now if they saw what I saw. I saw dogs roaming at will, passing through the few strands of wire surrounding the area. And where are all the quote, **"tombstones in it to rebuild the whole city of Stambul."** I saw half a dozen – at most.

Memories even amongst friends are sometimes short, and just over fifty years later Britain was at war with its former Crimean ally, Turkey. And something must have happened to the **"the beautiful cemetery, where now lie so many of England's bravest sons, no less than four thousand -**

Turkish War Memorial at Cape Helles, slightly further north than the British one. Origin: Author from seaward.

----**sleeping there."** It never gets a mention – anywhere.

Returning from the Crimean Cemetery, I found myself to be the last person to board the bus - filled with people from all over the British Isles and further, for the return to central Istanbul. I got a tittered response when I inquired, "Is this bus going to Ballymena?" They all appeared to know where Ballymena, Co. Antrim, was.

The ship sailed during the night across the Sea of Marmora, and on going on deck the next morning, I was surprised to find that the town of Gallipoli lay on our starboard bow. The ship was stopped and lying very close to the shore. This was puzzling – there was no obvious reason for this – but perhaps a pilot was boarding or departing. Presently we moved on, heading for the Narrows where in 1915, a net was strung across The Dardanelles in an effort to trap the British and French submarines making their way up towards the Sea of Marmora.

This was where, as George Plowman the leading signalman of the British submarine E11 recalled, "It was a case of backing up the electric motor fuses with wire and charging the net until it burst." As earlier mentioned, one British submarine, the E7 (Lieut. Cmdr. Archie Cochrane), was lost here when a piece of wire from the net became entwined in the submarine's propellers. The entire crew was taken prisoner. Cochrane, a grandson of former Admiral Lord Beresford, escaped later in the war, became an M.P. at Westminster, and was a Commodore of convoys during the Atlantic battles of the Second World War. The Dardanelles is about forty-one miles long, and about half way down, on the European side, is one of the remaining forts that, at one time, were in plenty along the shore. This fort is known as Kilhd Bahr, and looked in fair condition. No guns were to be seen now and something else was missing – a large sign which used to be mounted high on the European shore, and easily read from seaward. It showed a date – 18.3.1915. Until recently, it was a subtle reminder, that on that day, the British and French concluded (after losing three battleships to mines) that it would not be possible to capture the Dardanelles by sea power alone. But the large sign was now nowhere to be seen! Could this have been political correctness, as the European Federation beckons?

Lieut. C.W. Clark, Rathmore, Antrim, late of the North Irish Horse and the 54th. Anglian Divison. Photo: Courtesy of William Clark, Donegore.

A visit had been arranged to see the main battlefields on the Gallipoli Peninsula, but disappointment was our lot. A number of people were getting their wreaths ready, when it announced from the bridge that it was not found possible to put us ashore owing to a storm brewing the Anzac and Suvla Bay beaches,on the west side of the Peninsula. So we sailed away from the Gallipoli Peninsula – as the British had done before in December 1915.

Sometime I hope to visit the Cape Helles beaches where my Great Uncle William Cameron from Kellswater, near Ballymena, had landed from the ss "River Clyde," when serving with the Dublin Fusiliers in April 1915. Not far away is Suvla Bay where my old friend of yesteryear, Charles Warwick Clark from Rathmore, Antrim, had landed with the 54th. Anglian Division at Suvla Bay, on the West side of the Gallipoli Peninsula, Turkey - see above.

He was Invalided out in December of that year with frostbite in the feet, two days before the general withdrawal of the British and Commonwealth troops, and spent Christmas Day on Lemnos Island, "where the Greeks wouldn't give me an orange." He recovered in time to take part in the battle of the Somme with the Royal Irish Fusiliers, on the First of July 1916. His name, Lieut. C.W. Clark, is on the First World War Memorial in High St. Presbyterian Church, The Steeple, Antrim, Co. Antrim. He died in 1983.

Great Uncle William's name is on the 1914 - 1918 War Memorial in the Presbyterian Church at Kells, Co.Antrim.

President Kemal Ataturk's remarkable Memorial. The script set up, is as on the Memorial.

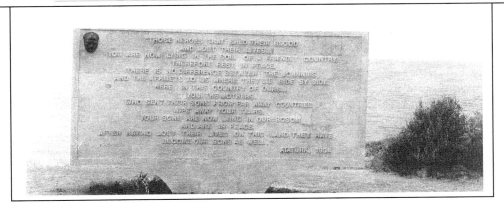

A remarkable monument indeed.

President Kemal Ataturk's Memorial. Script set up is as on the Memorial

" Those Heroes that shed their blood
and lost their lives
You are now lying in the soil of a friendly country.
Therefore rest in peace.
There is no difference between the Johnnies
and the Mehmets to us where they side by side
here in this country of ours…
You the mothers
Who sent their sons from far away countries,
Wipe away your tears:
Your sons are now lying in our bosom
and are in peace.
After having lost their lives on this land, they have
become our sons as well." **Ataturk,1934.**

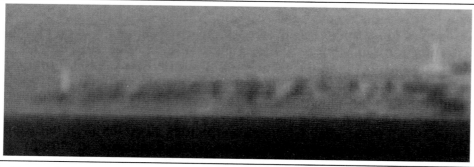

Above: At the tip of the Gallipoli Peninsula - a poor photograph perhaps, but it was taken from a mile to seaward and using a throwaway camera. To left, can be seen the Lighthouse. To right, the British War Memorial, just above where the "River Clyde" was beached (too far out unfortunately for the attacking troops.) Thus, on the 26th. April, 1915, British and Allied landings took place, largely between these two landmarks.
The carnage was such that the sea was red with blood and losses there of the most severe.
Origin: Author 1976.

Left: William Cameron, Dublin Fusiliers at Gallipoli 1915.

Left: Author's Great Uncle William Cameron, from Kellswater, Ballymena, late of the Dublin Fusiliers – the "Dubs" as he called them. It is thought he was one of a small detachment landed of the SS "River Clyde," as the main body of the Dublin Fusiliers were directed to land elsewhere.
(see earlier photos of the SS "River Clyde" at Cape Helles in April 1915.) He was later part of a section transferred in support of the Suvla Bay landings in August 1915.
A very tall man, he was a sniper with his unit. He had earlier served in the Royal Marines and at one time worked in the construction of the American railways.
Origin: Service Photograph

The Mediterranean Expeditionary Force was under the command of General Sir Ian Hamilton, operating from a British Royal Navy cruiser off shore. The Gallipoli Landings were both a disaster and a defeat for British and Allied forces. The operations cost these forces about 40,000 causalities. Eventually in the wake of any progress on land and mountings losses sustained by the British and French of ships at sea, Hamilton was removed from this post. It is believed that he never held command in combat again. The only consolation was that the subsequent Allied withdrawal was carried out without loss, it is believed, being sustained.

many years of absence - and with it, the imposing temples of Bacchus, Jupiter and Venus, and places like Beirut, and Byblos, (the latter word from which "Bible" is thought to have been derived).

The stunning Jeita Caves which extend six kilometres into the mountains, were all available for discovery. But a cracked windscreen in the bus I would travel in - see photograph on the previous page and also on a later page, all seemed to say, "Make haste slowly!"

 The Gorge of the Dog River north of Beirut, Lebanon, is where passing victorious armies from Ramesses the Second, to those of Allenby in 1917, have indeed sought to leave a record of their passing. Construction work made it impossible to park our bus near the Gorge, and photos of, eg, the two plaques seen on the previous page, were only possible by sighting them, somehow, in our bus wing mirror and also through a damaged windscreen! See these photos as taken.

I had three things on my own shopping list: - The Jeita Caves near the Gorge; the Square of Martyrs, Beirut, and the Gorge itself at the mouth of the Dog River. Here all the conquering armies that passed that way from Ramesses II to General Allenby in the First World War, had left their inscriptions. These are said to be seen as either simple scratches, or more permanent ones like the plaques shown on the photographs. These plaques are attached to the walls of the Gorge's rock formations through which the Dog River flows and becomes Beiruit's water supply.

I would have been very keen to have seen the Litani River to the south, where the 11[th.] (Scottish) Commando – within whose ranks was my late friend, Jimmie Storie, originally from Ayr, fought their first battle. Also with them was their piper, Jimmie Lawson, still living in Kirkaldy, Scotland and with whose hearty self I have a yarn from time to time. Here their battle, which was against the Vichy French in June,1941- the "Battle of the Litani River," incurred heavy casualties for them there.

It was here that Blair Mayne from Newtownards, Co. Down, with them in that same battle against the Vichy French, was mentioned in dispatches. Later in the war he was recommended for the Victoria Cross, having won the DSO four times. He shared that latter distinction with Lieut. Col. Alistair Pearson, commanding officer of the 8[th.] Battalion, the 6[th.] Airborne Division to become, arguably, the most highly decorated serviceman of the Second World War. Captain James Walker RN also had four DSO's.

It was, sadly, that at the Litani River, the 11th. (Scottish) Commando lost Col. Peddar, their first commanding officer. His daughter, now aged over 90 years, still keeps in touch with their piper, Jimmy Lawson, both now also well into their nineties. See Ch. 20 for more on Jimmie Storie and the 11[th.] (Scottish) Commando.

See also *"Antrim and Beyond"* Part Two (*"They served in time of war"*) by author - in which the death of Col. Peddar is recalled by Len Mitchell, a Medic serving there who was detailed to care for Col. Peddar after he was shot in the head at the Litani River.

 Sadly, Len Mitchell is now no longer with us either.

In the recent conflict in the summer of 2006, it appeared that the main objective of the Israeli Army was to clear the ground of opposition fighters - from the Israeli border with Lebanon, to the Litani River. The Litani is shown here flowing South, where it eventually reaches the sea about fifty miles from the Israeli border.

Arrival in Beiruit in 2004:

Upon arrival, transport was there to take travellers to those areas they wished to see. Cement bulk carriers, loads of scaffolding, timber, blocks – a thousand and one items were rushing to rebuild war torn Beirut at an astonishing rate. The bus on which I travelled made its way through this melee and after some thirty minutes or so of battle, was passing the mouth of the Dog River, the place I had wanted to see. The high south bank against which the relatively small river tumbled, appeared to consist of limestone stone. Erected upon this stone face could be seen various reminders of those who had passed that way ie plaques, perhaps a metre or more in length - actually erected upon the vertical face of the bank. See sketch map of that area on.

Due to the excessive industrial traffic on the road, and the congestion due to road accidents etc, our driver was unable to park anywhere close, and photos had to be attempted through the windows of the bus. The results shown are not too good, *but half a loaf is better than no loaf!*

Another twenty minutes and we were at the famous Jeita caves in the Nahr El-Kalb Valley. The Grotto of Jeita, the source of the Dog River from which Beirut gets its water supply, is formed of two galleries. The lower gallery, discovered in 1836 (and opened to the public in 1958) is crossed by an underground river, fed, it is believed, from the Dog River. It was possible that day, for some of us to go underground for a boat ride over about 500 metres of the 6,200 metres already explored.

Underground River Boat. Origin: Touristic Jeita

The temperature was a pleasant 16° C and it remains constant, apparently, throughout the year. The upper gallery was reached by a cable car known locally as a "ropeway". The views were picturesque indeed, and it was possible to walk into the system of tunnels – complete with hand rails and lighting, for perhaps half a mile - although the caves and tunnels actually penetrate the mountain side for over 6 kilometres. The overall spectacle is described in local tourist information as "a crystalline castle of magical fascination and one of the most impressive natural sites in the world."

Waters have indeed, since the dawn of history, issued from the mountains to carve out these fantastic caves and galleries, imbued with colours and forms of infinite variety and subtlety. In the main, these forms are those of the *stalactites* (formations of lime shaped like an icicle hanging from the roof or sides of the caves), and *stalagmites* (again formations of lime, built up in the shape of a cone and on the floor of the cave – caused by water that contains lime dropping from the cave roof onto the floor). Drops of water that "freeze," become *stalactites* – thus their appearance as icicles hanging from the roof.

One indeed could only stare in wonder at this thing of Creation framed through the ages with magnificent reminders of the wonder, beauty, and diversity of natural forces.

Back for a brief visit to Beirut the bus stopped close to the place I hoped to see again after so many years – the Square of Martyrs. The Square was so called, because this was the place where the Turkish authorities executed fifteen local men (possibly Armenians) in 1915, because of alleged collaboration with the British Forces. I remembered it as a large square, surrounded on its sides by all kinds of shops or business premises, and having various statues of riders on horseback etc situated in line up and down the Square. We had stopped at a junction of four streets, and one bore the legend "Square of Martyrs." But this street led, not to the Square of Martyrs that I remembered, but to a landscape flattened over the area of a football pitch – the Square of Martyrs had been on the line between the two warring factions in the civil war – and sadly had been completely destroyed. More sadly still, is the news just breaking on a day in late November 2004, that Pierre Gemayel, the thirty four year old Christian Minister for Industry in the Lebanese Coalition Government, has just been assassinated by gunmen in Beirut.

This assassination has renewed fears for the survival of the Coalition Government – indeed the threat of civil conflict now appears in 2006 to loom close once again. As already recalled, when walking through the streets of the bustling Beirut of the early 1960's, Stan Pacer – a naturalised Pole, torpedoed twice in the Battle of the Atlantic and our third engineer on the S.S. "Grecian," had that advice for me: *"Bob, this is a very old place - don't get knocked down here – nobody would ever want to know who you are!"*

The Dog River Gorge

Above: **Plaques - enlarged photograph of that shown later on, and taken at the Dog River Gorge, north of Beiruit.** (caught in the bus mirror.)   Origin: Author: 2004

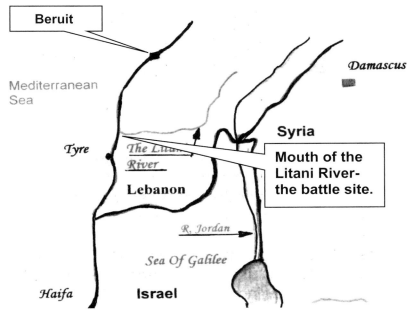

Above: **Sketch map showing the place where the Litani River reaches the sea – and the site of the battle there.**
Note: At this time, Lebanon was part of Syria, and known as such.   Origin: Author 2004.

Lebanon (contd.) Reference Stan's advice about walking in Beiruit!

Well, it didn't happen then, but it very nearly did during my next visit - fifty years later, that is, the visit currently being being described - just now!
I was determined to have a video recording of where the Square of Martyrs once stood - and where I once stood, gazing at those statues of men in armour, mounted on horseback on solid concrete pedestals of cubic form – with the latter rising fully six feet above the ground. Now I was recalling the backdrop of all the busy lives being lived out then - all around that square. Some vendors were selling red "Vino" wine by the bucket, others using mechanisms (not unlike that of a small vertical drill) squeezing halves of oranges to provide pure orange juice to sell in plastic beakers, and sellers of multifarious ingredients to satisfy a thousand Arab recipes – a vibrant part Arab part French society, with street names in both Roman and Arabic script. In recalling to mind these things from fifty years ago while pressing the record button on the cam corder, I didn't notice that a 35 ton concrete transporter – (there seemed to be cement or concrete mixers everywhere one looked in the revitalised Beirut), was reversing into the gateway I was standing in!
A shout from a Lebanese bus driver made me all too suddenly aware of the thirty five tons of concrete carrier that was lumbering my way. The resulting video however had caught it

all – including the warning shout of the bus driver. An interesting recording ! I then had someone (a member of the passer-by battalions that exist all over the world), to photograph the mixer and myself – just in case I would forget and do it again!

Left; This cedar plaque from Lebanon (reduced in size) was carried home in the old ss "Grecian" in 1961 – a wooden cedar wall plaque only, but there were few real cedars to be seen in and around Beirut even by then.

As I departed from the land of the cedars, I thought of how the cedars of Lebanon have been around for a long time – although not today in the abundance of former years .

Above: All that is left of the Square of Martyrs- an area of perhaps the size of a football pitch and is now a temporary car park. Author 2004.

Sadly, in the aftermath of the recent conflict with Israel (resulting in the demolition of large parts of Beirut), the cement mixers that I witnessed will have to do it all over again - reconstructing much of what had been achieved in that frenzy of activity I witnessed, at the Dog River Gorge in 2004 and have just remarked upon. See photograph above.(What would we travellers do without the helping hands of these anonymous "passer bys" ?)

King Hiram's presentation of cedar wood to King Solomon :Solomon's Temple was close to where the Wailing Wall is in Jerusalem. Now first read all about King Hiram's contributions to King Solomon in the Bible – see First King's Ch. 5.

Thus Hiram, King of Tyre, supplied some cedar wood and skilled stone masons to King Solomon when his Temple was being built.

It is still possible today, to visit the sarcophagus of Hiram in Beirut, but alas, I had no opportunity to do so then.

Chapter 9

Jordan
A Suez Canal Transit.

It was now, however, time to start heading to my final area of interest in this part of the world. I would find this in the footsteps of an archaeologist turned soldier, one T.E. Lawrence, but better known today as *Lawrence of Arabia* . This interest would take me through the Suez Canal again, but this time southwards. I was now leaving Beirut with T.E. Lawrence's wonderful book, "Seven Pillars of Wisdom" on hand, as the M.V. "Discovery" was headed for Port Said.This book has been designated a Classic of World Literature.
 On arrival, arrangements were in place for those passengers wishing to visit Cairo and the Great Pyramids of Giza. Having been to these places previously, I did not put up my hand but spent a leisurely day in Port Said, pondering upon the history of the Canal and the things I was seeing from the ship's rail - like the breakwater, possibly the one built by De Lessops when construction of the Suez Canal was beginning. Nearby also was the old lighthouse, now bypassed by numerous buildings and, it seemed, a considerable distance now from the sea. There was sharp contrast between the many modern buildings side by side with the older ones in the Turkish Ottoman style – the latter now showing their age. Further down the docks towards the entrance to the Suez Canal proper, were the offices of the Suez Maritime Company and the Harbour Police. There was a small slipway on the Eastern side, where some small ship building and repair work was being carried on – and all around, were those trying to sell all kinds of ware - brass lamps, carpets, beads, trinkets, leather goods, all persistent in their persuasions that these things were musts that one should never be without! But now I needed a leather wallet, and the wallet that I bought there in 2004, is still going strong today - in 2017. Even the magnetic clasp is still working! But absent on that day was a McTavish – an Egyptian, able to speak fluent Glaswegian! And there had always been a McTavish at Port Said!

  *   *   *   *   *

The MV "Discovery" which had been secured at the end of a pontoon bridge as is the custom at Port Said, cast off at around two am for the passage to the Great Bitter Lakes – there to anchor with the rest of the southbound convoy to allow the northbound convoy to proceed. The departure was watched with great interest by many of the passengers. I happened to have secured a vantage point on an observation area just above the wing of the Bridge, and since the Suez Canal Pilot and our Captain spent much time on the Bridge wings i.e. out in the open below the observation area. It was possible to hear their conversation, lean over, and ask the odd question.
Presently, I found myself standing beside a very interesting man. His name was Hammond, and he was a retired master mariner on ships of the Royal Fleet Auxiliary – support vessels that supply the Royal Navy, in peace time and in time of conflict. He had served in the Falklands conflict, and in fact had towed the wreck of the "Sir Galahad," a Royal Fleet Auxiliary vessel, out into deep water, where it was disposed of. The "Sir Galahad" was caught without air cover while discharging stores and the Welsh Guards, and was bombed by Argentine aircraft.
Mr. Hammond had many interesting things to say indeed. However upon entry into the cuttings of the Suez Canal proper, a fog had suddenly come down but the ship did not appear to slow – the normal convoy speed being understood to be 8 knots and I remarked to Mr. Hammond about our "pressing on" in these conditions. He too seemed puzzled by our

speed, eventually informing me, that although he had passed through the Canal on numerous occasions, he had never seen fog there.

"But I have been caught in sand storms – so violent that ships have had to stop, with boats being deployed from the banks to attach securing lines, so that the ships remain in the centre of the channel. I wouldn't like to be taking a ship down through this lot tonight," he said. He suggested that the skipper must be using radar to be able to navigate so confidently.

This was later confirmed by our own skipper as being the case – "No problem at all," he said.

Thus the unstoppable march of progress in technical advance.

Note: The Suez Canal was constructed largely by the removal of sand, although in places in the southern part of the workings, some blasting of rock was necessary. Sand, in lacking vertical stability, tended to drift towards the centre of the cut and in cross sectional profile would be seen as vee shaped. That is why ships moving in the Suez Canal must keep to the centre line, especially those of deep draught. It is also the reason why ships docked at Port Said have to use Pontoon bridges and secure in deep water towards the centre of the waterway, and why Mr. Hammond's ships were constrained to anchor in the middle of the Canal by ropes during sand storms – otherwise they might drift aground on its sloping sides.

Aqaba Fort and Wadi Rum - In the Footsteps of "Lawrence of Arabia."

Eventually the transit of the Suez Canal was completed having waited in the Great Bitter Lakes to allow a North bound convoy to sail northwards unimpeded. The final port of interest to me was Aqaba, (see earlier description of Petra). This Jordanian port - Jordan's only port, is at the head of the Gulf of Aqaba (or the Gulf of Eliat if you happen to come from Israel). Eliat and Aqaba lie at the head of the Gulf – and are separated by only a few miles.

As was mentioned previously, Aqaba and Aqaba Fort were occupied by T.E.Lawrence and

The Sinai Peninsula, Akaba and Eliat
Origin: Author 2016.

Prince Faisal during the 1914-18 War – in fact in 1917 (some spell Faisal as Fiesel). This was the early part of the epic events that were to make T.E. Lawrence - later to be Col. T.E. Lawrence DSO, a household word in many parts of the world. He was later named "Lawrence of Arabia" by a well known American journalist. Lawrence would help Prince Faisal's Arabs drive the Turks from Arabia. A graduate of Oxford University, T.E. Lawrence was involved in archaeology in the Middle East (where he first met Gertrude Bell, the English woman whose own Middle East experiences were very complimentary to his own) before the First World War, and he became skilled in desert ways and language. These latter acquisitions were surely the key to T. E.'s success in helping to co-ordinate the Arab Revolt. Just how important a role he played, depends on who the commentator might be – Arab historians tend to ascribe the more important role to Faisal, later to be king of Iraq.

Part of Lawrence's early professional work, however, involved surveying in Sinai, which although a Province of Egypt (through which runs the Suez Canal with all its importance to British commerce), it was nominally under Turkish rule. Modern thinking is that his survey work there was but a cover for intelligence gathering considered essential for the safe guarding of the Canal. Indeed this fear was entirely justified when Turkish troops had to be beaten back following their attack there upon the outbreak of war in 1914.

My object of being in Aqaba again, was to complete unfinished business there – namely to visit Wadi Rum, a place in the desert associated with Lawrence, the road to which I had passed some years before when travelling to Petra - see Chapter 6.

In his writings, Lawrence has revealed that during the First World War, he once visited Petra one moonlight night!

I also wanted to see the Fort (or castle) at Aqaba.

Wadi Rum :

In Akaba I joined a group of people on a bus, all with the same intention as myself – to visit Wadi Rum. This bus was to take us to a location known as the "Rest House." This lies East off the road to Petra. It is a local establishment for refreshment (local food), some shopping facilities, and two old railway carriages dating from Ottoman times. One speculated if these might be carriages salvaged from a train wrecked by Lawrence. The Bedouins of the area were literally all around with their sheep and camels. There, after some refreshment, we were invited to leave our bus and clamber aboard our transport. This consisted of a motley collection of jeeps, Land Rovers, and Nissan pick-up trucks – all devoid of tyre treads and headlamps without bulbs in their sockets!

"We were riding for Rum."

from "Seven Pillars of Wisdom," T.E. Lawrence.

I managed a precarious position on a Nissan pick-up which had some light angle iron rails attached across the open rear and sides of the pick-up's body. I soon found out the reason for such precautions as we proceeded wildly across the desert sands at speeds bordering on the unsafe and hanging onto those rails with my eyes shut at times. With mounting concern, I began to cast a fearful eye on the very suspect welding where these rails were attached to the pick-up's body. But nothing came adrift and we headed on for Wadi Rum, the desert crossed by Lawrence and the Arabs on their way to capture Aqaba in 1917.

Wadi Rum desert is sometimes known as the "Valley of the Moon," because of its surreal landscape. The "Wadi" part means that it is the dried up bed of a former river. It is quite a bed – sometimes a quarter of a mile wide and surrounded on the sides by towering mountain ridges of the most strange and weird shapes – a wadi with walls. The mountains loom up from vast areas of pink and white sand.

Wadi Rum had a profound effect on Col. Lawrence. He described it in the "Seven Pillars of Wisdom" – already mentioned in the history of Petra, as "vast and echoing – and where a squadron of aircraft could manoeuvre" - presumably safe from hostile eyes.

We stopped at the place known as the "Spring of Lawrence," where water can be seen springing from a rock, before being piped into a watering place on the desert floor.

Lawrence above, in typical Arab dress and Wadi Rum - at the "Seven Pillars of Wisdom."
(From an old Jordanian post card).

Recently, while watching a T.V. documentary, I recognised this very spot – a square watering trough on the desert floor. Close by on the rock faces, are inscribed many inscriptions and portraits - some dating from pre Islamic times.

 Now one was drawn to try and focus on the probable scenes that would have been taking place here in 1917. Hundreds of Arabs, of different tribes – mostly clad in flowing garments, camels, Lawrence, Faisal, and all preparing for the attack on Aqaba – spelt sometimes as Akaba.

Perhaps some British officers of the "Camel Corps", with Crossley or Rolls armoured cars , would be joining them. Here however, it was possible to align one's focus on more tangible things – things still associated with Lawrence. One was a certain elevated ridge, pointed out for us by our guide, and where apparently at times, Lawrence would seek solitary time to rest or think and perhaps plan another attack.

In fact from his own account, it was at this ridge that he would ascend "for peace and reflection at times." Or one might observe and consider a wild fig tree, that, arguably, could have been gazed upon by Lawrence, or drink from the spring referred to in recent lines.

Author at the " Seven Pillars," Wadi Rum, in the Jordanian desert, 2004. At this point, there is a break in the "walls." Unfortunately, the sun was behind them as well!
Source: Author (taken by our guide 2004.)

 But what were the "Seven Pillars?" Did they exist, or was it only a fanciful title for a book dreamed up by Lawrence? We were soon to find out.

After the adventure in the desert was over and refreshment - mostly of the salad variety, was offered at the Rest House – (no sheep's eye though), we started on our return to our air-conditioned bus.

Shortly afterwards, the bus stopped and our guide invited us to step outside for a photo opportunity. We were still in the Wadi Rum, its "walls" still stretching for miles. "There," he cried, " There are your Seven Pillars."

Sure enough, there it was - at a break in the desert walls, was a section of mountain with seven peaks in order of diminishing height – what a formation, and indeed, what a photo opportunity! Lawrence would obviously have noted this unique structure – but is this where he found the title for his famous book. As far as is known, he never mentions the physical "Seven Pillars " at Wadi Rum as the origins of the title. A more interesting possibility is that it was the title of the earlier smaller book written in1914, but destroyed by him, for some reason.

As already referred to, it is thought by some commentators that it was derived from the Scriptures, thus:

Proverbs Ch. 1, v9:

" **Wisdom hath builded her house, she hath hewn out her seven pillars.**"

This thought indeed, has some credibility and as already been mentioned, Lawrence, coming from a non-conformist family, had indeed taught in his Sunday School before the war, and just might have been aware of this verse. In passing, it is interesting to record that after the First World War, his mother and one of his brothers (he had lost two others in the war), became missionaries in China, but he, apparently, did not approve of them doing so. The sun was setting when we returned to Aqaba, passing the fort forever associated with Lawrence and Prince Faisal's Arabs. Faisal was one of the sons of the Sherif of Mecca, and he was later to become King of Iraq, eventually suffering assassination there in 1951.

Aqaba in Jordan.

Aqaba is identified with the Biblical city Exion Jeber, mentioned in the Old Testament. As a port, its role goes back to the time of King Solomon and the Queen of Sheba (1st. millennium B.C.). In more recent times, the city was occupied by the Crusaders, the Mamelukes, (rulers in Egypt, 18th./19th. century), and the Ottomans.

The Ottomans, or Ottoman Turks, were driven out by Lawrence and Faisal's Arabs in 1917. Different historians give different weightings to the respective roles of Lawrence and the Arabs in actually causing the fall of Aqaba Fort. It seems possible, that the Turks had decided to move out, rather than face a full assault, otherwise the Fort, (which was built by the Mamelukes), might still be occupied by the Ottomans!

Having arrived in Aqaba, I spent the most of a day, wandering about the remaining structure of the Fort (sometimes referred to as Aqaba Castle) and whose main entrance is now adorned by the Hashemite coat of arms (the latter dates from post First World War period). Lying close to the sea front at Aqaba, the fort is of low construction, and in fact, quite difficult to spot. It lies below the level of the present main road which passes by, shaded as it is by quite a few palm trees etc. The area in total is less than one acre, surrounded by a wall, except where the main structure, e.g. living quarters, are part of the wall.The fort has a fairly large open area within, but nowhere does it appear to be more than two stories high – ground and first. Its adjacent building was where, I was assured by a local shopkeeper, Lawrence lived for a period of five months.

A Brough Superior motor cycle. It is possible that this Brough was the last one belonging to Lawrence - see closing paragraph. Origin uncertain.

Above: Author at Aqaba Fort (or Castle), forever associated with "Lawrence of Arabia," Col. T. E. Lawrence DSO. Built by the Mamelukes, it overlooks Eliat in Israel and today is at places below the main road. In the time Lawrence was there, it was in the country of Arabia (today's Saudi Arabia) but after the First World War, Saudi Arabia gave Jordan a strip of land which extended to the Gulf of Aqaba, thus providing land locked Jordan with an access to the sea.
Origin: Fellow tourist 2004.

Above: The entrance to Aqaba Fort, complete with the Hashemite Coat of Arms, those of the Hashemite Shariff of Mecca in Arabia (Pre 1914 – 1918). His son Prince Faisal, led the Arab revolt during that period, and became King of Iraq. He came to England for Lawrence's funeral in 1935, but was himself assassinated in Iraq in 1951. Origin: Fellow tourist 2004.

Above: The Egyptian Airport of Sharm El Sheikh, at the southern tip of the Sinai Peninsula. Shortly after the author passed through these gates, a party of French tourists did likewise, and boarded a French Boing 737 airliner – in all 150 people. Minutes later, the aircraft crashed into the Red Sea. There were no survivors. On the week previous, the Swiss authorities had refused to allow this aircraft to overfly their country because of its mechanical condition.
Origin: Author 2004

Departure From Aqaba

So departing Aqaba on the M.V. "Discovery," landfall was soon made again at Sharm El Sheikh, at the Southern tip of Sinai. It was the departure airport for the United Kingdom (see photograph above). It was also goodbye to Wadi Rum and Aqaba Fort, both with their associations with T.E. Lawrence, the Oxford Academic, a hostilities only soldier, and an officer who at first refused to accept the D.S.O. when awarded it. He said that he had, through no fault of his own, misled the Arabs into thinking that they, in defeating the Turks, were fighting for freedom to run their own affairs for the first time in hundreds of years. The "Sykes Picot Agreement" ensured that such freedom (for most), would not come until after another World War.

Lawrence was to eventually accept the decoration.

Lieut.Col. Lawrence DSO, was a complex man in time of war and peace. Perhaps he was even more so in the years following the war. But his name is associated with many places – like Aqaba, Maan, Damascus (which he actually governed for a few days) and – ah yes, a place called Derna in Syria. Note: All the land mass between Turkey and Arabia during this time, was known as Syria.

The failure of the British and French governments of the day to listen – perhaps with similar care and closer attention to the views of Lawrence himself on Eastern affairs, has, one hundred years on, consequences for us today.

 The "Sykes Picot Agreement," was an arrangement which carved up much of the former Ottoman territory that had stretched from Turkey to the Arabian Sea. It created straight border states rather than nations and was a sticking plaster solution covering the wounds of centuries of Ottoman misrule.

It has ensured that almost every Arab state subsequent in being, experiences periodic, endemic and violent turmoil.

" Clouds Cottage," the home of T. E. Lawrence. With his friends, meals were not cooked as such – if someone was hungry, they "just opened a tin." Who knows what role Lawrence might have played in W W Two, had he lived Source: Cecil Millar, Templepatrick, Co. Antrim.

Note: Wadi Rum in the Jordian desert, had, by 1917, been made famous by the exploits of T.E. Lawrence, Col. T.E. Lawrence DSO – better known as "Lawrence of Arabia." This mountain shape at Wadi Rum (a dried up river bed with towering walls on either sides) is also known as the "Seven Pillars." In 1914, Lawrence wrote a book called "Seven Pillars of Wisdom" but little is known of its contents. As already mentioned, it is now thought that he took the title from the Old Testament (Proverbs Ch. 9 and V1-----"Wisdom hath builded her house, she hath hewn her seven pillars." As mentioned earliier, coming from a non conformist family, Lawrence at one time taught in his local Sunday School and is likely to have been well versed in the Scriptures. That book was destroyed by Lawrence, but after the First World War he would write his classic " Seven Pillars of Wisdom," autobiographical and largely about his time in Arabia during the war there.

The peculiar service life of T.E. Lawrence, "Lawrence of Arabia" from the end of the war until he retired in the early 1930's is much too complex to cover here - the title "Lawrence of Arabia" was apparently first used by an American War Correspondent – as earlier referred to, when introducing a film presentation he had produced about Lawrence.

One final observation on Lawrence: He had met the famous English – almost mysterious Gertrude Bell, a daughter of the famous Bell steel producing family (later to become Stewart and Lloyd's) when first working as an archaeologist in Syria prior to the 1914 -18 War. Miss Bell was herself to become a famous, experienced, traveller/explorer in Arab lands, a historian interested in archaeology and eventually a political figure of amazing stature in Middle Eastern affairs in the 1920's.

As earlier mentioned, their lives were to become complimentary to each other and one almost senses how Lawrence would listen carefully to her observations on the then current world scenes that they were passing through.

When finally retired, it was to his cottage in Dorset, "Clouds Cottage." There he and his friends would meet to talk and walk about, "eating out of tins."

It was from "Cloud's Cottage" that he set out one morning on his Brough Superior motor cycle and shortly afterwards died following a road accident close by. He had owned eight Brough's at different times, and was riding the eighth one on that fatal morning. The funeral of Lawrence, following that motor cycling accident in 1935, was attended by the highest in society (including Winston Churchill), and one understands that this eighth Brough Superior - the one he was riding on that fatal morning, is one of those now on view in the Imperial War Museum, Lambeth, London.

Had he lived, what interesting, dangerous and important roles would he have carried out in the Second world War?

Chapter 10

Different ways of travel to places of interest -

(And the voyage of the MV "Velarde.")

Most travellers on holidays use scheduled services – by bus, train, ship or air to reach their destinations. Some in fact have holidays on a train – full board for days or weeks - especially on the long hauls of the USA, Canadian or Russian railways. Less affluent travellers – perhaps in some African countries also make lengthy rail journeys. Here these may have a more commercial goal but with lesser daily bread, accommodation, and - a rolling stock infrastructure a trifle dodgy! Western cruise ships would be full board of course, but what, if the places of desire are well off the beaten tract where such services do not exist?

Other solutions do exist in places. One possibility is to travel by sea to remote places by taking passage on cargo ships which are on supply duties - if no conventional ferry, liner or cruise facilities exists to such places. Addresses for such bookings can usually be found in magazines like "Sea Breezes" or "Shipping" etc. Remote places, for example, might lie in the latitude of Southern Africa - east for Mauritius or west for St Helena. It would mean that one would have to fly to, for example, South Africa, to make a connection for such an undertaking. Nevertheless, opportunities exist here, to visit remote ports *not normally* used by conventional passenger services.

West of South America, one could find their goal in the remoteness of the Galapagos Islands – virtually on the Equator, off the coast of Ecuador but commercially accessible. It is now also on the cruise ships' itineraries. Further south in the Southern Hemisphere there is even more remoteness at Easter Island – 30 degrees south although now with some airport facilities. Pitcairn Island, lies on the same latitude but with only a tiny dock to accommodate the island's fishing boat needs etc. It is extremely difficult to get permission to land on, for Cargo vessels to these latter out of the way places, will mostly be in the business of supply – with possibly a return cargo of some primary source produce or other and - maybe only calling three or times in a year. The problem of limited docking facilities - such as, for example at Juan Fernandos Island (now known as Robinson Crusoe Island in the South Pacific Ocean and thirty degrees south) usually means that visiting vessels tend to be on the small side - with limited accommodation for passengers or perhaps the tenders of visiting cruise ships. (There may now an Air Service from Chile to the latter.)

It is possible to book for just part of a cargo ship's round trip e.g. a section in the middle of a trip, or the first or last section, if the round trip is not required. Some cruise companies do likewise, especially if the full cruise is of long duration e.g. a round the world cruise. Occasionally, conventional cruise companies have "cruises to unusual places" and indeed the "Voyages of Discovery's" Company specialise in excellent cruises that mean just that. There is however another way to get around – and indeed with pay.

If you have adequate qualifications and suitable previous experience, then, with some time available – eg a job with long vacations, or a job with shorter vacations but with very flexible arrangements where you can vacate at short notice or indeed even if you are retired, you could be a holiday relief crew member of a merchant ship. In the following pages, there is an account of how the author did just that very thing as a relief engineer at sea and see a country which he had never visited before.

 Somewhat amazingly in this age and generation, that country was Spain!

 Finally, you can use a bicycle, yes, "Get on your bike." The Author has used the latter possibility. Two are included in one of the final Chapters of this book, with memories of adventures in cycling to see some interesting places.

Just now however, are some experiences on a working holiday as a Relief Engineer at sea. This would involve doing something to keep in touch with the tools, since rapid advances in technology were constantly taking place in recent years. I was curious to see such at first hand.

*   *   *   *

This is the account of a trip made by the author during a summer vacation on a motor ship named the M V "Velarde," MacAndrews and Company, Royal Liver Buildings, Liverpool. The author was then a Lecturer in Mechanical Engineering in Lisburn Technical College (later known as Lisburn College of Further and Higher Education).

The M.V. "Velarde."

By now summer had arrived, and with it a long vacation when a lecturer in Mechanical Engineering at Lisburn Technical College in Co. Antrim – and it would be all of ten weeks. The normal vocational months of July and August usually provide for about nine weeks and three days of vacation for most F.E. lecturers. But, due to an alteration in my timetable to facilitate the teaching of a special one off course for adults during the summer term, my timetable was spread over three days per week (starting early each day at 8.30 am and finishing my week at 5 pm each Wednesday. I therefore finished the last week in June two days earlier than normal, and these two days in June added to those of July and August, gave me ten clear weeks in all. For me, it was an interesting time table change indeed, but alas, in the next twenty four years at the chalk face in Further Education, one which was not ever repeated.

*   *   *   *   *

I had been offered a Fourth Engineer's position with MacAndrew & Co, Ltd., Royal Liver Buildings, Liverpool, as a holiday relief engineer for one of their engineers wanting a trip out during August - see the following telegram. Accordingly, early in August I thence repaired to the dock known as Canada 3, Liverpool, from where MacAndrews traded in the Western Mediterranean – especially to Spain. I was there to sail as Fourth Engineer, first to Bilbao in Northern Spain, and then to the Western Mediterranean, passing Gibraltar on the way. There were five engineers on board.

 It was on a Monday that I had travelled overnight to Liverpool on the MV "Ulster Prince" from Belfast. Canada 3 dock is a fair distance west from the Pier Head in Liverpool, so a bus was called for, and according to my "diary" of that day, I found the MV "Velarde" lying at No 2 shed. The "Velarde" was a fine looking ship, and was indeed referred to as the "Yacht," an impression not unconnected with the fact that all MacAndrew's boats had white painted upper works. The hull down to the Plimsol Line was white, and below that line the hull was painted green. The funnel was amidships, indicating that the engine room was also so positioned – (which tends to be more comfortable for the engineers when a ship is pitching). With an engine room aft, those working there get the full "benefit" of the maximum pitch in a fore and aft pitching sea.

I reported to Mr Masson, the Chief Engineer – he had just recently left B.P. tankers after sixteen years there as a chief. He already knew that I was a "temporary," but lifted one eyebrow – at least, upon hearing that I had just left a classroom. He would have had some concern I'm sure, because as Fourth Engineer, I would be looking after his watch – the 8 am until 12 noon watch and 8 pm until 12 midnight watch. I am sure that Mr Masson initially had indeed misgivings about having a teacher taking his watch, but after he saw my Discharge Book and noted that I had acquired some diesel experience - and had a little chat with me, I think he was a little more assured. Previously my experience was mostly with Steam turbine and Triple Expansion steam plant.

"Well," he spoke at length, having looked again at the Discharge Book, "I'll take you along to the Second – then I'll give your book to the Old Man."

111

Communications: – Positive and sure! how it used to be done by a Telegram:

It now seems unbelieveable but, when an urgent message had to be delivered – such as one relating to a position of employment, the communication relating to above was actually done by using a Post Office Telegram. This was because not every home had a land line telephone (and mobiles had probably not been invented although calculators had been!) Thus a Telegram was usually delivered in rural areas by the postman on his bicycle - as was the normal post as well of course.

Red Post Office vans were not common there until the late 1960's or 1970's, but Belfast was noted for its fleet of Telegram Boys on BSA "Bantam" two stroke motorcycles!

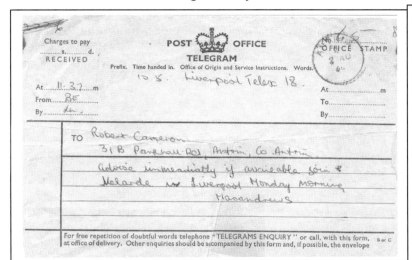

Communications by a telegram, 1960's style. This telegram is MacAndrews reply to my earlier communication advising them that I would be available for doing the relief trip for them during my summer vacation when teaching in Lisburn Technical College.

It says,

Advise immediately if available join Velarde in Liverpool Monday morning. MacAndrews

(no dots or commas etc !)

THE M.V. "VELARDE" The "Velarde" was a cargo ship that looked like a yacht, and, as already mentioned, was known as such in the local "trade." MacAndrews traded in the Western Mediterranean – especially Spain, but occasionally traded also in Italy. For the next trip, the MV "Velarde" was to sail first to Bilbao in Northern Spain, Basque country, and then enter the Western Mediterranean passing Gibraltar of course on the way. Other ports scheduled, were Cartagena, Barcelona, and Valencia.

The Second Engineer, responsible for the day to day management of the Engine Room was a Scot by the name of Don Frazer. Like others in the Merchant Marine, Don had, as we say, "got around." He had been with Shell, B.P., Gulf Oil, Bank Line – he had even done a spell on a weather ship, out in the Atlantic.

I seem to recall that these weather ships were old ex-Royal Navy corvettes or destroyers, with triple expansion machinery.

"Nice place that," said Don, commenting on the Atlantic station, "the scenery is out of this world." He was an excellent chap. He told me that the engines in the "Velarde" ran like clocks, and that I would have Jack, a very experienced donkeyman with me. (A donkeyman was a rating who looked after auxiliary services like oiling, running up compressors, pumping bilges and cleaning filters etc.) Many donkey men would have been with a ship for a long time, and often had a very useful knowledge of engine room procedures and where everything was located. Ron was proved right – Jack was a great man to work with and, as will be revealed, he left me with something important and impelling to think about.

Just now, Ron had got a message – I was to proceed to the Shipping Federation Offices at Cornhill, Liverpool, and sign the ship's Articles – Articles "A" or Articles "B"- see as follows. I proceded thence, my memory recalling a previous occasion when I had last been there many years before.

I had then been there at Cornhill to sign on the Articles pertaining to the old S.S "Grecian," an Ellerman Papayanni Lines vessel, in the company of Mr Goldie, her Chief Engineer and her Third Engineer, George Hollis.

```
The Shipping Federation Ltd.,
Officer's Pool,
Mann Island,
Pier Head,
LIVERPOOL 3.


Dear Sirs,
        Bearer, Mr. R CAMERON  has been appointed. Asst. ENGINEER
on our m.s." VELARDE          in   LIVERPOOL.
    Please issue this gentleman with the necessary papers to
enable him to sign on vessel's Articles.


               Yours faithfully,
        MAC ANDREWS & CO. LIMITED.,
```

Now nostalgia for those days was my only companion, accompanied to some extent with the thoughts that sometimes attend the signing on of a new ship – especially about another new engine room layout and ship's routine to get to know - and quickly, and how would one cope?

In the U.K. when an engineer signs on ship's articles, it is usually for the round trip ie from A to B and return – and usually to the U.K. Of course ships can be diverted to a port not normally visited - as when the ship is going into dry dock abroad for its annual survey, and with the crew being paid off there, and flown home. A ship may also have to re route in response to an emergency at sea - eg a fire aboard another ship, or to assist another which perhaps is in even danger of sinking. There is always the possibility of a change in schedule in respect of a commercial opportunity. Another may be when a ship is delivered to a ship breaking firm abroad – a one way trip with the delivery crew flying home. Incidentally, "A" and "B" articles relate to working agreements, eg whether overtime is paid, and to other agreements / conditions etc.

However, ships in a line of trade known in the business as "tramps," one can never be sure of how long the trip will be. These ships would literally trade the world's oceans carrying cargo here and there and often being away from the U.K. for a year – or more. Usually, the crew on such a voyage of over one year away from the U.K., would be exempt from paying income tax!

During the afternoon, I entered into the usual pre-sailing activities that go on in the engine room of any ship about to go on "stand by." For the technical, the two main engines of the "Velarde" were of German manufacture – M.A.N, J- type, single acting, turbo charged four stroke diesels, with hydraulic couplings and single reduction gearing to a single propeller shaft. The port and starboard engines each had ten cylinders and of about 5,000 H.P.

But now of course the main thing was to find my way around – where were the lubricating oil pumps, fresh water cooling pumps, oil coolers, fuel filter and transfer pumps - and, essentially, the diesel generators and procedures for putting them on the "board." I would find that there were two main DC (direct current) generators and one stand by DC generator.There was also a small emergency generator which was located on the Boat Deck. Usually when full away, one main generator would be of adequate electrical provision, but one would never be sure of when the Bridge would suddenly ring down and request another generator to be put on the Board. This usually happens when leaving or

entering port. Here extra power might be needed for things like lowering or raising an anchor as when cargo is discharged into a barge alongside in deep water or warping the head or stern of the ship when closing with the dock side. Warping is (or was) the terminology used to describe occasions when a rope (sometimes referred to as a spring) is thrown ashore where its loop is placed over a bollard. The other end of the rope would normally be around the drum of a special capstan in the bows. As this capstan revolves, the ship pulls the bows inwards and closes the dock side. A similar rope and procedure secures the ship's stern to the quay side. When a ship is departing the dock, someone
(maybe the Second Mate) will shout "Let go the for'd spring." The for'd mooring rope near the bows will then be pulled up over the top of the bollard by a person on the dockside and thrown into the water where it is wound back onto the drum of the capstan! Still held fast at the stern, the ship's head is free to swing outwards towards the dock exit as perhaps a slow ahead engine movement is rang down to the engine room. When the direction of the ship's head is judged appropriate, the after rope (or spring) is disconnected from its bollard and secured on board. The ship is then free to move to the great beyond.

 Strangely, the main engines would be the least of my concerns – it was unlikely that they would give any trouble – even after running without stopping for days between ports.
A watch keeper (if he puts himself forward as one), is usually on his own on cargo ships (on passenger ships there is usually a legal requirement for two engineers to be on duty per watch).So if he is alone on watch, he has to know where things are, and act if a Bridge request requires a response. He also needs to know how to respond to some alarm going off.
Since there is usually a "stand by" unit ready to go at the touch of a button or the opening of a valve (as is likely on steam), one might think that this is no big deal. But it could well be!
A lub oil pump alarm going off in the engine room of a ship at two o'clock in the morning just after the donkeyman has brought down the "Smoko" (the tea and toast), can be a most disorientating experience. I had this experience once, on, as it so happens, on a MacAndrew ship - the MV "Velazquez." After the "dust" settled, I later regaled some of my colleagues as to what I experienced. If I recall aright, I described it as having a thousand Bansidhe (pronounced Banshees) doing the the slosh, with MacBeth's three witches, (and those other three boys who came to sort out Scrooge) - all joining in, and creating a racket. Since components are designed not to break down, alarms are not going off on every day of the week, and many watch keeping engineers have seldom experienced such an alarm . All the greater shock when it happens! But a sense of humour helps.
Sometimes the Bridge would communicate to just convey some information like," There is fog expected soon," or " There is heavy traffic ahead." These messages would be meant to warn the engine room staff to expect some engine movements – known as "manoeuvring." But, a very common request would be for "water on deck," the latter usually for deck washing purposes.
Shortly, I met the Third Engineer – his name was Larry and he came from Liverpool.
 As related, in the U.K. when an engineer signs on ship's articles, it is usually for the round trip ie from A to B and usually return to the U.K. I was just hoping that the "Velarde" would be back before the end of the month – I would be expected to attend a staff meeting in Lisburn Technical College just before the students returned in September.
MacAndrews had its origins in 1770, when a young Scot, William MacAndrew, from Elgin in Scotland, came to Liverpool, and eventually started fruit importing, his business being with Spain, Portugal, and the Azores. While now their ships seemed to be mostly called after Spanish noblemen, they earlier had some strange but interesting names in the past, like
 " War Bagpipe," "War Fife," "Nineveh," "Lusitania," (1880), and even one called "Larne!" These were all steamers. Now one real character I was about to meet was one Jock Sinclair, the skipper – the "Old man." I would learn from him, that he was a Presbyterian from the Shetland Islands, and that he had a farm with one thousand sheep. He soon realised that I was concerned to be back by the end of the month, and played some right pranks on me.

Some Memories of MacAndrews' Engine Rooms

Summer vacation

Above: Author on the engine room manoeuvring platform, having joined the MV "Velarde" to see a bit more of the world! The "Velarde" was powered by twin MAN diesels, supercharged with Brown Boverie exhaust turbine blowers.

A tale of two ships' engine rooms.

The engine room controls on two of MacAndrews' motor ships – that of the MV "Velarde," above, as presently described; On right, those on the MV "Villegas," on which ship I was to do a trip during the following year's summer vacation. The MacAndrew ships were mostly named after Spanish noblemen. Both these ships had four stroke diesel trunk engines – no piston rods.

Another Summer vacation

Above: Manoeuvring platform. Here the following year, author has joined the MV "Villegas," MacAndrews and Co., Liverpool. The MV "Villegas" was powered by two four stroke eight cylinder MWM U-Boat trunk engines – (no piston rods) unsupercharged, and made in Augsburg, Germany. The engine room telegraphs were placed close enough so that both engines could be controlled by one engineer. An account of this trip appeared in a book by author called **"Before that Generation Passes " 2001,** see page 164 there.

Left: Tom Birch, Chief Engineer of the MV "Villegas," probably the nicest man to work with or under, in my lifetime. I would meet him the following year, during the summer school vacation then.
Origin: The late Capt. Jim Bothwell, Whitehead, Northern Ireland.

The Approaches to Liverpool and its Docklands

Sketch Origin: Author 1968

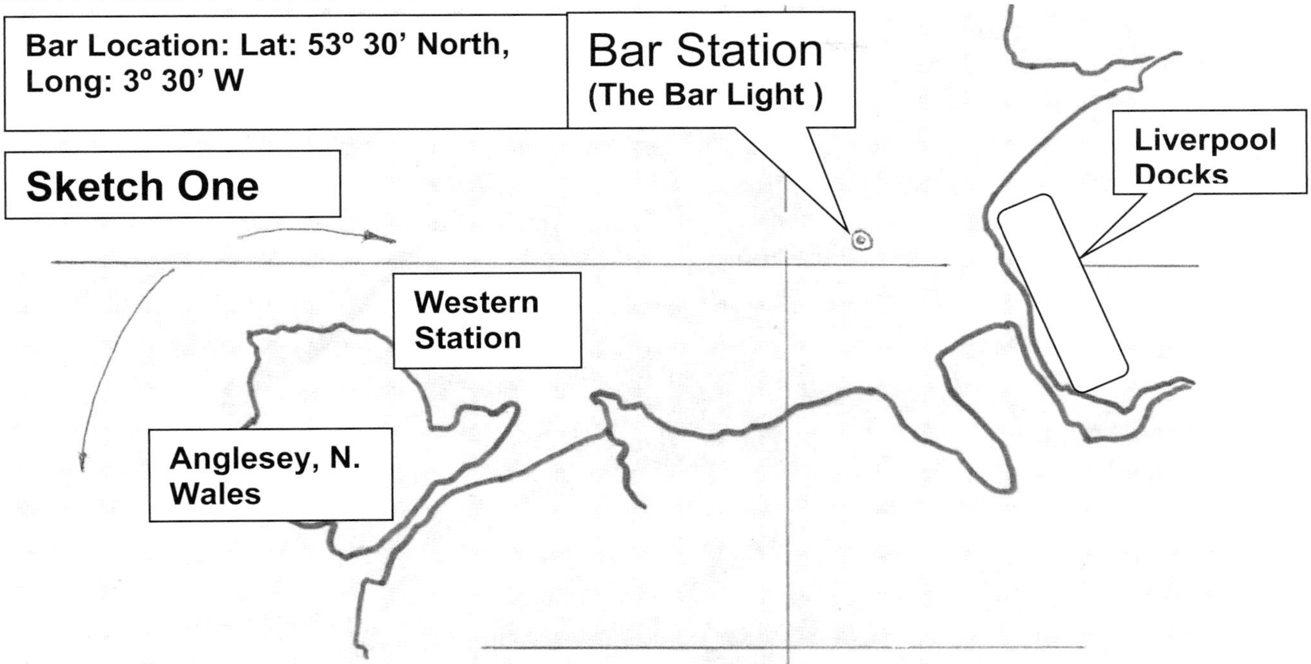

Bar Location: Lat: 53° 30' North, Long: 3° 30' W

Bar Station
(The Bar Light)

Liverpool Docks

Sketch One

Western Station

Anglesey, N. Wales

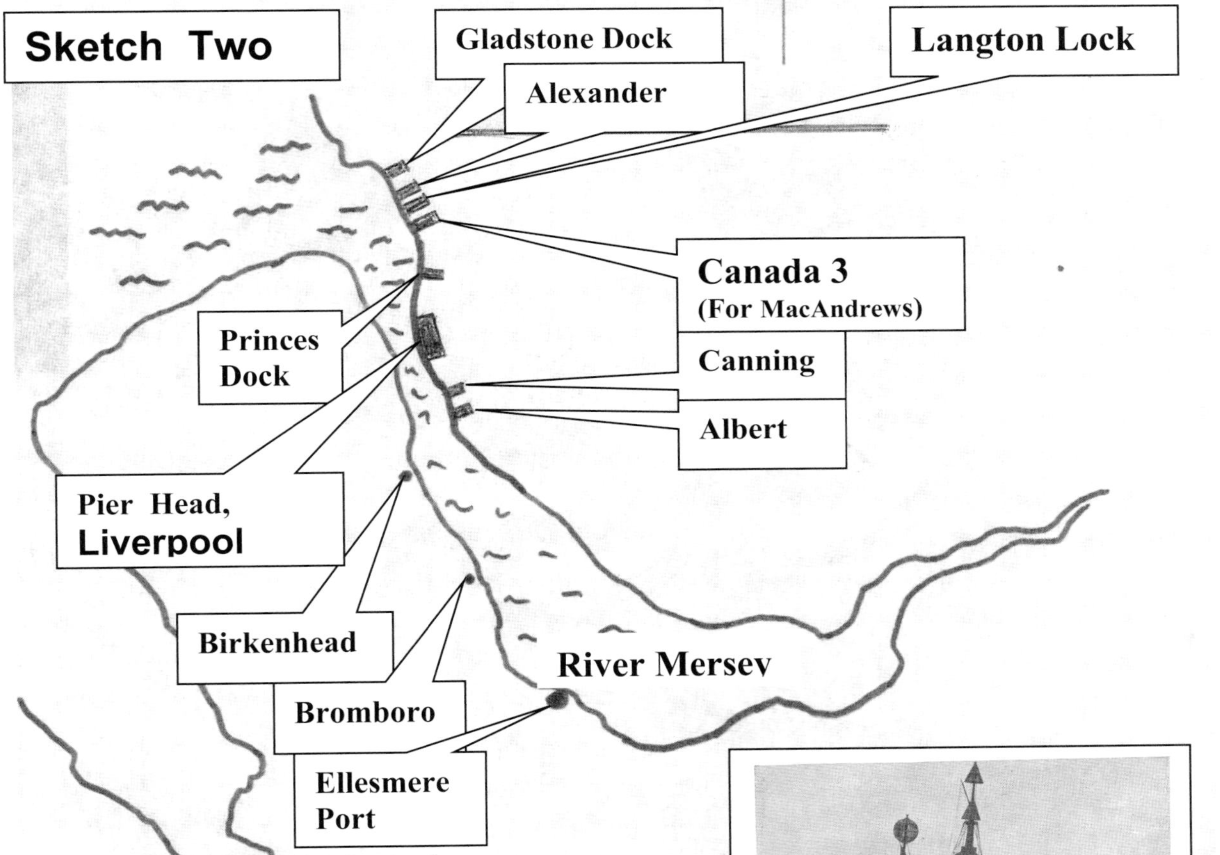

Sketch Two

Gladstone Dock

Alexander

Langton Lock

Canada 3
(For MacAndrews)

Canning

Albert

Princes Dock

Pier Head,
Liverpool

Birkenhead

Bromboro

River Mersey

Ellesmere Port

Right: A Lightship, similar to the "Bar Light," but identity and origin unknown.

Script contd: Ref, Jock Sinclair.

Even when crossing the English channel coming home, Jock caused a bogus piece of information to get around that we had to divert to Hamburg in Germany!

Having said that, he was a most pleasant person with whom I had a chat from time to time. A memory of another MacAndrews vessel – was the MV "Villegas,"

I was to meet the "Villegas" and her Chief Engineer, Tom Birch one year hence. See two pages back for more information.

*   *   *   *   *

Early in the afternoon, I saw a familiar board placed near the gangway.

It bore the legend, *"Shore leave expires at 20:00 hours."*

As well, watches would commence shortly – I would be on duty as an engine room watch keeper at 8 p.m. – my first watch on the MV "Velarde."

I wondered if it would go smoothly, if it would be free from alarms, no lubricating oil pumps breaking down, no fog, no excessive demands from the bridge. I couldn't run home anyway! I watched the Second as he descended the engine room steps – what news did he have – was there a delay?

"We have to wait for the Irish Boat," he said. This would be the Belfast boat and It left at 20.00 hours (8pm) so we would be going out on my watch and the Second would be with me during the stand by period, it being customary for port manoeuvring to be done by the Second Engineer. Of course, the engine room could get a ring from the Bridge for an engine movement (s) at any time in a 24 hour period, and this would be attended to by whatever engineer might happen to be on watch. During manoeuvring, we would also be joined by the "leckie," the ship's electrician. Electrical faults - say in a ship with electrical steering gear during a "stand by" period (or at any time) must be addressed immediately – the ship may be technically "not under control."

Presently, the telegraph rang "stand by," followed eventually by a ring for the first engine movement. Each main engine control – we would be manoeuvring on only one engine, consisted of a wheel with two protruding handles, clockwise for ahead, and anti clockwise for astern movements.

Don handled these with easy confidence – a turn of the wheel opened starting air to turn the massive engine over – I believe the port engine was being used, and further movement of the wheel opened fuel to the injectors – and all ten cylinders burst into song. I was soon busy, looking after a number of things – like oil and water temperatures. The engine speed when "full away," would be of the order of 250 R.P.M., and that of the propeller shaft, reduced to 125 R.P.M.

There was a lot of traffic about the Mersey that night and there was also some fog. Don stayed with me until "full away" and then departed. By "full away," is meant that engine manoeuvring is finished and the throttles are set at maximum cruise speed. Emergency full speed would be somewhat higher if required. But before Ron left me, he gave me a little note setting out my course of action should certain things fall out of place. Don Frazer, was responsible for the day to day running of the engine room, and was a good man to work with. He was one of those – big enough to inspire confidence in one's self by appearing that he feels confident that you can do your job without seemingly to be constantly checking up on you. I found Mr. Masson the chief to be in the same mold. I also seem to remember that Don thought a lot of the robust M.A.N. engines, which were turbo charged (supercharged) by a Brown-Boverie exhaust turbo system. I believe these exhaust gas turbos revolved at 20,000 RPM – possibly as high as 30,000 RPM. They had a fair scream and were known locally as the "blowers."

Eventually a gentle lift of the bows told me that we had left the Mersey behind, and I had arrived in the Irish Sea.

Left : Mr Masson, the Chief Engineer of the M.V. "Velarde" left, with Larry, the Third Engineer. Note the clinker constructed life boat, never seen on lifeboats nowadays. They are now more likely to be known as survival craft – and completely closed in!   Origin: Author.

By noon the following day, we were approaching Land's End, and by midnight of the same, the "Velarde" was off Ushant, a light house island, and the most westerly part of France. Its lighthouse heralded the start of our journey across the Bay of Biscay – to the port of Bilbao in Northern Spain. After - happily for me, a reasonable passage weather wise across the "Bay," we arrived off Bilbao on Wednesday, 7th August. 1968.

We then proceeded up the river on which the port was situated, passing a swing bridge similar to Tower Bridge, London, on the way.

Watches being broken, all the engineers resumed day work – and we were all engaged in changing the valves of the main engines. Unlike most small diesel engines, such as one would find in a bus or lorry and where valves and their springs are usually located in the cylinder heads, the marine diesels employ separate valve housings complete with valve springs, collets, inlet and outlet cooling water seals and connections etc – all as part of a unit attached to the cylinder head by a bolt on flange with the cooling water passages isolated by a seal as appropriate. A block and tackle was used to remove the heavy valve housings and swing them clear of the cylinder heads.

Above : The second mate takes a "sight" of the sun at noon time, using a sextant.
Origin: Author 1968

A spare set of valve housings, overhauled and with valve faces already ground in, were available for each cylinder being attended to and were now fitted to the cylinder heads being worked on. The valve housings that were removed would shortly be overhauled, set in storage and ready when required to replace the other set just fitted into the cylinder heads. The M.A.N. engines were sturdy and functional – if square corners were not in the way, the Germans didn't waste time and energy removing them in manufacture and these engines looked strong and reliable.

For me, the contrast between what I was now doing – in this environment with my new companions, with the smell of diesel oil, and that of the classrooms I had recently left in Lisburn Technical College, could not have been sharper. Indeed I questioned – was this a dream? But as, with the help of my donkey man I reassembled a valve housing complete with its rocker gear and with the tappet clearance set at one millimetre, a misjudged hammer blow on a thumb nail assured me that it was all real!

Then it was "smoko" time, that hallowed time in all engine rooms, when labour is set aside for the coffee (with condensed or other form of preserved milk). Then, on again to labour. (None of the engineers were smokers.)

Eventually it was noon, and in the tradition of all "fourths," I prepared to take the noon readings – the depth of fresh water and fuel oil in various tanks, all sounded by dropping a steel tape with brass sinker down the pipes leading into these tanks. In port or in good weather a simple reading is easily taken. However, if the ship were to be rolling in heavy

The MV "Velarde," MacAndrews, Liverpool. She was known as the "Yacht."
Origin: Author

seas, it would be essential to drop the sinker when the ship's position during the roll was judged upright - with the oil mark on the tape showing the true level in the tank. These are important recordings. One day, towards the end of the trip, I found Mr Masson the Chief, pouring over the recent noon soundings.

"There's something wrong," he said, "we seem to have more fuel today in the port bunkers, than we had yesterday – do you think you could have made a mistake?"

I checked the sounding, and discovered that I had indeed taken down an incorrect reading. Now such an unusual discrepancy might have indicated sea water entering somewhere e.g. into a water tank or, in this case, a fuel tank – it was important to get it right.

Leaving Bilbao later that afternoon and proceeding down river, I was off watch, and was surprised to see the extent of Spanish shipbuilding – the river looked like the shipbuilding on the Clyde of bygone years. Alas this prosperity was not to last. We were now moving West, before turning South round the "corner" of North West Spain. Eventually, Finisterre Light at Cape Finisterre was passed, then Cape St Vincent with that white building, the convent on the cliff tops. Eventually, Cape Trafalgar, associated for ever with Admiral Lord Nelson, showed up, with its white cliffs, just visible on the distant coast. Our first port of call after passing the Straits of Gibraltar, would be Cartagena, then Barcelona and finally Valencia. Sharing my watches was an excellent donkey man, Jack. As mentioned, a donkey man had engine room duties that might include cleaning filters, pumping out bilges or greasing moving engine parts as required.

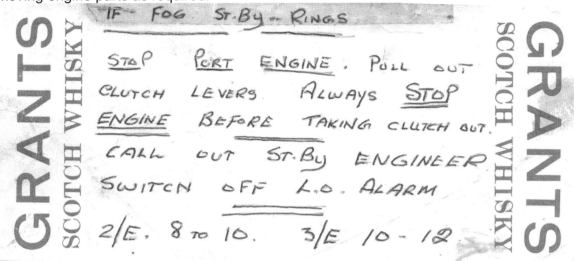

Jack was approaching retirement and had been at sea most of his life, including service with MacAndrews during the Second World War. I would also have an acquaintance with another donkey man, as each day at five o'clock, I, again in the manner of all fourth engineers, covered the tea break for Ron, the Second. It was usually a case of just "being there" for a short time. One of my routine jobs on my own watch, was to purify diesel fuel oil and transfer this oil to the daily service fuel tanks in use.

This entailed the use of the transfer pump - part of a De Laval fuel oil purifier, which lifted oil from the "double bottom" bunkers and after purification, transferred this oil to the daily service tanks, port or starboard. To every watch keeping exercise that Don anticipated I was likely to be involved in - like pumping paraffin to the galley oil tank (and there was no overflow outlet on it !), changing generators or, as just mentioned, the purification and transfer of fuel from bunkers to the daily service tanks port and starboard as required etc., he always left me notes of precise instructions which I never had difficulty in following. It is surely astonishing, that two of these typical notes from Don have survived, and are thus produced. (In preparation for this account of seafaring on the "Velarde," I discovered several other similar notes - also telegrams informing me of vacancies that were available to me during vacations if I were available – I must rank as a champion horder ! See above.

Ron's note pads were typical of the day – sponsored by those who processed the barley, rye, and fruit of the vine into liquid form. Apart from being a very pleasant guy to know, he was also indeed a very intelligent engine room manager of its day to day running, and had taken on board that I was "here today and away tomorrow" and didn't trouble me with unnecessary detail and instruction!

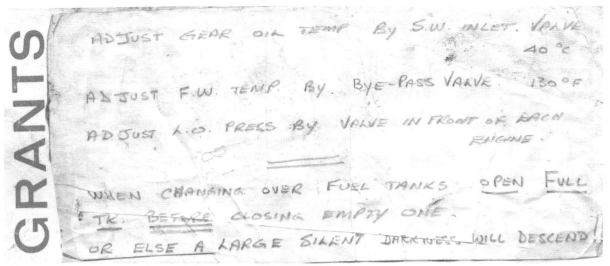

GRANTS

ADJUST GEAR OIL TEMP By S.W. INLET. VALVE
40 °C

ADJUST F.W. TEMP. By BYE-PASS VALVE 130 °F

ADJUST L.O. PRESS BY VALVE IN FRONT OF EACH ENGINE.

WHEN CHANGING OVER FUEL TANKS OPEN FULL TK. BEFORE CLOSING EMPTY ONE.

OR ELSE A LARGE SILENT DARKNESS WILL DESCEND!

Above: Ron's instructions for me relating to keeping oil and cooling water temperatures at the proper levels, and other helpful things for me to look out for. Also see above for a good example of his rare sense of humour in namely, ref "changing over fuel tanks!"

As a result, I never had any problem in "steaming the ship." Ron had just made sure I knew what to do, and in any emergency, who else was available at any given time to assist.
I was also very impressed with that German M.A.N. layout – the main engines never missed a beat. But it's also amazing how an engineer at sea can keep himself informed about things there, by using the senses – sight, touch, smell, hearing and taste. For example, the exhaust temperatures of the main engines are important indicators of each cylinder performance. If the average exhaust temperature is say 650°F and suddenly one **sees** a cylinder showing an exhaust temperature of 580° F, it might indicate a deficiency of fuel being injected – in this case there is usually a local adjustment that can be made for each cylinder which can increase the amount of fuel being injected into that cylinder. It is sometimes referred to as a "micrometer" adjustment. If however, the temperature has dropped to 450° F, this might indicate faulty injectors or worse, a serious situation – there is little or no compression and combustion taking place. Another example for one's senses: A diesel engine fresh water cooling water pipe return, say at 130°F, could comfortably be assessed by **touch**. If a low pressure oil warning alarm should go off – one would definitely **hear** it – and often it would be accompanied by a flashing light (this helps the "hard of hearing!") Something overheating might be detected by **smell,** and old steam men wouldn't have been adverse to even **tasting** boiler feed water, to detect and estimate the presence and quantityof excess salt. Are not our senses wonderful things to be grateful for?
Eventually, we passed Gibraltar – unfortunately it was dark as I came off watch at midnight and so had to content myself with just seeing the lights on the Rock. Our next port would be Cartagena.
The Third Engineer seemed to know a lot about Cartegena. "You see that place," he said to me one day, "well, after the Spanish Civil War was over, every night for months afterwards, a little boat used to leave here with prisoners on board. It went out to deep water – and returned empty. And what's more, it was from this port the Russians carried off the gold of Spain." Presently, Jack my donkey man, informed me that Cartagena was thirty hours from Gibraltar, but during one watch before then, the telephone rang: **"Third Mate here. There's fog about."**
I consulted one of Ron's notes and just then the telegraph rang for "Half Ahead." I stopped the port engine and adjusted the starboard engine R.P.M. accordingly.
Jack started the air compressor – in case of any manoeuvring, it is essential to make sure that the air bottles are kept fully topped up.

Then I had a visit from the Chief. "Keep a good eye on the job – if you get any more movements, give me a ring."

Fog is a terror at sea – the general rule then being observed was to proceed "Slow Ahead," sounding the fog horn every minute. However the fog cleared and soon with "Full Ahead" the "Velarde" thundered on in bright sunshine to Cartagena.

Sometime after tying up, a rope ladder was thrown over the side and borrowing Ron's swimming trunks I went in for a dip. Howiver I soon noticed how dirty the water was – there was more in the water than swimmers and soon I was back on board again.

A short distance outside the harbour gates - on dry land, stood Spain's first submarine – the "Perla." It looked the part, but apparently was not very successful as a submarine – see later page for photo the "Perla."

Routine work continued in the engine room the following day, and I was allocated that time honoured task of checking the bottom end bearings and other attachments in the crankcase of the port engine for tightness or otherwise. It was a case of opening the crankcase doors and in with the turning gear – which latter consisted of an electric motor driving a small low speed helical pinion which engaged with appropriate gear teeth cut on the flywheel rim. It thus was able to move the heavy crankshaft into any position required. Then, getting inside the crankcase of each cylinder, hammer testing of the large hexagon nuts securing the keep of the big end bearing to the connecting rod end commenced . These nuts were perhaps six inches across the flats and by striking the flats of the nuts with a 2 -3 pound hammer helped to detect any sign of them slackening. As in previous experiences of this exercise on another motor ship, I had never found any slack nuts on our M.A.N. main engines. I had seen a photograph, however, of what happens when a loose connecting rod disconnects from a bottom end journal on a running engine. The damage is unbelieveible and it is referred to in Engine Room parlance as "putting a leg out of bed!"

Our next port was Barcelona, about thirty hours "steaming" from Cartagena, and our final port would be Valencia. In Barcelona opportunity was taken to visit the replica of the "Santa Maria." In the original, Columbus had discovered the Americas. It was also an opportunity to stroll up Las Ramblas, a wide thoroughfare of shops, flower sellers etc., often now on the tourist itinerary for visitors to Barcelona.

Above left: The replica of the "Santa Maria" in which Colombus had discovered the Americas.

Sadly, as part of this book was being finished on this, the last week in August 2017, terrorists choose to carry out an attack upon Las Ramblas, resulting in serious casualties. Apart from walking up Las Ramblas or seeing the replica of the "Santa Maria," I cannot recall anything of other startling interest in Barcelona, and I could say the same for Valencia which port we would eventually sail from for Liverpool. The beach at Barcelona is some distance from the city.

Author on "Velarde," as it passes Gibraltar, with a warship in the background. Orig: Some crew member.

We had also carried on our deck, some barrels of I.C.I. petroleum additive – very dangerous stuff, as a trip on the MV "Villegas"(during the next Summer's vacation would draw attention to.) However, our consignment had been off loaded at Cartagena. After Barcelona, we came to Valencia to complete the loading of onions and melons. While there, I had a visitor – an unusual character, for I had met one Henry Rees, a Spaniard of Welsh descent and who carried on a spirit business there – wine, bacardi, muskatelle, vermouth – you name it, he could supply it, in half gallon or gallon glass demijons and all protected in wicker baskets. He spoke good English and told me that his Welsh grandfather had set up the business in Valencia. I made a modest purchase of some wine and on the day of our departure from Valencia, I was greatly amused to witness Henry arriving at the dockside on a large tricycle towing a trailer in which there was an enormous cargo of wines, whiskies, rum – mostly in those wicker covered glass containers, called demijons. Now, I was to pay a small amount of custom duty on my modest purchases, but I doubt if yon lot coming on board was ever declared at Customs - it would have cost a fortune as some containers held five gallons! I was to do several trips with MacAndrews over the years when on vacation, and later I would see one Second engineer making his way on watch into the engine room with a large bottle of rum by the neck . He was not going to drink it there, though! He was more likely to have been hiding it. My memory recalled that time on the SS "Rathlin Head" when arriving at Liverpool, Customs Officers discovered a few bottles of whiskey in below a diesel generator in the Engine Room.The Head Line was fined something like £17 but those petty smugglers were Sunday School teachers compared to the villain smugglers on board the MV "Velarde!"

Author: Just up giving the boys on the Bridge of the "Velarde" a helping hand! Orig: A Crew member

Valencia was a hot place, and part of my duties in the port, was that of refrigeration engineer. This was the only experience I was ever to have of this important duty. The temperature in the holds was mostly controlled by running the "fridge" compressors from time to time.

By this time I was hoping for a straight run home - I had my day job to attend to!

So I was much relieved to hear that we were to sail direct from Valencia to Liverpool – on Sunday 18th August, which was duly accomplished. The following day about three o'clock in the afternoon the great grey rock of **Gibraltar** hove in sight.

We passed, I suppose, about half a mile from the breakwater that protects the harbour anchorage.

I could see the "Mission to Seamen" building at end of the pier, a two storey building - and easily identified.

I had been to Gibraltar many years before, and would visit the port once again in the not too distant future with MacAndrews. Some of their ships carried a few passengers – I can recall a couple, man and his wife on the "Velarde." Since I finished work each day at noon, I often joined this pair and others off watch for sunbathing on the boat deck. Earlier, I had also discovered a little deck on top of the wheelhouse which was even more perfect for sunbathing in port! It was like on a par with those blissful nights in Malta when on the SS "Grecian" as earlier recalled, when I worked alone at night under a large, low hung moon and swinging stars, fixing equipment that the Arab dockers had broken during the day. I then

123

shared the world with the duty fireman and donkeyman, frying eggs and bacon at two oclock in the morning! It was in fact, quote " nearly enough to make one believe that life is worth living after all – joke" unquote. During these afternoons, I also had the company of the Third Mate and sometimes the Fifth Engineer - see photograph. Indeed, even from time to time in these sunny climes, I was engaged as earlier mentioned in conversation with the skipper, Jock Sinclair. I recall amusing incidents with him, but years later, I learned that he had been lost at sea - in the Caribbean. Note: On average over fifty ships, each larger than a fishing trawler are lost at sea each year! But there are certain other losses whose memory we should never be allowed to forget. Jack's story now tells of one of these. One night, homeward bound and off the French Biscay coast, my old donkey man, Jack, returned after calling the watch - I suppose around 11.45 pm. He seemed upset, so I asked him if he was feeling all right. He was all right, except that he had just had an emotional reminder of wartime and his mind was on a sad incident that had happened then. It would also stay with me.

Left: The "Perla," Spain's first submarine, sitting outside the port area of Cartagena, Spain, showing the bows end. Built in the 1880's with twin propellers, she looked the part, but there is little evidence that any success ever attended in her role as a submarine.
Source: The late Capt. Jim Bothwell, Master Mariner, late of Whitehead, Co. Antrim.

"You know, Bob," he began, "when I was up top there – we're just off Ushant Light now, I was thinking of someone - you remind me very much of him, with your mannerisms and the things you talk to me about. He was the Third Engineer I shared the watch with in that ship, in 1941. He had just asked me – as you have just done, to call the watch - about here off Ushant Light. Being in wartime, we were well out off the coast. Just before four o'clock am, a torpedo hit the engine room when I was up top calling the watch, and the third, poor chap, was blown from the manoeuvring platform upwards. We found him lying on the funnel uptakes. But he was done for – such a nice lad, and not a mark on him. **He was a lad just like you.**" See later note – a sequel to Jack's story recalling being torpedoed.

Above: On the "Velarde" with the ship's Electrical Officer – and a book! Origin: Fellow crew member.

Above: With theThird Mate, back left, and the Fifth Engineer, back right, and Cape St. Vincent in the background.
Origin: Some nice crew member!

We were soon making good progress across the Bay of Biscay, a place renowned for its dreadful storms and where their energy finally disapates in surrender on the shores of France.

   This time indeed these storms were asleep as the "Velarde" stealthily progressed towards the shores of England. Up untill a short time before, however, the day had been bright, but now there were some signs that the weather was closing in.

Just at this time I found myself recalling Jack's recent wartime recollections. They had certainly brought home to me, the awesome sacrifices made **for us** by the men of the Merchant Navy during the last War. It does no harm to be reminded that 30,000 men lost their lives in the effort to keep the life lines open, to bring in the food and oil on which Britain depended absolutely. Without that effort, I might be writing in German or Japanese today – if at all!

*   *   *   *

But now the bay was becoming misty, although, as said, the crossing had been in calm weather and in daylight, but it thickened around the Scillies. Soon the engine room was on stand by, and we were proceeding at reduced revolutions. However, time and distance lay

The MV "Hibernian Coast" at Liverpool.

behind us, and we arrived while on stand by off the "Bar" light, Liverpool, at almost 2400 hours on Thursday 22nd. August 1968 - see sketch map of the "Approaches to Liverpool." The Pilot would board before long, but according to the Engine Room Log which I saw the next morning, the "Velarde" did not start the River Mersey transit until 0230 hours. I was of course turned in by this time, but the "Velarde"

The MacAndrew House Flag

didn't tie up at Canada 3 Dock until eight o'clock the next morning – for some reason, a somewhat lengthy "stand by!" Before this time, I was up and out on the deck watching proceedings, and on passing the end of a dock, I saw something that called for a second look. A black coaster. A black coaster with a large vee on the funnel – I couldn't believe it, because it looked like a vessel called the "Hibernian Coast." Later, when having a break from whatever I was doing, I made my way to the * MV "Hibernian Coast." No mistake it was indeed the MV "Hibernian Coast."What nostalgia!

It was indeed the "Hibernian Coast," on which I had sailed briefly as Third Engineer sometime after leaving the SS "Grecian." I thus proceeded up the gangway, walked into Engineers' alleyway and then to the Engine Room door. Alas, the door was locked. Then I looked at the ancient old emergency, manual steering wheel on the poop over the rudder post. I had actually watched this being used by the sailors one storm lashed Sunday morning to bring the ship into the Spithead, which lies between the Isle of Wight and Portsmouth. This all happened after we had lost our electric steering gear following

extensive flooding when a massive following sea had climbed aboard in the midst of the wicked gale that was raging at the time and also flooded the seamen's quarters.
 I then remembered Van Den Ent, her old Dutch Chief Engineer, and then - the other Dutch engineer who had joined us in London and then created that racket in a cafe in Dublin – memories indeed. The M.V. "Hibernian Coast" looked as if she was going to the knackers yard.
Then I walked off down her gangway – once more. (The tale of the MV * "Hibernian Coast" and "that other Dutch Engineer," is recalled in **"Before that Generation Passes,"** by Author, published in 2001.)

Returning to the MV "Velarde," I prepared to take my leave of this fine vessel and a couple of days later, I said good bye to my new colleagues of past weeks. I was also glad that I had still been capable – or just about, of stepping out of a school classroom, to take over the Engine Room watch on a strange ship – on a motor ship, deep sea. My only regret was that I had forgotten to get a reference from the Chief Engineer. MacAndrews appeared happy enough to have the pleasure of my company during several vacations in the coming years - I think I was something of a novelty for them, but they were very good to me. I was there primarily to supplement my knowledge of "hands on" experience in modern heavy engineering plant, and up to date usage of various tools and pieces of equipment. (I was introduced to things like the hydraulic torque spanner, something ingenious for example, when tightening down cylinder head nuts - precisely.) But as a family man, just at this time involved in building a house – I was always pleased to accept my wages!
Returning on the Liverpool boat to Belfast two days later, I was sitting down shortly in Lisburn Technical College in time for the opening staff meeting of the new session presided over by Mr. David Wright, our principal.
 He wanted to see me. Now, what could he be wanting?
Actually, he just wanted to apologize to me – he had mistakenly omitted my name from the staff list! I think I just said, "Oh, that's all right - Mr. Wright!"

Note : Reference to Jack the donkey man's story on being torpedoed: *My late friend, Captain Jim Bothwell, Master Mariner, who once sailed with MacAndrews himself, kindly sent me a short account of all the MacAndrews ships lost at sea. My search through this indicated that Jack's torpedoed ship was likely to have been the MacAndrew's steamer "Ciscar II, " of 2,436 Tons Gross, her Master being Captain Hughes.*
Outward bound for Spain on August 19[th.]1941,the vessel was torpedoed and sunk off Ushant in 49°.10 N., 17°. 40 W. (which was indeed keeping well out from the coast.)
Of her crew of 39, 20 were lost.
*One of these latter was the Third Engineer of whom Jack the donkeyman had said "--- **he was a lad - just like you."***
I have often wondered who he was, where he had come from and, that had I been born earlier I might have been him - taking the watch in his place.
I have also had difficulty in getting my head around the fact, that 30,000 seamen lost their lives at sea in the Second World war.

Note : This has been a sobering thought for me since - and is why I have included that part of the Preface from "Antrim and Beyond, Part Two - " They Served in Time of War," as the Preface of this book. *Author.*

Down the tunnel:

Left: The propeller shaft and tunnel of the MV "Velarde.
A solitary place:
The tunnel, a somewhat lonely walk for the engineer on watch to make to, where the propeller shaft of the MV "Velarde" revolved in such splendid isolation. Here, part of the watchkeeping Engineer's responsibility is to check the oil lubricated bearings – as seen in the forefront, in case they overheat and also the Stern Gland, where the propeller shaft passes through the hull, and where a trickle of sea water was allowed through to help lubricate the lignum vitae bearing.
Origin of photo: Author.

Question Time:

" How did you know that? " said the man.

I had been greatly interested to see from " Velarde's" deck (as recalled above), the old coaster, the M.V. "Hibernian Coast " in Liverpool, albeit in "mothballs," and where I spent a brief period as Third Engineer years before. She was an uncomfortable beast!
Some time later - perhaps a couple of years so, I attended a wedding with my wife, in Sinclair Seamen's Presbyterian Church in Belfast – the bride being the youngest daughter of a sea captain of our acquaintance.
It would always be an interesting place for me to go to, because my father and mother were also married there.

    *   *   *   *

Later at the reception, I was sitting opposite the late Captain Campbell Kerr, who was recalling to someone beside him his early days on a coaster called the MV "Hibernian Coast. "
Campbell had been a "hawse pipe" man. This means that he had been raised to command, from the ranks of an AB – ie he was an able bodied seaman on deck, before becoming an officer.

"Did the Mate, by any chance, come from Bangor in North Wales?" I inquired.

"Yes, he certainly did," Campbell replied, *"But how did you know that ?"*

Chapter 11

The San Blas Islands.
Regions of the Rain Forests (Central America)

RAIN forests are very large, dense forests found in regions – usually tropical, where rain is very heavy throughout the year. The regions are found between 20 degrees North and 20 degrees South of the Equator and in all the continents - except Europe. Characterised as places both steamy and hot and where the sun seldom penetrates the canopy of the tall tree. There is one exception to this general rule, and strangely, this is where these conditions are found in Rain Forests in South Eastern Alaska, in the U.S.A.

I set out for brief visits to Colombia in South America, and the Rain Forests of Panama, and Costa Rica. But on the way, the ship I was travelling on called at a group of islands – where time indeed seemed to have stood still.

*   *   *   *   *

The San Blas Islands (Nov. 17[th.] 1999.)

This is a group of islands, about 40 in number, which lie mainly in and around the Gulf of San Blas, on the Atlantic side of Panama. A swath of tropical forest on the mainland completes the San Blas territory, which is peopled by the Kuna tribe of San Blas Indians, and their population is estimated at 40,000. The islands are extremely low lying, which the Kuna stabilize with chunks of coral dredged from the sea and topped with sand.

For the most part, these people are self sufficient in matters of food, shelter, and transportation. Visits are made daily, either to attend to their farms - possibly vegetable farms on the mainland areas, to cut wood, hunt, or carry water locally. The Kuna may also sail to outer islands for water (mainly a job for women) or to beaches where fishing is more productive. Coconuts and other fruits – lemons, oranges, pineapple, mangos etc, have to be gathered, and smoked fish and smoked iguanas seemed much in evidence. Something of great interest I discovered was that Kuna society was a matriarchal one i.e. a form of social organisation in which the mother is the ruler of the family, the descent of leadership being traced through the mother. When a man marries, he goes to live in his wife's village or perhaps in her parent's home.

I met a most interesting man when I visited San Blas. His name was John Mann, an ex-marine (American), and he had spent about 27 years being with the Kuna Indians of San Blas. He was the author of a book, the proceeds of which were in aid of the little school for the children of the Kuna - see its front cover on p130. I was to visit the school in due course. But first, I had to get ashore and this was accomplished through the use of the ship's survival craft (lifeboats) to ferry passengers into a small dock on the island of Porvenir. Now the previous day, on our 20,000 ton vessel, the SS "Emerald " we had gone through that very thorough and time honoured ritual – Lifeboat Drill. We were to find out shortly that the Kuna did not have either lifeboats or lifeboat drill!

 But they soon showed plenty of business acumen. They lined up with their gaily painted dug out canoes, which seemed to have been made out of logs perhaps four or five feet in diameter. They reminded me of the huge Elm logs that threatened to destroy the party on the old SS "Grecian" when, during the crossing of the Bay of Biscay, they decided to "shift cargo."

The Kuna were indeed quite keen on business, and soon we were aboard these dugouts – each possibly carrying six or eight passengers – plus the boatman himself. Time had not stood exactly still in marine matters here, because each canoe was fitted with an outboard motor and rejoiced in the name "cayuko" (motorised dugout canoe). But there was more than a trace of irony around as we set out for a tour of these islands: We would be travelling

128

in shark infested water (see next page), with no life jackets, and with our "skipper" using a tin can to bale out water – all this in a dugout with little freeboard. Looking back now, I cannot believe that we had partaken in such a caper. For, on the previous day as already mentioned, we were exercised in that time honoured ritual - Lifeboat Drill, being thus adorned in life jackets, whistles, lights etc and happily, not a shark in sight!

However we were now afloat, and spent twenty minutes or so touring around without mishap, and then approached the island cemetery - but not to land on it, that being forbidden. This was a strange place indeed. The natives inter their dead here in their hammocks. The graves are not filled in, but are given a little thatched roof by way of cover. I could not be sure, but I thought that I knew why those large birds that I saw hovering about seemed so well fed!

A display of dancing was in progress as we returned to Porvenir (see photograph), where the music was supplied on the "hoof " by the men of the dancers – playing their "reed" like mouth organs, or recorder like instruments etc. I bought one of the latter, and some time later, proudly displaying my potential talent, offered myself as an addition to a steel band in Montego Bay, Jamaica. However, having only had experience of playing in our local pipe band in Antrim, I was not, regrettably, able to encourage "further inquiries" there, and with no room in the Inn, I decided to keep my day job! See photographs later.

However, it was interesting to notice that the instruments used by the Peruvians as shown in the photograph of their group, were similar to those of the Kuna musicians. See the following photographs and later comments on the Pan Pipes.

Returning again to the dancing, it was then that I noticed something very striking indeed: As earlier revealed, Kuna Society is a matriarchal one.

Perhaps that is unrelated, but all the females I saw, seemed to have a striking resemblance to each other - whereas the males did not appear to share similar characteristics and features at all.

Souvenirs - what about souvenirs?

The Indians had limited home produce for sale, but I bought myself a couple of nice shells for the hearth back home.

Well the San Blas Indians had put on a show of dancing. Wearing hats, the men supplied the music "on the hoof," using what looked to me like " reed mouth organs" where the reeds were probably made from bamboo stems with the pitch of each adjusted by length. (It is most likely that they were pan pipes played along with their version of our recorders.) I purchased one of the latter and later, tried to join a band In Jamaica. Watch this space!.

Above: The San Blas Indians put on a show of dancing. Wearing hats, the men supply the music "on the hoof," using what looked like " reed mouth organs." See further comparison and comment on "Pan pipes."

Below: A contribution from Siabibi in a signed copy of John Mann's book.

This is our new baby and she is sleeping, I hope. *Mimiya* is singing and rattling and swinging the hammock. *Mimiya* sings better songs than I do but my father says I sing louder than she can. The baby is called *Mimisipu* because she is so pretty.

A big needle and a little string were pushed through her nose just yesterday and she didn't even cry. The string is still there. When she is old enough to be careful not to lose it she will have a gold ring like mine.

My grandmother has the biggest nose ring in this village but everybody wears little rings now. They cost so much money some people don't have nose rings anymore. There is nothing else to draw in this picture except the basket. It has a top and you can not see what is in it, but I will tell you. It is a sewing basket and in it there is cloth and thread and scissors for making *molas*.

That is our cat — next to the basket.

To Bobby
from John
San Blas. Panama
Nov. 17. 1999

SIABIBI'S
SAN
BLAS

AN ILLUSTRATED NOTEBOOK*

BY
JOHN MANN

Above: "Cast off for'd." Our skipper is about to take a group out in shark infested waters in his dugout canoe. His baler – a tin can, is possibly in his left hand – a sharp contrast to the ultra modern ship's tender (survival craft) that brought the group to the islands! Author, holding camera – and with the faithful yellow/blue bag on his back, but not a lifebelt in sight! Life boat drill, what's that then?
For this photograph in colour –see the front cover. Source: Ship's photographer

Left: The natives of the Kuna islands await the tourists to show them arounds their islands
Origin: Author 1999

Above: Repeat picture from two pages back to view along with the picure below: Author saw and heard these San Blas Islanders playing instruments which he described as " pipe mouth organs." But it is more likely that their proper name was indeed, Pan Pipes. We can see what Pan Pipes look like in the photograph below, and these seem similar to those witnessed being played on Porvenir Island. It helps to show that movement to the beat of music, is world wide. It is called it dancing – indeed a universal enchantment!

Origin: Author 1999.

Above: The book in which the photo of these Peruvians appeared, identified their instruments as Pan Pipes.
Origin: This photograph was found in a book called, "The Story of the World in Pictures." It was published by Odhams Press – and not later than the early 1930's.

Above: Peruvian Indians are seen playing an instrument like that used by the San Blas Indians and indeed were seen at San Blas and referred to as "reed mouth organs."
In the book where this photo came from, however, the caption to the photo of the Peruvion musicians, refer to their instruments as Pan Pipes. Where does the name Pan come from?
Pan, is revered in mythology as the Spiritual Diety of the animal world, and to whom they might look to for protection, for example. He appears in mythology as a figure standing upright , wearing horns and playing the Pan Pipes, an instrument that most people would be hard pressed to describe. However, the mouth organ analogy is technically not too far away. But one can read about Pan and how his interaction in the animal world might take place.

In the book, "The Wind in the Willows," by Kenneth Grahame, once every child's favourite story and written in allegorical parlance, there is a scene where a baby Otter gets himself well and truly lost. Searchers include his father and such respectable animals as the Mole and the Water Rat. As they look for him along the river bank, they presently hear the sound of music. With the Mole rowing their boat and the Water Rat navigating –"Row closer, Mole, row closer," they eventually find the baby Otter asleep at the feet of the Diety of animals – Pan with his pipes. Grahame's superb description of the scene, highlights that animals indeed hear things that humans would also like to hear - but cannot do so!

What the Oxford Dictionary says: **" Pan Pipes – A musical instrument made from a row of short pipes."**

        *   *   *   *   *

Final Comments: In addition to Pan Pipes, the San Blas people also played instruments of the recorder variety with which European school children are familiar, and one of which the author bought as a souvenir (but see later for adventures with it in Montego Bay, Jamaica!)

Although often associated with classical Greece, the Pan Pipes are to be found being played in many pastoral places throughout the world. Peru and the San Blas Islands are in the same Longitude belt.

Question: What have the following got in common?
    San Blas Indians; Members of a pipe band;
    Natives of Peru;
    Answer: They all play wind instruments

  ●   *   *   *   *   *

Now for a brief departure from the general theme of this book:

My memories of that introduction to the Pan pipes and the other wind instruments of the San Blas Indians - plus my forlorn "attempt" later to join a Steel Band in Jamaica (see later!), helped recall to mind a relatively unheralded and forgotten bit of travel – an epic of "they that go down to the seas and do business in great waters." (It certainly would qualify as another method of travel to see the world - volunteer for a mission full of hazards and - travel to Distant Lands.

The Voyage of the MV "Clyde Valley."

* Denis Young, the Drum Major of Antrim Pipe Band was a member of the volunteer crew who under took to crew the former gun runner of 1912, the SS "Clyde Valley" back to Northern Ireland from Canada, as the MV "Clyde Valley" in 1968. Most of the crew who eventually brought the ship back across the Atlantic, came from Northern Ireland but some were Canadians. Why has it taken so long for such a feat to remain untold?

It is only now that some details have become available as to what an epic voyage it was, and what it took in a combination of courage, determination, outstanding seamanship and marine engineering to accomplish a successful landfall for this old vessel, built in 1886.

132

Antrim A.B.D. Memorial Pipe Band:

From left, standing: Pipe Major John Noble, Norma Burrows, Raymond O'Neil, Adrian Steel (standing forward), Tom M'Cosh, William M'Elhill (rear) , Author, Matt McCullough, Drum Major Denis Young. Front seated: John Gray, Lloyd Jack, Ronnie Preston, John McNeil, Darren Hogg.

  * *Denis Young, former seaman, was a member of the crew that sailed the former gun runner when registered as the S.S. "Clyde Valley" from Nova Scotia, Canada, back to Larne, Northern Ireland in December, 1968.* Denis Young was the Drum Major of Antrim ABD Pipe Band.

  * *William M'Elhill (extreme back), was a veteran of the Korean War and late of the Argyll and Sutherland Highlanders).*

  * *Norma Burrows, is now a much travelled artist with world wide exhibitions.*

The SS "Clyde Valley" was re engined after 1912, and returned to Larne, Co. Antrim, as the M.V. "Clyde Valley" in 1968.

Above: The MV "Clyde Valley," outside Larne Harbour in County Antrim, prior to docking there in December 1968. Likely Origin: Ballymena Times, Thurs. Dec 1968.

The Voyage of the MV "Clyde Valley."

This was the epic voyage of the MV "Clyde Valley," when sailing from Nova Scotia, Canada to Larne in Northern Ireland. She was it seems, a ship built in 1886 – using iron, not steel. Her date when registered was thought to be 13th. Sept. 1886.

Having got the Old Lady reconditioned enough to satisify the Canadian Authorities of her condition as satisfactory to withstand the rigors that would be before her, she set out. But the problems that emerged were soon to be immence.

The crew tried an initial start from Sydney, Cape Breton Island to Northern Ireland but they suffered a breakdown and had to be towed back to Trepassey Bay by a ship called the "Montmorency." However the tow slipped and the tow was resumed by a trawler, the " Zaley."   Setting out again, a major main engine failure occurred and she had to be towed back again by another trawler, the "Zinder." For this major repair to be done – it may have involved a seized main engine, she then set out for major repairs in St. Johns via Cape Race and Cape Spear under tow from another trawler, the "Zeeland." This major work completed, she then set sail again for Larne.

 Their problems were not over, however , because shortly afterwards, she suffered a total loss of generator power, with all electrical circuits becoming defunct. She had to return to land again through continuously very heavy weather.

Did they give up? No, things were repaired again and - even sails were organised as they crossed the North Atlantic and secured at Carrickfergus Co. Antrim at 19.50 hours on Saturday,14th. December, 1968!

Above: The MV "Clyde Valley" prepares to face the North Atlantic again, and took advantage of the "westerlies" to hasten her journey to Northern Ireland - note the sail!   Courtesy of Denis Young, crew member, Nova Scotia, Canada.

Some of the volunteer crew of the MV "Clyde Valley" take a welcome break after their voyage from Nova Scotia, Canada. Engine trouble forced them back on three occasions – but they made it at the third attempt. Extreme left, Denis Young, Antrim, G Buchanan, Leslie Barnes, Edward Gilkinson, William Connor and extreme right, Second World War veteran, Captain William Agnew, Kilkeel, Co. Down.

Origin: Ballymena Times, Thurs. Dec 19th.1968.

As related, there were several occasions when the vessel had to return to port and after at least one of these, there was a lengthy repair to be carried out. There were also some changes in crew personnel. Below are the names of what is thought to comprise the final crew which brought the vessel to Larne in Co. Antrim.

William Agnew	Master
William Pollock	Mate
Shane Connor	Second Mate
Noel Heal	Third Mate
G. Buchanan	Chief Engineer
Leslie Barnes	Second Engineer
Edward Gilkinson	Third Engineer
Norman Kelly	Boatswain
Dennis Young	D.H.V.
John Poe	Supernummery

When the lights go out!

Information is just not at hand at present to verify if emergency lighting was available or not, but a totally blacked out ship is a nightmare few would want to be part of.

Jamaica : We were now headed for Jamaica . I had acquired an instrument not unlike a recorder while at the San Blas islands and decided I would offer my musical talents as soon as I set foot on Jamaican soil.

My dream comes true at last! My audition to become a member of a Jamaican Steel Band!
The guy beside me is beginning to wonder where I came from. He maybe thinks I am a white ghost!   Origin: A kind passerby.

Now well into my audition: His mate, the second guy across has downed tools and is straining his ears – was that a false note he heard?
(What did those guys really think ?
     Origin: The same kind passerby!

Above: An audition was the first test of my offerings and things did not go too well. However, having only had experience of playing in our local pipe band in Antrim, I was not, regrettably, able to encourage "further inquiries" there - no room left in the Inn.
To make a long story short, I decided to keep my day job ! See above – every picture tells story.
          *   *   *   *   *

The Panama Canal:

A little pre view : In 1904, as the U.S.A. was taking an interest in a canal across Panama, the Colombian state of Panama declared independence – which **Colombia** of course opposed - and flexed its muscles.
An American gun boat appeared, and this helped Colombia modify its opposition, and for the next one hundred years, the U.S.A. became the dominant influence in the region. They built the Canal, managed it and this would help to revolutionise the world's commerce in the years to come. They also would control a ten mile strip of land on either side of the Canal part of which consisted of a stretch of Panama's Rain Forest.
I would now shortly be approaching that very place – **Panama**. The canal that was eventually built across that narrow strip of land, a mere fifty miles or less, surprisingly travels slightly towards the East – from the Atlantic approach. A look at a map of the country of Panama will reveal this peculiar feature of the Canal.
The Panama Canal would help shorten the distance between New York and the Western States of the U.S.A. by 5,000 miles. A land route crossing Panama in conjunction with the Chagres river, was the path followed by generations of adventurers, from the Spanish conquistadors of the early sixteenth century, to the miners of the American gold rush of later years. Some of the latter were to benefit from the construction of the Panama Railway across the Isthmus in 1885.This railroad was about fifty miles long, and in1914, a waterway would largely follow the line of that little railway. It would be known as the *Panama Canal.*

Chapter 12

Panama and its Canal.

(From the Atlantic to the Pacific)

From the Atlantic Ocean, the approach to the Panama Canal is made by way of what is surely one of the world's great wonders and a prodigious man made engineering feat. By six o'clock on the morning of our arrival there, and when it was still somewhat dark, passage was being made along the channel leading to this man made wonder– the Gatum locks. This consists of a set of three locks in fact , which in sequence, lifts a ship up eighty nine feet, from the Atlantic Ocean to the Gatum Lake. The lake provides thirty miles of plain sailing, following the line of the submerged Chagres River.This latter is important, because the ground which the lake covers is strewn with submerged villages and other potential hazards to shipping – the discarded debris of a mighty engineering feat, from a wheel barrow to railway engines. We would be doing a complete transit of the Canal, from the Atlantic to the Pacific Ocean in a ship called the **MV "Regal Princess."** But we must now leave the **"Regal Princess"** outside the Gatum Locks while we borrow an account by the author of a visit to the Rain Forests of Panama made some years earlier on a ship called the **SS "Emerald." But we will return to the "Princess" shortly!**

*   *   *   *   *

So, at this point, we digress for a short time to examine something in this very region which could also be described as a prodigious feat, a feat of Nature, namely the Panama Rain Forest.

In 1999 I had had an opportunity to see the Panama Rain Forest for myself.

To do this, it was necessary to approach it from the Gatum Lake via the Gatum Locks using the afore mentioned **SS "Emerald."** Our little expedition, organised by the Thompson Travel Group, who at times have included in their itineraries places to visit of unusual interest, took place some time before the Americans handed the responsibility for running the Canal over to the Panama Control Authorities in Dec. 1999.

The Construction of the Panama Canal : A short history.

It had been the dream of many – for over four hundred years - to find a suitable route joining the Atlantic to the Pacific. Surveys were carried out across Colombia, Panama (a province of Colombia), Mexico, and several others places on the "neck" of the Isthmus. In Nicaragua, a one hundred mile route across was considered, because on that proposed route was Lake Nicaragua, fifty miles long. Panama, however, – also known as the Isthmus of Darien, was the shortest – about fifty miles across.

Being thus about only fifty miles from the Atlantic Ocean to the Pacific Ocean across Panama led De Lessops, the builder of the Suez Canal (during 1859-69), to lay plans to build a sea level canal, and the first French engineers arrived in 1881. Their subsequent failure, was brought about partly by the mosquito, (the carrier of malaria and yellow fever), the death of at least ten thousand workers, and the problems caused by the Chagres River. Some American estimates later put the French losses at over twenty thousand, and mostly black workers from Caribbean countries.

Work by the French officially stopped in December, 1888, although a French Consortium would still own the rights, as agreed by Colombia. They would do a little more work on the project, before parting with those concessional rights and the remaining plant, to the Americans for forty million dollars.

In 1904, the Americans came in, defeated the mosquito by methods of hygiene, and dammed the Chagres River to create an artificial lake. This latter provided a straight passage for about thirty miles, with suitable locks built at the entrance (the three Gatum Locks) and at intervals in the latter section of the canal towards the Pacific Ocean. The lake was to be known as the Gatum Lake, 164 square miles in area. On the Atlantic approach, the first of the locks were, as above, the three twin locks at Gatum, and where a ship would be lifted about eighty five feet to the level of the Gatum Lake. Twin locks means that two parallel locks can work two ships at any one time – and going in the same direction. After the passage of 30 miles across the lake, there was a very difficult section – about eight miles long, the Culebra Cut or Gaillard Cut. This was where a cutting through the lowest dip in the mountains of the continental divide (where falling rain either deposits to the Pacific Ocean or to the Atlantic Ocean) had to be made, although even at this point it was still three hundred feet above sea level and the French managed to remove about twenty per cent of this lofty section. The Americans expressed amazement that the French had achieved so much, given the conditions and equipment that the French had been working with and under.

The cutting referred to above, was known as mentioned, as the Culebra Cut, but it was to be later known as the Gaillard Cut, named after Lieut. Col. D. D. Gaillard who was at one time in charge of this Central Division. He retired through ill health sometime during construction, and he died of a brain tumour, in Dec., 1914. The Culebra Cut was the scene of constant landslides, responding to which, the engineers kept widening the base and seeking to find the angle of repose for the sides of the canal at Culebra, that would satisfy the voracious appetite of the Culebra for mud slides that blocked the 'cut' for months at a time, often burying expensive plant in its avalanche. It was to prove an elusive, lengthy and expensive task.

The canal would be blocked here on a number of occasions in the future. In October 1914, the central channel was closed. In Sept.,1915, another avalanche blocked the canal for many months. Even as recent as 1974, an avalanche, estimated at one million cubic yards entered the canal – and, as in the Suez Canal, dredging continues routinely to this day."

Extract concludes

A ship entering the three Gatum Locks is lifted about 85 feet from the level of the Atlantic Ocean to that of the Gatum Lake. It then can travel about 30 miles across the Gatum Lake to where three other sets of twin locks were constructed . These locks enabled ships to be lowered down to the Pacific – a single twin at Pedro Miguel, and two twin locks at Mirroflores. Again, a twin lock simply means two single locks side by side, thus allowing two ships to pass through the locks at the same time. It has been calculated that each single lock contains the same weight of concrete, as that of the stone in Cheops, the Great Pyramid of Giza in Egypt.

Each lock chamber is one thousand feet long by one hundred and ten feet wide, and stands eighty one feet high (6 stories high). Each lock is an edifice in concrete of gigantic proportions, with a side wall thickness of forty feet, and in places, a floor foundation of similar dimension.

The excavation alone of the Pedro Miguel twin lock started in 1908, and took almost one year to complete, one million cubic yards of spoil having been removed. Concreting started in 1910 and went on without let or hindrance until the Pedro Miguel was completed in1913 – with a further one thousand cubic yards laid in 1914. Almost one million cubic yards of concrete was laid at the twin lock of Pedro Miguel, and miles of old French railway lines were used as steel reinforcement for the concrete.

The first vessel to sail through the canal, was a cement boat at work in the canal – the "Cristobal," on August 3rd. 1914. This was a rehearsal for the passage of the first commercial vessel to pass from ocean to ocean, at the official opening of the canal in August 15th. 1914, just before the First World War. This vessel was the S.S. "Ancon," which made the passage in just over nine hours.

There were few vessels in 1914 that were large enough to justify using the full lock – 1,000 yards long, so intermediate gates were installed so that a smaller lockage was available if required, using less fresh water in doing so. By the year 2,008, there were over seven hundred ships across the world that are too large to pass through the Panama Canal. Each full lockage involving sending a ship through the locks from ocean to ocean, uses fifty two million gallons of fresh water. The waters of the Gatum Lake are not of infinite existence – they depend largely on the Panamanian Rain Forest, which acts as a giant sponge. It is well that it is so, because the yearly rain fall is of the order of one hundred to one hundred and thirty inches. One can see how important it is, that this rain forest remains – standing!

In 2004, the cost to transit a ship of large size from ocean to ocean is of the order of fifty thousand dollars - indeed sometimes much more. The last time the 'Q.E. Two' passed through, the cost was $42,078! Finally, a word about the lock gates. These are in pairs, each half known as a leaf, the pairs closing to mitre in a shallow vee. For safety and security reasons, each pair is backed up by another pair, and as already mentioned, there is an intermediate set of lock gates for shorter lock requirements.

Each leaf in itself, is an enormous construction in itself,. An outer steel plate covering is riveted to a girder framework – after the manner of constructing an aircraft wing, watertight and buoyant.

The leaves are sixty five feet across, seven feet thick and from forty seven feet high – as at Gatum, to eighty two feet high – as at Mirroflores, the latter here taking into account the variation in the higher tides of the Pacific Ocean end. The gates therefore vary in weight, with each leaf at Mirroflores – closest to the Pacific tides, weighing seven hundred and fifty tons! For maintenance purposes, and since they float, they are towed into a drydock, about every ten years, after the manner of dry docking a ship. The total weight of steel in all 92 leaves(of the twin lock), is over sixty thousand tons – more than in the "Titanic!"

The part de Lessops plays in Panama Canal History:

Ferdinand de Lessops was really a French diplomat – not an engineer. His drive and vision, however, helped bring the remarkable undertaking of building the Suez Canal in Egypt to fruition – he became the hero of Suez, that canal opening in 1869. His eventual defeat at Panama was firstly, due to his insistence that he would build a sea level canal like Suez in Egypt, when he had not solved the problem of the wide ranging Chagres River and secondly, the high mortality – from malaria and yellow fever, among the workers.

In fact, in 1883 alone, over 1,000 deaths took place, and by the mid 1880's, four train loads of corpses travelled each day to the burial grounds. It is reported that a ghoulish trade developed – sending barrels of pickled corpses to medical schools all over the world. One wonders at all this gruesome business, but apparently a question much asked – possibly in entertainment circles, was, "Is de Lessops building a canal, or a graveyard?"

The passage of the Gatum Locks - the SS " Emerald."

Going back now to the SS "Emerald" in the twin lock at Gatum, we had for company a "Panamax" i.e. the maximum **size** of ship able to pass the locks. This "Panamax" was seen to have a clearance of one metre or less, at each side, with, it seemed, containers piled higher than the Bridge. The passage through the Gatum locks took over one and a half hours, and soon the great man made lake was stretching away across isolated islands, past ships riding at anchor - and through to the ragged edges and mists of the Panamanian Rain Forest. Soon the ship was at anchor, and with the ship' s survival craft (life boats) being used as tenders, passengers were soon ashore, close to the premises of the Panama Yacht Club.

The intention now was to visit the Panamanian Rain Forest. Those on the visit boarded a bus which passed over the lock gates on its way to the Chagres River. Then the visit to the Rain Forest was finally accomplished by passage in a boat down the Chagres river and east of the Gatum Lake spillway. The boat eventually stopped at a suitable place for the travellers to step ashore and * walk amidst the wonders of the Rain Forest of Panama.

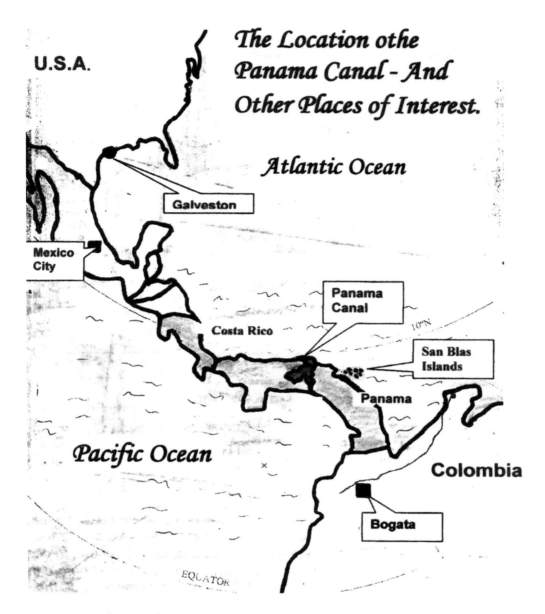

The Location othe Panama Canal - And Other Places of Interest.

U.S.A.

Atlantic Ocean

Galveston

Mexico City

Panama Canal

Costa Rico

10°N

San Blas Islands

Panama

Pacific Ocean

Colombia

Bogata

EQUATOR

Map for The Location for the Panama Canal, the San Blas Islands, Costa Rico and the Sky Divers of Mexico. It should be noted that the line of the Panama Canal is slightly South East – one is further East after passing from Atlantic to Pacific, than when one set out from the Atlantic side!   Origin: Author 2006.

* By contrast Costa Rico does not permit walking in their Rain Forests!

See "Fourth Coloured Selection"(P210) for above map, and the following P141 - to be seen in Colour.

The Rain Forest of Panama contd.

The river they had travelled on, was the same Chagres River that had been used by the Spanish conquistadors to transport the stolen treasures of the former Inca Empire of South America to Spain - and possibly as far back as the sixteenth century.

Thus gold was once transported - past right by where one was about to stand on the banks of that River which also, during the California Gold Rush in the 1880's, had served as a short cut for gold rush fortune seekers coming from the East Coast of the United States. No doubt my short journey down the Chagres brought to life the history of this water – one could imagine those who had gone before along these waters to conduct their business. The guided nature walk through this lush tropical Rain Forest show case, highlighted such a variety of exotic birds, plants, iguanas, howler monkeys, two toe sloths (sleeping upside

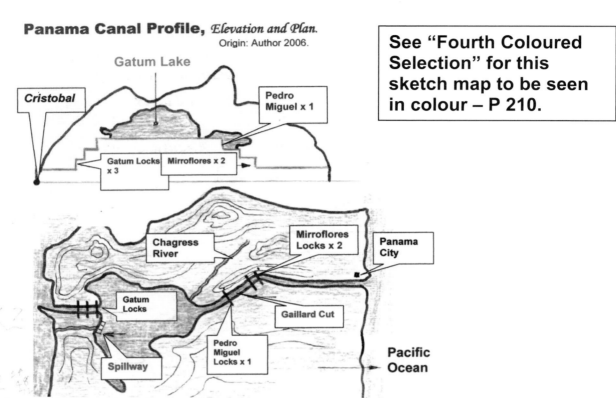

Panama Canal Profile, *Elevation and Plan.*
Origin: Author 2006.

See "Fourth Coloured Selection" for this sketch map to be seen in colour – P 210.

down) showed why this part of the world is so widly recognised for its biological diversity. It also highlighted something else of great significance – the Rain Forest tourism, and how it is managed. Panama like other countries, as I was to learn, has discovered that a standing forest will earn the nation much more standing than a heap of dead wood shipped out to augment the living rooms of Japan.

During the trip down the Chagres – about two hundred yards or so wide it widened further into small lake and our guide informed us that sharks had been known to appear (but how this happened was not explained.) Caymen and crocodiles are common in Panama as are jaguar, turtles, wild pigs, giant frogs and giant ospreys.

The plants of the Rain Forest benefit medicine. Drugs for the treatment of leukaemia and cancer, and medicine to help modern surgery, have been developed from Rain Forest products.

The reference to sharks later led the guide to speculate further that under sea passages might account for their presence. But of course, the river outlet is controlled by the mighty wall of the Gatum Dam and water leaves by way of its spillway.

Rain Forests are rarely exploited wisely. Loggers only want about 5% of the trees, but the damage they do accounts for about 65% of those remaining.

There are plants in the rain forest which might help to develop better varieties of rice which might be more resistant to disease with a higher yield, and the amazing copaiba trees, recently discovered, which yields a heavy oil, suitable for use in truck engines. Is it not amazing?

Finally the slash and burn policies adds to the amount of carbon dioxide in the atmosphere, and we are now told, of course, that such policies contribute to global warming. Slash and

141

burn of course, is often used to clear such a forest in order to provide pasture for cattle – which in turn supply the burger trade. One was permitted to walk in the Panamanian Forest – at least where I was, but such an intrusion is not kindly looked upon by some other countries who possess Rain Forests, and who are seeking to preserve their Rain Forest from foreign bodies. Today, the Canal Zone has been handed back to the Panamanians, the U.S.A. lease having now expired, and the Panamanians may now introduce stricter measures to further preserve their Rain Forest. Irregular walking may soon be restricted or simply not permitted. Having seen our last sloth retreat unsociably further up into the canopy – and the last troop of monkeys chatter objections to our presence, we made our way back to our boat, and the Chagres River. A bus eventually delivered us back to and across the canal to the Panama Yacht Club, where, to our surprise, some light refreshment was available - for all. The refreshment, it seemed, was by courtesy of the Panama Yacht Club, to whose premises, we had been taken by the bus. The Yacht Club was also where we would find our ship's lifeboats to return us back to the ship. *Note: From time to time, bridging is arranged across the canal to facilitate traffic.*

Now it just so happened, that the refreshment was served close by their lively and well stocked "souvenirs for sale" display!

Message: There are no free lunches in life. It is quite true!

Presently in the ship's life boats - now being used as tenders, we made our way back to our ship - still anchored in the artificial lake at Gatum.

This brief sketch is much too inadequate to fully describe a Rain Forest. It is vast but has an ordered way of life. There is an endless variety of trees and plants striving to gain the sun, reaching perhaps, one hundred feet - some nearly double that. Those branches (the canopy), breaking into the sunlight burst into leaf and attracts creatures that feel comfortable and safe in the heights. Other species dwell lower down – indeed some creatures dwell on the forest floor. As indicated earlier, when rain falls – as it very often does here, the trees and plants act like a giant sponge, soaking up the water. The trees allow the water to pass out slowly to feed rivers and other systems. But the wholesale removal of trees allows the water to run off quickly – taking the soil with it.

Since, as mentioned before, each time a ship passes through the Panama Canal in a full lockage, about 52 million gallons of fresh water is lost to the sea,and there was real concern during the nineteen eighties, that the artificial lake might run out of water, if the cutting down of the Panamanian rain forest (their rain maker) was not controlled.

But the "rain maker" seems to be in good health today – the warning may have been heeded in time!

The Return to the Atlantic from Gatum Lake.

 Going now in the reverse direction, we were lowered in the locks to sea level again, and were soon proceeding north, if time permitted, to our next magnificent Rain Forest setting – that of Costa Rica and the Atlantic port of Puerto Limon. In Panama we had witnessed the last days of the Americans running the Canal Zone – shortly they would be leaving the Panamanians to run the Canal themselves from - **Mid Day, December 31st 1999.**

The latter may indeed have views as to how the rain forest is run as well! " (This ends the account of that visit to the Rain Forests of Panama.)

☆   ☆   ☆   ☆   ☆

While this ended our little "expedition" to the Panama Rain Forests, the "Emerald's" sailing schedule had left sufficient time to make a visit to nearby Costa Rico, and have a brief encounter with the Rain Forest there. It was not to be missed!

The Rain Forests of Costa Rico.

Time and space are not available here to adequately describe the experience of travelling in this small country. It might be described as a Third World country but before much longer this description may not apply. Costa Rico has been committed for some time now, to spending a massive 22% of its GDP on education - and it had dispenced with its army. (One understands that in any nasty situation that may arise, a large friendly neighbour will drop a few shells in the right places – and return later to pick up the pieces!)

*   *   *   *   *

Although warm, it was raining heavily the next morning when we arrived in Puerto Limon, Costa Rica, and as we had to set off almost immediately on a three hour journey to the Rain Forest, drastic measures were called for. The ship's store of rubbish disposal bags was raided and by pushing one's head through the bottom of a plastic bag – hey, instant water-proofing was obtained. My own bag was of a brilliant yellow hue – it has now an honoured place in my garage - see the photograph! With some new friends from Co Tyrone, Northern Ireland (who were on the same business as myself) and our guide, I posed for a photograph at the Rain Forest in my yellow smock - and feeling awhile like a Priest from Inca days. For some reason, it was the only still photograph I have showing people in the Rain Forests on the Atlantic coast of Costa Rico.

Our route lay through banana country, and it was noticeable that on each tree in a typical farm, the banana truss was also enclosed in plastic - in something like a bin liner ! Only one truss of bananas grows on each tree. Our guide on the bus explained that this plastic cover was to protect the banana from damage from insects – the damage mostly being to appearance, and each farm had a different colour of protective bag – no mistake in who the owner was here! It was noted that small streams were permitted to flow across the road, but Costa Rico is still a developing country. Bridges and under road piping will come later. It was also very interesting to look at the local enterprises e.g. wayside garages, if we happened to stop near one, and also to look at the type of cattle – cows etc, grazing in the fields. These were in the main, smaller than British or Irish breeds, some with that "rump" at the base of the neck more typical of Indian cattle. Our journey actually took three hours, and I was to be very glad of my trusty blue and yellow bag and the flask of coffee it contained close at hand. They have travelled with me for many years !

Travel through the Rain Forest was by means of an aerial tram, which, attached to a stout steel cable, moved withthe cable in a more or less horizontal line. Since the ground below us consisted of little hills and valleys, sometimes one was above the canopy (the leafy tops of the trees in the forest) and at other times passing through the trees at almost ground level. As with the Rain Forests of Panama - as observed on prevous page, these comments are much too brief to properly describe a Rain Forest.

Left: Dressed in the latest fashion for wearing in the Rain Forest (when it is raining), I am joined by two friends from Co. Tyrone and our guide for the day.

Origin: Another kind passer by.

The Rain Forests of Costo Rico (Contd.)

Wild life seemed less in evidence than in the Panamanian rain forest near the Chagres River, but the opportunity to gaze at the multitude of plants and trees was superb. Of interest, as our guide explained, was that when a tree – even a large mahogany falls – as when blown down, etc., it is allowed to remain on the floor of the forest. There, with insects taking up 'residence,' a new food chain develops, and, as the tree rots away, nutrients are returned to the ground. Quite often, the guide would point out the hardwoods, like mahogany, ebony, and others, that, had they been growing in other Rain Forests in the world, might have been destined for a drawing room table – or a wardrobe. But here they were safe.

Above: I meet one Michael Molchoff, son of the former White Russian General, Lieut. General Molchoff.
Source: Author 2006

Sometimes the guide - with an eye for such things would point out a snake in a tree which our unpractised eyes could barely distinguish from the branch on which it was lying !

As Panama probably will, (when in the near future they gain full control of their country), the Costa Ricans already see that a standing Rain Forest will earn more income over the years, than a pile of timber awaiting shipment to far off markets During the tour, our guide was following the letter of the law, when he pointed out to a passenger in our car, that smoking was not permitted in the Rain Forest. It is sad to think that each and every day, Rain Forests are being destroyed somewhere, and reports indicate that huge areas of the Rain Forest in Brazil are being lost daily on a disastrous scale, the area lost per year estimated to equal the area of France.Usually only a few people benefit financiall , but the overall loss is incredible. As already stated, in extracting the 5% of the timber they want – mostly hardwoods, the loggers destroy an estimated 65% of the forest through the creation of roadways or in dragging their spoils around to transit sites. Not only is the forest, created over hundreds – maybe thousands of years a casualty, but the people of the rain forest – as in Brazil, are also so. This is because they are unable stand up and oppose successfully, those who are invading their forest and threatening their way of life. They have been shot, poisoned and worse – they have been infected with diseases like measles, flu or whooping cough, with which they cannot survive as they never have been in contact with them before. Finally these forests are great providers of oxygen – "oxygen" makers as well as "rain" makers, yet these benefits are being cancelled out by another by product of the loggers. The slash and burn policies practiced to clear the land for cattle ranching – presumably to provide more beef burgers, adds to the amount of carbon dioxide in the atmosphere and adds to the atmosphere's temperature increase. This could have consequences for Polar ice caps – it has been predicted that in fifty years time, the sea level could rise by ten metres. The consequences do not bear thinking about.

Shades of the Czar of Russia ! It was at this time that I met some very interesting
people – see photograph, left. These were two Russians and their families whose parents had fought on the side of the White Russians with General Kerensky against the Bolsheviks as late as 1922. One was Boris, and the other was Michael, Michael Molchoff, in fact the son of the White Russian, Lieut. General Molchoff. The latter and his family had to flee Russia via Vladivostok, Korea, Yokohama in Japan, and finally to San Francisco, in the good old U.S.A., where the General first got work on a chicken farm!
They were making the transit of the Panama Canal to San Francisco – see previous page for photograph.
One morning, having breakfast with my new Russian friends (they were only three or four years old when their parents fled Russia), an interesting rapport in humour took place between Boris and Michael:
  "Remember," said Boris, " your folks gave my folks a hard enough time of it!"
Now what could this mean – they were both on the same side, were they not? Yes, but surprise, surprise!
 Michael's family were members of the Tsar's Russian Orthodox Church, while that of Boris were Quakers – Russian members of the Society of Friends. This was interesting indeed!
 Note: The Society of Friends was founded by an Englishman, one George Fox at Cumbria in the Lake District of England in 1652. George Fox had protested that people should have the right of a personal relationship with God, rather than one dictated through the channels of the bishopric of the Church of England. Not intimidated when hauled before a judge, he addressed the judge saying, "You should be quaking at the name of the Lord."
The judge is then supposed to have shouted " Take this quaker back to gaol."
Well, let's hope that someone recorded the judge correctly!
 This concludes our interlude in the rain Forests of Panama etc and now for the major part of this Chapter – to experience a full transit of the Panamma Canal.

*　　　　*　　　　*　　　　*　　　　*

A Full transit of the Panama Canal.

(From the Atlantic to the Pacific)

We have now returned to join the good ship M.V. " **Regal Princess**," of Princess Lines, whom we last encountered in the approach channel to the Gatum locks, Panama Canal. We then went on extended leave to revive memories of a past visit to the Panama Rain Forest . Now on the 27th. of April, 2006, as dawn was breaking, the M.V. " **Regal Princess**," was in one of the Gatum Twin Locks of the Panama Canal. We had for company at the locks, a large tanker, the "Ruby Mar," which accompanied us in the other half of the "twin" – all the locks in the canal being double, and side by side. A little over a couple of hours later, the ship had been raised 89 feet and was through the locks and heading slowly past the islands in the Gatum Lake.
The air was becoming hot and humid, with mists hanging above the vegetation of the Panama Rain Forest on the shore and beyond. See profile sketch map and route plan of Canal (five pages back) which actually follows the course of the Chagres River - now drowned by the waters of the Gatum Lake.
A clearly defined channel leads through these islands and as just mentioned, actually follows the submerged bed of the Chagres River. These islands were once the tops of hills in the Panamanian Rain Forest, now submerged in places by the Gatum Lake. Also submerged is the remains of Indian villages, as well as construction plant left on site by the builders of the Canal.

145

The route now followed the original bed of the Chagres River, with a couple of left legs and then a right, as the ship was manoeuvred between two large land masses. Here progress was stopped three times, as way came off the **"Regal Princess"** in order to give right of passage to other vessels, the first of which was a tanker, the **"Jade Mar."** This was obviously a sister ship to the **"Ruby Mar,"** the tanker which had just accompanied us through the twin Gatum locks. The second was a medium sized, six hatch cargo vessel, with with an entirely unpronounceable name - probably a Russian.

What was interesting about this vessel, was the lifting gear over the hatches – four vertical tubular pillars, arranged in pairs and funnel like in appearance. These were derrick cranes, with the main weight bearing member slung between two pillars and they could, no doubt, handle a fair lift.

Above: At the Gatum Locks, Panama Canal, where an electric locomotive known as a "mule" is waiting to receive the light lines (ropes) which lead the heavier hawsers from the ship. The main function of the 'mule' is to centralise the ship in the lock during transit. Main engines are also used.
Origin: Author 2006

Above: Leaving Gatum Locks, both gates are opening, the one to right has white rails on top, the other presents a dark face – note the ship following the " Regal Princess." Soon the ship will be in the Gatum Lake and will travel over thirty miles before reaching the Pedro Miguel single twin lock thus commencing the descent to the level of the Pacific Ocean.   Origin: Author 2006

Around noon the ship was approaching that part of the Canal which had proved so expensive in men's lives and materials to build – the Culebra Cut. During the time of construction, the Chief Engineer responsible for this section of the Canal became ill and retired through ill health, dying shortly afterwards. His name was Gaillard and the Culebra section was later renamed the Gaillard Cut, in his memory.

The Cut was through a pass between two mountains. But, it was still 300 feet **above** sea level. Even when this 300 feet was removed, the Canal proper would have to be built – another 50 feet deep. The Cut would eventually stretch for 8 miles – and it would be plagued for years with landslides.

The "Gaillard Cut"

Today, passage is through an apparently relatively wide gorge in the mountains of the Continental Divide (where falling rain either flows to the Atlantic or to the Pacific.) Then under the New Bridge, which is soaring high on the Pacific side. Passage then progresses to reveal spectacular terraced rows (a method used to reduce or minimise land slides) in the towering embankments at Gaillard Cut.

This is where so many men struggled and indeed died when seeking to find the " angle of repose" for those embankments that would stop the heart breaking landslides that blocked the canal – sometimes for months at a time.

Large cruise liner waiting to be lowered in the single twin Pedro Miguel Locks

Happily for us today, there is an abundance of still photographs and also some 8 mm film – the latter now of course, in video or in CD form.

It is difficult indeed today, to realise that the " wide gorge" at Gaillard is in fact an eight mile long artificial canyon, almost half a mile wide in places at the top, perhaps three hundred feet wide at the water line and at one point four hundred feet deep (cut through a mountain three hundred and fifty feet above sea level, with the Canal itself being fifty feet deep.

Out of this "canyon" over one million cubic yards of soil and rocks were removed which included the use of six million pounds of dynamite.

Eventually we passed through the final stretch of the Gaillard Cut and came to the single twin lock at Pedro Miguel. It was also where the Panama Railroad begins to run parallel with the which allowed the final drop to the level of the Pacific Ocean. Here lying off our starboard bow was a cargo vessel – and there was something familiar about this vessel.

Yes, it had the same "four funnel" pillar lifting gear – the derrick cranes that had been seen on that other similar vessel, seen earlier in the day. But this one had a pronounceable name – it was " Murmansk," and a Russian indeed!

With the Pacific Ocean in sight, the canal continued by way of the double twin lock of Mirroflores which allowed the final drop to the level of the Pacific Ocean.

Having passed Mirroflores, and with the skyscrapers of Panama City rising behind the port facilities on the left, our good ship shortly passed into the Pacific Ocean. The temperature had been a steady 29° all day.

Passage now resumed for San Franscisco, calling into Puntarenas on the Pacific side of Costa Rico. Here it was convenient to visit again the Rain Forest , this time using a cable system which allowed the cable car to follow the contour of the ground. As compared to the Costa Rico Atlantic Coast, there was a noticeable lack of wild life, but there were very large numbers of trees of the maghogany variety there and crocodiles were seen in a river – in fact the first I had ever seen. This reminded me of the occasion when travelling in Jamaica, I passed a large notice reading, " Keep out – trespassers will be eaten." It was a crocodile farm !

Proceeding further north, calls were made at several Mexican ports including Acapulco to see their Cliff Divers. Verdict: Crocodiles and Cliff Divers may be worth seeing but, hardly worth going to see !

Arrival in San Francisco :

Finally we were in San Francisco, past Alcatraz Island, the former prison , where it is thought, only one prisoner ever escaped from. All this on a very wet day in San Francisco at the Fishermens' Wharf close to the USS submarine , "Pampanito," a Pacific veteran. In the extreme distance at the end of the pier was the SS "Jeremy O'Brien, see Chapter 2 for a close up photograph. This is the last **ocean** going survivor of the World War Two "Liberty" class of Merchant ships.

Note: The Liberty ships - like the **SS "Jeremy O'Brien,"** were American cargo vessels built from around 1943, and powered by triple expansion steam engines. These ships, of up to 10,000 tons were constructed from prefabricated welded sections, these having been built all over the UnitedStates. They were assembled at various ports and provided the necessary shipping to carry the supplies and hardware to Europe to bring the war to a successful conclusion. One was thus assembled - in four days.

A later version of the "Liberty" ships were the " Victory " ships, slightly larger, faster (up to15 knots to help avoid attacks by German U-Boats) and having either steam turbine , triple expansion steam reciprocating or Diesel propulsion.They had also, additionally, certain structural refinements to help provide extra speed and more flexible hulls. The earlier "Liberties" had problems of hull fractures, and problems associated with brittle fracture.

Crocodiles in a river off the Pacific coast of Costa Rico. Orig: Author 2006

In an Aerial tram, high up in the Costa Rican Forest, off the Pacific Coast. Trams are seen at different levels – note cable. Origin: Author 2006

Author at the Twin Locks at Mirroflores, Panama canal. Orig: Author

Extreme distance, left:The SS "Jeremy O'Brien." Background: The USS "Pampanito," and front, author on a very wet day in San Francisco. Origin: A kind American passer by.

The Twin Locks at Mirroflores, a ship in the one to left, the other " twin" at right. Origin: Author

Chapter 13

A Submarine Experience -

Viewing Shipwrecks on the Sea Bed.

Six years after my partial transit of the Panama Canal in1999, I returned to Caribbean waters having arrived at the Island of Aruba. I was on the island of Aruba (a place formerly under Dutch influence), to experience a dive in a commercial submarine, which provided an opportunity to examine the sea bed, its fish and the coral there. But there was something else to see that interested me more - the wrecks of two ships lying there, a few miles off the coast of that island and what was flagged as a "mystery " aircraft ! Unfortunately, during the

dive we were advised not to use a flash, as the double glass ports might cause reflection. I took the advice - and none of my photographs came out, except one – see that later. However, the cam cording came out perfectly and the sea was awash with all kinds of weird shapes and colourful coral creations, and with all the varieties one could wish for of colourful fish, although the colours of these did not show up very well on the camcorder.

My first sight of "Atlantis 6,"on morning of dive. Origin: Author

Below, left: Someone boarding Atlantis 6.
Origin: Author 2006

In the early part of the day on which the dive was made, a visit had been made to the Aloa Vera farm and factory, where those products that are kind to one's skin are processed from the cactus like plant of that name. The Aloe Vera plant, about one foot in height, has a thick, fleshy core about the size of and not unlike a large banana. This, the fruit of the plant, is protected by leaf like spines.

It is pulpy in texture, and is removed using a knife. It is not unlike a banana and although it can be eaten, we were recommended not to do so eaten, as it sometimes has disagreeable after effects. I don't believe that we were shown all the processes which produces the cream, save when it came to the end products! Here we were given the "works," and shown finished products galore, packaged in many alluring ways in neat little baskets. But, there were no free meals or samples! However I made a few

Aruba: This farm is the home of the Aloe Vera plant. Origin: Author 2005

purchases – seeing I "was there." Afterwards I had a tour of the island. It is largely of a desert nature, with little scenery to compare with what we are used with in our islands although the fine weather is typically Caribbean. A former Dutch colony, at one time the island prospered when Columbian oil was available for refining, but such stocks have now run out. However, what they still have in Aruba they flog it to death!

149

Every large rock to be clambered up, yes the tourists flock there like a moth to a light. Or their one weather beaten bush with a simply unpronounceable name will be paraded and proclaimed as a must on a tourist's itinerary - specially for anyone interested in botany . And this all along with creations of nature like the "natural arch" – well, the choice can be yours ! All are there for one to be photographed against.

When people travel long distances and then arrive at their destination, they want to see what's there to see. So they sign up to what is available on the local tourist menu and - pile into the buses. I did likewise, and literally "went out to see a reed shaken by the wind." Nonetheless, I admire the tenacity with which the people in Aruba flaunt what little natural resources they have. The buses always seemed to be full! Oh! the weather is beautiful.

*   *   *   *

Atlantic 6 surfacing.

The submarine Atlantis 6 was operating several miles off Aruba, and while sitting in a waiting room, awaiting the boat that would take me out to it, I had an opportunity to observe who my fellow "submariners" were going to be. Glancing around, I was somewhat amazed to find that in age, gender, shape and size, they would have been typical of those that one would meet in any High Street. Beside me was a young lady – in her early twenties. Beside her was a man and woman, the latter of such generous proportions, that the crew were to have trouble later getting her eased down through the submarine's hatch! But she was made of stern stuff and did not let a few extra inches mar the day!

Upon reaching the submarine's operating area, we arrived just as Atlantis 6 emerged from the depths and the returning passengers reassuringly appeared pleased with the trip. When we went below and took our seats, our observation port holes were already under water.The waters were calm, and we did not experience much of a transition upon diving except that there were quite a lot of sounds.These appeared to have to do with the blowing of tanks, and the whirring of electric motors controlling speed and depth, etc. Soon we were seeing coral and tropical fish in abundance.

Eventually, first one wreck of a ship appeared – then another, and such was the condition of both, that I was only able to identify the bows section and the forward windlass of one of them. One lasting impression remains – and that is the extent to which a ship disintegrates in contact with the sea bed with the masts making the first contributions to the debris trail.

Although the capacity available in Atlantis 6 was double that actually on board, we were asked to sit on one side, and listen to a commentary there relating to what was seen on that side. This perhaps made it easier for the commentator! These commercial submarines are remarkable vessels, and are now widely used in the tourist industry, although no doubt they would have been originally designed for industrial usuages and later adapted for tourism purposes. Such applications like digging trenches for pipe line laying or survey, telephone cable laying etc. or indeed searching for missing objects like that atom bomb once lost off the coast of Spain - spring to mind. With such large port holes, there is thus a limiting factor in the depth one is permitted to safely descend in them, but we were down at one stage to150 feet. But nonetheless, what one can see "down below " even at modest depths, is truly astonishing and exciting. Accessibility through modern technology, has, in the last decade, made possible for Mr. Everyman things that only a short while before, were dreams for him. Oh ! The "mystery" aircraft did not show up.

The photographs tell the story. I discovered that the crew came from Indonesia, and the Captain told me - if I understood him correctly, that he had served in military submarines there.

150

Left: The under water camcording film made in Atlantis 6 turned out quite good. But using a camera inside the sub. (without a flash as recommended), was a failure. Above: The only exception was the one above – the only photo to come out. Does one see a skull?

Origin: Author 2006.

Aruba: " What went ye out for to see? " Well, this is where the bus took me – to see the Natural Arch! Seen between author and the man in the white hat. Yes, its that piece of coral with the sea rushing in beneath! Origin: A kind fellow traveller

"I'm here now and I'll have to go through with it!" About to dive in Atlantis 6 as the skipper looks on from his cockpit in the bows, which was sealed off from the main cabin during the dive. Origin: The same kind fellow traveller! See Third Coloured selection – forward.

The World War Two German U-Boat, U-534, type 9C 40, sunk by the RAF in May 1945 and raised after lying on the sea bed off Denmark for 50 years. Courtesy of John Lawton, C/man, Historic Ships Museum, Birkenhead.

Our jovial skipper gives us the "thumbs up," and we all hope he knows what he is doing. *He looks a happy man.* Source: Same nice person!

151

I thought of my old friend, George Plowman DSM, whom we have met already – he was the leading signalman of the British submarine, the E11 at the Dardanelles in the First World War. It would have been nice to have been able to tell him of the dive. The E11's recommended diving depth was a little over one hundred feet in 1915, although this was often exceeded!

(See Chapter 7 for George Plowman DSM and the British submarine, E 11.)

It was recorded in 1915, that Commander Bruce in the E12 dropped to 250 feet after being entangled in a net at the Dardanelles in 1915.

The sea is not man's natural environment – it is still possible to descend there – and stay!

Presentably the "Atlantis 6" regained the surface, and we each were presented with a certificate to testify as to our daring do! I was now bound for San Francisco and my route was via the Panama Canal! This would be my first complete transit of the Panama Canal, but a common experience nowadays for many.

Before leaving this tale of the Atlantis 6, some might wish to know what emergency procedures might have been invoked in the event of some mishap occurring while under water.

On Atlantis 6, amidst the blowing of tanks and the whirring of electric motors etc. we were given substantial instructions as to emergency procedures but I had just hoped that they would not be necessary to put into practice. There were many many things to be remembered!

So, farewell to the deep.

Left: My friend Bruce Johnson - and a step back in time: A replica of the "Hunley" – named after its designer, which was an American mid nineteenth century pedal powered submersible. It was finally lost with its designer - along with its third crew. It was recently discovered with remains of that crew intact – still at the pedals.   Courtesy: Bruce Johnson, San Francisco, USA.

Above: Some of my fellow travellers of the deep.

Left: The Atlantis 6 passengers waiting for their"Dive" certificates.   Origin: Author

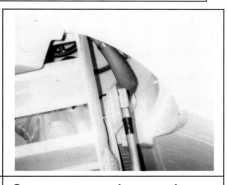

Some crew member opening the hatch – note the wheel and part of a spoke.
Origin: Author 2005

Some Memories of British Aviation

1

The Shorts SA4 "Sperrin," with one Avon top, and one Gyron lower, in the port engines. See next page.

2

The Short SC1 on a tethered vertical lift off. See next page. Queen's Island, Belfast.

3

Anti Submarine, attack: Short "Seamew" production line. A "Britannia," top right.

4

First vertical lift off for the British Aerospace P1127 later the" Harrier." See next page.

6

Production line at Short's of the De Havilland "Comet" Mark 1. This was the leading fuselage. See over.

The Short "Sunderland."

5

Sunderland EJ164 lost S. Atlantic on 3.10. 1944 See next page. At rear: A Short Stirling.

7

The PR9 Canberra production line at Shorts. See next page.

Courtesy: Messrs Short Bros. and Harland Ltd, Belfast.
Courtesy: British Aerospace, Dunsfold , Surrey.

8

Above: The Short "Sealand," a small ten seat amphibian of the early 1950's.

9 The Belfast – a heavy lift freighter

1 The SA4 Short "Sperrin" was a research aircraft, two being built. But had the more advanced technology of the V bombers failed, the "Sperrin" was capable of delivering an atomic bomb. When an apprentice, , the author worked on the SA4 during the engine convertion at Shorts, Aldergrove, on one of the aircraft. See photo.This retained two Avon engines top, and two De Havilland Gyrons bottom. The aircraft in photo is flying with conversion at this stage on the port side only. Courtesy in 2001 of Short Bros. and Harland, Belfast.

3 The Short "Seamew" was envisaged as an anti submarine carrier based aircraft. It was a turbo jet with contra rotating propellers although the one in the photo overleaf has a single propeller.Only 16 were built and in a fatal accident at a Sydenham Air Display, a test pilot lost his life. See third coloured selection.

The Short "Sunderland" was a maritime reconnaissance flying boat, the early versions of which had four Bristol "Pegasus" radial pushrod operated air cooled engines, supercharged and producing 950 HP. Its armament included machine guns (0.303 to 0.5 calibre bullets), Hispano 20 mm cannon and bombs or depth charges – the latter indispensible in the Second World War operations against the German U-boats. Later versions were fitted with AmericanTwin (double banked) Wasp Engines.
Courtesy of Short Bros. & Harland Ltd., 2001

5 The PR9 Canberra was essentially a photo reconnaissance aircraft and was built after the original contract for 140 Canberras was completed, considerable re tooling being required. Author worked on some of the tooling required – one, a large structure, inside of which the new fuselage would be put together. It was called a "jig."Some PR9's survived to take part in the present Afghan conflict – over fifty years along the road!

7 The Short "Sealand," was a small ten seat amphibian-from 1948. Powered by twin Gipsy Queen engines, 25 were produced. Courtesy of Short Bros. & Harland Ltd. 2001

2 The world's first vertical take off and land aircraft – the Shorts SC1. It made its maiden conventional flight on 2. 04 '57 and first vertical to forward flight on 6. 04. 1960. Courtesy of Short Bros. and Harland Belfast 2001

This is the Hawker P1127 on its first vertical lift off. Its tether is somewhere in line with the rear wheels. The cable at the rear is a telephone cable to the pilot, who was Bill Bedford on this history breaking "flight." Developed into the "Kestrel," and then finally the "Harrier." At Dunsfold Aerodrome. Courtesy of BAe Systems, Dunsfold, Surrey. **4**

The De Havilland Comet

The photo overleaf shows the leading Comet 1, Mark 1 of the production line in Shorts on which the author worked as an apprentice (and which he described as his happiest days in Shorts) : Courtesy of Short Bros, Belfast, 2001.

Note: The "Comet," was the first all jet and pressurised passenger aircraft in the World. Designed, and first produced by De Havillands, it was sub contracted out to Shorts in Belfast.
Work was suspended on the Comets following two catastrophic fuselage failures in flight – to G-Alyp and G-ALYY within three months of each other. In the author's book "Before that Generation Passes," a chapter contains an indepth technical examination of this failure - and gives prominence to the interesting findings of the accident report by the **6** Ministry of Transport and Civil Aviation. Courtesy of Short Bros. & Harland Ltd. 2001

The "Belfast" was a heavy lift aircraft built for the RAF. It was based around the wings of the "Britannia," a passenger airliner designed by the Bristol Aero Company. The Britannia itself had a fair capacity for freight, the author having spent some time on its freight door (panel 22512) – it would allow entry of a jeep! Courtesy of Short Bros. & Harland Ltd. 2001 **9**

Above: The water wheel at Moylinney, Muckamore, (the one seen behind the sluice gate in right.)This outstanding example of Victorian Industrial composite construction - wood with iron, is being allowed to lapse into the earth. Recently, in – 2016, a German visitor stood there. His comment: " 1886 or there about. But why is it not being refurbished?" Sadly since this photograph was taken, the wheel, now in 2017, has suffered advanced deterioration, and the very special repair on sluice gate lost to view.   Origin: Author 2003.

Left: Part of Antrim and District's wonderful industrial archaeology - a gear tooth repair. But all of is being left to nature's way of disposal (– leave it there and it will likely go away!) But some people would like it to stay - maybe in a public museum!
                Author, 2003.

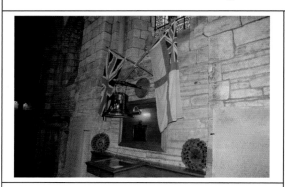

The bell of HMS "Royal Oak," torpedoed at her moorings on the evening of Sept.,14th. 1939 in the secure anchorage of Scapo Flow, in the Orkneys. Sunk by the U-47, Cmdr. Günther Prien, over 800 of her crew perished.
Photo: Courtesy of Richard Doherty, author of "In the Ranks of Death."

A 6 foot dia. V- pulley wheel -- another superb icon at Moylinney Mill and how the problem of the then brittle cast iron spokes was solved !
                Origin: Author 2003

Below: The British and Commonwealth cemetery on the desert sands of El Alamein, Egypt.
                Origin: Author 2007.

The British Aerospace Hawk. Courtesy of British Aerospace, Dunsfold, Surrey.

The rear propeller driven Lear Fan Jet. The Company once set up business in Belfast to tool up and make its components.
Courtesy Lear Fan Company.

The Blue Mosque, Istanbul, situated on the Bosporus, with six minerets, it ranks third in the Moslem faith.In 1915, Cmdr. Nasmith (E 11) took its photo at periscope depth – a first in under water photography.
Origin: Author: 1974.

The two blade propeller of the "Fox."It was driven by a 16 HP steam engine, but with limited coal bunkers! But what an engineering heirloom? Origin: Author, Aberdeen Marine Museum.
Author 2012

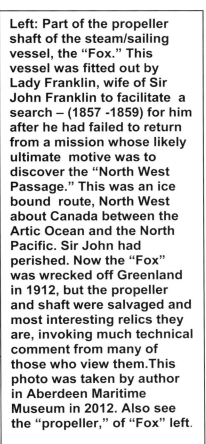

Left: Part of the propeller shaft of the steam/sailing vessel, the "Fox." This vessel was fitted out by Lady Franklin, wife of Sir John Franklin to facilitate a search – (1857 -1859) for him after he had failed to return from a mission whose likely ultimate motive was to discover the "North West Passage." This was an ice bound route, North West about Canada between the Artic Ocean and the North Pacific. Sir John had perished. Now the "Fox" was wrecked off Greenland in 1912, but the propeller and shaft were salvaged and most interesting relics they are, invoking much technical comment from many of those who view them.This photo was taken by author in Aberdeen Maritime Museum in 2012. Also see the "propeller," of "Fox" left.

Author at the twin Mirroflores Locks, Panama Canal.   Origin: 2006

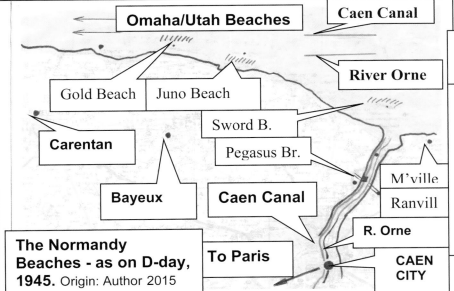

Omaha/Utah Beaches

Caen Canal

River Orne

Gold Beach   Juno Beach

Carentan

Sword B.

Pegasus Br.

Bayeux   **Caen Canal**

M'ville

Ranvill

R. Orne

The Normandy Beaches - as on D-day, 1945. Origin: Author 2015   **To Paris**   CAEN CITY

A potter at work,on a Greek Island,1974.   Origin: Author

156

Anti pirate water cannon

The MV "Voyager" (A "Voyages of Discovery ") vessel had quite a lot of anti pirate security on board, especially when transiting the Arabian Sea and Indian Ocean areas. Razor wire was much in evidence. Also see the water cannon, top right.

Origin: Author 2013

Below: At Belfast the "Nomadic,"the one time tender to the "Titanic."
Origin: Author 2013

A lady of Djibouti: The population of Djibouti (formerly French Somali) is of 27% French and the remainder of two indigenous tribes, one of Arab ancestry and the other of African origins.
Djiboutie is a prosperous Country.
Origin: Author 2013

Author with an 80 ton Moai on Easter Island.
Origin: A passer by. 2007

Round Tower, Antrim, Co. Antrim, N. Ireland. Standing 28 metres tall it was likely a monastery bell tower. Orig. Author.

Post W W Two anti submarine Short "Seamews" fly over Belfast.
Courtesy of Messrs. Short Bros. and Harland, 2001

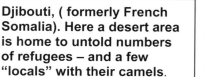

Djibouti, (formerly French Somalia). Here a desert area is home to untold numbers of refugees – and a few "locals" with their camels.
Author 2013.

Right: Typical Egyptian art work. Their pictorials seem to use a mixture of isometric and orthographic projection.
Original: From Cairo – here copied.

Typical Egyptian Art.

157

The island of Aruba is not overwhelmed with many of the earth's wonders of Nature – but one they have is their Natural Bridge (seen between author and the white hatted man), an overhang of coral with the seas rushing through beneath. See this and have a life! Origin: A kind passerby.

The San Blas Islanders – off Panama, dance for their visitors. The music appeared to come mostly from "reed mouth organs," typically of Peruvian culture, with the lead player left.
Origin: Author 1999

Aruba in the Carribean – home of the Aloe Vera plant from which comes the well known brands of lotions for ones skin. Origion: Author 2006

Before the submarine dive – " I'm here now and I'll have to go through with it!" The Skipper is watching – he has seen it all before. Origin: Another kind passerby.

A pleasure cruise in a dug out canoe with an outboard motor, no life jackets in shark infested waters, and with our San Blas skipper in a red and black uniform. Author holding camera, with arm raised. As on front cover of book. Origin: A Thomson ship's photographer.

It is amazing that the San Blas Islands exist at all, as they seem to lie virtually at sea level - or a few feet above it . (Maybe we arrived at a high tide!) Origin: Author 1999.

Above: Typical Chilean sculpture seen in a Santiago Square, but the author at the bottom is completely real! Origin: Passer by, 2007.

Above: An interesting photograph of a large cruise liner, possiblity " Jewel of the Seas" awaiting to descend the single lock at Pedro Miguel, Panama Canal. Photograph taken from the "Regal Princess."
Origin: Author 2006

Author with daughter Moyna on this special occasion!
Origin: Mrs. Audrey McClean 1984.

A Light Ship, identity unknown but similar to that which at one time was positioned on the approaches to Liverpool – also identified as a Pilot Station for ships heading for the River Mersey, Liverpool and the Manchester Ship canal. Origin unknown.

Author with Sir Philip Foreman, Chairman and Manageing Director , Messrs Short Bros., PLC: " I don't know, Sir Philip, what it is like at the top – but its rough near the bottom!" Origin: Mrs.Audrey McClean 1984

The Leaning Tower of Pisa, Italy: It was originally built as the Bell Tower of the Cathedral, Piazza dei Miracoli.
Origin: Author 1993

HMS "Caroline" built in 1915, veteran of Jutland in 1916 and its the last surviving British warship to have had an active role in the battle.
Now recently refurbished, the "Caroline" resides in the Titanic Quarter, Belfast.
Origin: Author 2007

The Temple of Philae: Now raised from the River Nile to a higher level.
Origin: Author

A Breadfruit tree on the island of Raiatea, South Pacific. Unfortunately, this one was not in a ripened state!
Origin: Author

Shades of Agatha Christie : The passage through the Columns, Karnac, Egypt. Origin: Author

Above: Ardnaveigh House, Antrim, accidentally destroyed by fire, in WW 2. Courtesy: Mrs. Jane Edwards, Antrim.

Author with John Kerr at his 99th. birthday party.

Author reading a newspaper in the Dead Sea, Israel. Photo taken in Israel in 1977.

From left: Mark, Jean and Owen in Jerusalem.
Origin: Author'76

The "Seven Pillars" in Wadi Rum, Jordan.
Orig: Author.

Head Line Reunion, 2004. From Left: Andy Shaw, author's former Chief Engineer; John Hanna, Master Mariner; Robert Aiken, Master Mariner; Author.

St. Paul's Armenian Church, Damascus, Syria – on the "Street called Straight."Author.

Author at the caves at Kumran where the Dead Sea Scrolls were found.
Photo taken in Israel in 1977

The MV "Velarde," MacAndrews and Co., twin 4 stroke MAN diesels, 18 knots with exhaust turbo and hydro flex couplings to a single shaft. This was the first of the MacAndrews vessels on which the author was a relief engineer during some school vacations - trading to Spain.
See Chapter 10 –"Different methods of travel etc."

The MV "Villegas," MacAndrews, twin MWM ex U-Boat 4 stroke trunk diesels, unblown with fluid couplings and single reduction gearing to a single shaft. (As during holiday relief duties). See Ch 10.

Author on the manoeuvring platform of the "Velarde." The heavy red spoked wheels are the controls for Starting Air, Ahead and Astern movements, with the Engine Room telegraph above.

Author on the manoeuvring platform of the MV Villegas." The "L" shaped handles seen in front of the telegraph are the air starts, one per port and starb'd engines and Telegraph above.

Mr. Masson, Chief Engineer of the "Velarde," left, with Larry, the Third Engineer.   Origin: Author.

Left: The late Tom Birch, Chief Engineer of the MV "Villegas."
He was the nicest man I ever had the priviledge of working for – a Cockney, and a caring man - who liked his wee pint! See next page!

My dream comes true at last! My audition to become a member of a Jamaican Steel Band! (At least - I think that was said). The guy beside me is beginning to wonder where I came from. He maybe thinks I am a white ghost!   Origin: A kind passerby.

Now well into my audition, and his mate, the second guy across has downed tools and is straining his ears – was that a false note he heard? (What did those guys really think ?
Origin: The same passerby!

At the Langton Lock, Liverpool: In the foreground is the British diesel electric submarine HMS/m "Grampus," and in the background is the MacAndrew fruit carrier, the MV "Villegas." A failure on the astern cams of the "Villegas" almost caused the "Villegas" to ram the "Grampus" inside the Langton Lock. See Chapter 10.The man in the white cap is likely to be the Lockmaster. Origin: Courtesy of the "Liverpool Echo." (Author on a working holiday during Summer vcacation(Lisburn Technical) – as relief engineer on the MV " Villegas," MacAndrews, Liverpool.)

Just up giving the boys on the Bridge of the MV "Velarde" a wee hand !
Some kind fellow crew member.

Right: The camel drivers await the tourists at the Great Pyramids of Giza. There is an Egyptian security presense at the Pyramids to combat the terrorist threat (and at times the camel drivers themselves) persistant at times to sell their wares!   Orig: J. Marshall, London.

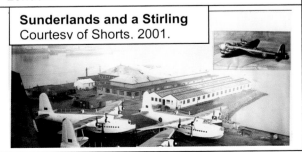

Sunderlands and a Stirling
Courtesv of Shorts. 2001.

A Short amphibious " Sealand,"one of twenty seven produced in early nineteen fifties.

Chapter 14

Polynesia :
The Chilean Islands of Juan Fernandos Island (now Robinson Crusoe Island) and Easter Island.

The Pacific Ocean was discovered and so named – *Mare Pacificum* from the Latin, by the Portuguese explorer Ferdinand Magellan. It is the world's largest body of water accounting for about one third of the Earth's surface, having an area of about 70 million square miles. It extends from the Bering Sea in the north to Antarctica in the south (almost 10,000 miles). Its greatest width is just north of the Equator – from Indonesia to Central America, a distance of just over 12,000 miles. The greatest depth of the world's oceans has been recorded there - the Mariana Deep, which is approximately 36,000 feet deep.

Below: Author beside a Sculpture in a Santiago Square. Origin: A passer by.

Also to be found in the Pacific Ocean are 25,000 islands, most in the southern hemisphere, and a great number composing the area being presently examined – Polynesia. In fact, there are more islands in the Pacific than in the total of the rest of the world's oceans combined.

Although Magellan found on this voyage that the Pacific Ocean was calm, and peaceful, it is not always so. The lands around the "Pacific Rim," as are indeed many of the islands about to be mentioned, are full of volcanoes, and subject to typhoons and hurricanes that attack all that stands in their way. Earthquakes often shake these lands, and tsunamis which are caused by underwater earthquakes, cause immense destruction, destroying all in front of them.

Polynesia – where is Polynesia?

Polynesia has often been defined as the area inscribed by a triangle whose South Western apex is New Zealand (about 40° south of the Equator), its Northern apex the island of Hawaii (about 20° north of the Equator), and the Eastern apex, Easter Island, (about 27° south of the Equator) - see the maps and sketches on the following pages. Referring to the islands presently described, it is true that most are small in area – as low as 2 to 6 square miles, with

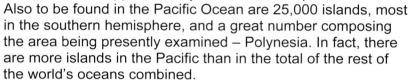

Above the Andes in Chile. Origin:Author 2007.

Easter Island about 63 square miles. However, they and the events associated with them have found an elevation in historical matters out of all proportion to their physical size.

Those islands visited were Juan Fernandez (Robinson Crusoe) Island,and Easter Island - both belonging to Chile; Pitcairn Island, British but administered by New Zealand ; Raiatea, Boro Boro, and Tahiti, these latter four belonging to the Society Islands group, and are nominally French possessions.

After arriving in Santiago, the capital of Chile, and travelling to the Chilean port of Valparaiso, passage was made to these islands by travelling on the "Voyages of Discovery" vessel, the M.V. "Discovery." As already mentioned,

Chile possesses the first two of these remote land masses, Juan Fernandez and Easter Island. Both are classified as National Parks, but not easy to access.

However, those who do make the journey, are richly rewarded with firstly, one of the world's most precarious ecosystems, namely, at Juan Fernandez Island, and secondly, a collection of the most amazing and enigmatic statues which are to be seen on Easter Island (Rape Nui in the native tongue).
Juan Fernandez (now officially known in Chile as Robinson Crusoe Island), is about 450 statute miles west of mainland Chile and was discovered by the Spanish Mariner, Juan Fernandez in 1574. (A statute mile is 5,280 feet in length and a nautical mile is 6,080 feet in length.)
Juan Fernandez is part of the Juan Fernandez Archipelago – three in number. All rise dramatically out of the ocean to soar almost vertically to peaks covered with the dark green foliage of pine forests whose very large pine cones cover the forest floor. This spectacular scenery is embellished with history, adventure and romance, and of course associated forever with the adventures of the marooned Scottish sailor, Alex Selkirk, who spent four years on the island between 1784 and 1788. Selkirk, it is said, was put ashore (at his own request, perhaps), after a dispute with the captain of the privateer "Cinque Ports" in 1784.
He survived by eating the flesh of the goats that then roamed the island. Pirates and freebooters at one time used the islands as hideaways and places of rest.
The island of Juan Fernandez is now served with good docking facilities for small supply ships.

To the "lookout of Selkirk,"- anothers forty minutes hard hill walking ahead!   Orig: Author.

By using the ship's tender, I was able to set foot on Robinson Crusoe Island, the home of Alexander Selkirk from 1784 until 1788, and I set off as soon as possible to try and reach Cumberland Point. Selkirk would often climb to a lookout (see photo below) above Cumberland Bay (Bahía Cumberland) in the hope of spotting a vessel. It was not until 1788 did his rescuer, Commander Woodes Rogers of the British privateers "Duke" and "Duchess"find him. Commander Roger's pilot was the famed navigator, William Dampier. Commander Rogers was reported as

saying that when the ship's pinnace (boat) returned to the ship " – it was with a man clothed in goats' skins who looked wilder than the first owners of them." Selkirk returned to Britain as a crew member with his rescuers – to become a celebrity in Scotland, and the real life model for **Daniel Defoe's** fictional character, **"Robinson Crusoe." Defoe**, strangely, sited his hero as being marooned on an island in the Caribbean.

Right: Author on the path to 'Cumberland Hill' Juan Fernandos Island, South Pacific. Origin: A fellow traveller 2007.

Chile established a permanent settlement on **Robinson Crusoe Island** in 1877.
In World War One, the island played a historic role when a naval battle between the German cruiser "Dresden" and the British cruisers H.M.S. "Glasgow" and H.M.S. "Orama" at Bahía Cumberland, resulted in the "Dresden" being scuttled. There is a German War Memorial in the local cemetery at San Juan Bautista.

See photo three page on.

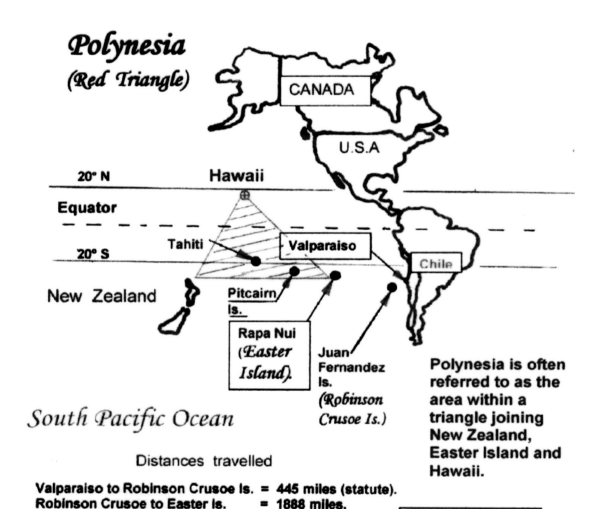

Polynesia
(Red Triangle)

CANADA

U.S.A

20° N   Hawaii

Equator

20° S   Tahiti   Valparaiso

Chile

New Zealand   Pitcairn Is.

Rapa Nui *(Easter Island)*

Juan Fernandez Is. *(Robinson Crusoe Is.)*

South Pacific Ocean

Polynesia is often referred to as the area within a triangle joining New Zealand, Easter Island and Hawaii.

Distances travelled

Valparaiso to Robinson Crusoe Is. = 445 miles (statute).
Robinson Crusoe to Easter Is.   = 1888 miles.
Easter Is. To Pitcairn Is.   = 1333 miles.
Pitcairn to Tahiti   = 1642 miles.

Origin : Author, 2007

Above: A large group of Maoi on Easter Island. Courtesy of "Voyages of Discovery."

Easter Island (Rapa Nui). It lies 2,330 miles
west from mainland Chile.

Origin: Author,

Moai Symbol: Principal sites are shown inland and also those facing seaward and mounted on foreshore.

N

Max. length at longest stretch 23km. (about 14 miles). **Sketches to different scales).**

Moai Sites

Rano Raraku, the main quarry for basaltic tuf.

Hanga Roa, below left, the main settlement on the island, and close to the airport.

Iko's ditch

Rano Kau Volcano, south of the airport.

Airport

The "Birdman Cult" competition - held each year at Easter Island to help solve the problem of community strife – as below.

Motu Nui Islet

Motu Nui Islet left, two and a half km. from Easter Island, and to which each clan representative every year paddled on a reed raft to await the arrival of the sooty tern sea birds. The first to return with a sooty tern's egg, ensured a one year's dominance for his clan over the resources of Easter Island.

Robinson Crusoe Island (Juan Ferndandos Island)

Origin: Author, 2007.

Bahía Cumberland
(Cumberland Bay)

San Juan Bautista

Selkirk had a lookout point high above Cumberland Bay where he often scanned the horizon for a ship.

Measures 22km. by 7.3 km. (**Sketches to different scales**). (about 14 miles by 5). It lies 450 miles west from mainland Chile

Origin: Author 2007

Easter Island.

Easter Island (or Rapa Nui in the native tongue), lies about 27° south of the Equator, and is located 2,237 statute miles west of mainland Chile. (This is about the distance between Spain and Newfoundland). Being 1,290 statute miles east of Pitcairn Island, it is considered the most isolated inhabited island in the world. It has an area of about 63 square miles (163.6Sq. Km.) and nowadays a population of 3,791 (2,002 census). It is triangular in shape and of that population, 3,304 live in Hanga Roa, the islands single settlement, with a small airport close by.
 Some published observations on the early settlers of Easter Island suggest that they arrived around 300- 400 A.D. and that some of the early work on the Moai dates from 800 A.D. Today, Easter Island has good, modern, telephone and postal services.

Chilean Guard
Author 2007

Author meets a Llama on the road to Valparaiso.
The Llama is on the right! Origin: Some fellow traveller, 2007.

   The Island was discovered by the Dutch naval commander Jacob Roggeveen on Easter Sunday 1722. He and his crew would appear to have been the first Europeans to land on the island and see some of the Moai, the tall stone statues – all with the same severe, enigmatic and frowning faces standing upright * in locations across the island.
The Moai have characterised the island ever since, and fascinated all who have gazed and speculated upon them likewise. The Dutch were astonished that such enterprises could have been undertaken by people - apparently devoid of the material supports supposedly necessary for the construction, transport and indeed erection of these stone monolithic figures.

Left: The Memorial at San Juan Bautista cemetery, Robinson Crusoe Island, to the German naval personnel lost in the naval engagement in1914 between the German cruiser "Dresden" and the British cruisers H.M.S, "Glasgow and H.M.S. "Orama" off Robinson Crusoe Island, resulting in the "Dresden" being scuttled. Photograph: Courtesy of Mrs. Mary Nicholson, England, March 2007.

Author photographed with one of the large Moai now upraised and installed on its platform on the sea front at Hanga Roa, the main settlement. Weighing perhaps 80 tons with a red "top knot" of another 8 tons and 30 feet tall, this Moai is unique in that it has eyes – most Moai have just sunken sockets and little of the original eyes as fitted, have ever been recovered .This one is also unique, in that it faces inwards!

Origin: An English tourist, 2007.

Some of these weigh 80 tons and stand the upwards of 30 feet tall! Forty eight years later, the island had another European visitor, the Spaniard Felipe González (who claimed the island for Spain), and four years later Captain Cook arrived.

Easter Island right, Motu Nui extreme left. Here Clan reps. wait for the sooty tern to lay their eggs in the days of the "Birdman Cult."

Orig: Author 2007.

Cook too viewed with incredulity the massive statues – although he noted that many were toppled. Later, in 1868, the English Dr. Linton Palmer [*]reported that not one statue remained standing on the island.

Easter Island is therefore famous for its amazing statues – the Moai, and there about 900 such there although about half of these lie unfinished in the great quarry at Rano Raraku. What could have caused the work to stop apparently so abruptly?

It may have been due to the devastating raids made on the islands by whalers and slavers – who carried off numerous islanders to work as slave labour. It is recorded that between 1862 and 1864, Peruvian sailors took about 2,500 men, women and children to work as slaves in the guano mines and plantations in Peru. Many died of disease there, and even when the islanders were repatriated (after intervention by the Bishop of Tahiti to the Peruvian Government), many died during the voyage home, and those who did return, infected the remaining islanders with diseases such as smallpox, tuberculosis etc. to which they had little resistance. It was a disastrous time for Easter Island.

Other explanations point to divisions between various clan factions. The toppling of the Moai may have had something to do with the possibility that the Moai represented the ancestral interests of each clan. The toppling of an adversary's Moai could have been a way of adding insult to injury. For maximum damage to a statue, it appears that efforts were made to place a large stone at the place where the head of a statue would hit the ground when toppled – thus inflicting damage when contact with the stone took place. Sometimes the head would be broken off completely, and during the visit now being described, severe damage was observed on the faces of certain Moai now upraised in standing mode.

Birdman Cult. It appears that the dangers resulting from strife among the clans as to who had control over the island's resources – including the best areas on land for cultivation and the best areas around the coasts for fishing was recognised – possibly as early as the 15th century. New ideas were thought up to allot resources, and in the Cult of the Birdman, a

competition was held each year to determine which clan would have control over these resources. A representative from each clan would clamber down a steep cliff on Easter Island and swim or paddle across to the small island of Motu Nui, a distance of about 2Km.

There he would await the arrival of the manutara – (the sooty tern sea bird), search for an egg laid by one of these, and make off for the main island again.

The first representative to arrive back with his trophy would secure for his clan control over the island's resources for one year.

This tradition was still being practised first Europeans arrived, i.e. the 18th century.

A small "modern" Moai borrows my blue/yellow bag and flask! Origin: Author 2007.

Carving, elevation and movement of the Moai.

It is indeed a mystery as to how these Moai were raised and transported to their platforms. One theory was that they were placed on wooden sledges and dragged there (which might help to explain how the island was de forested). Another suggestion was that rocking was used after the manner in which a modern washing machine is sometimes moved.

Returning now to our visit, on upon arrival off the little dock at Hanga Roa, the main settlement, the ship's tender put us ashore.

I proceded inland and visited some Moai around the local shoreline etc. but intended to have a full tour of the whole island the following day, the highlight of which would be a visit to the quarry at Rano Raraku, where hundreds of Moai lie in an unfinished state.

Easter Island might be said to have a sub tropical climate and one could see bananas growing quite happily in the open, some in cultivated areas but in other places they appeared to be unattended – possibly as part of a hedgerow. At one stage in my wandering, a rooster appeared to interest himself in my company and proceeded to escort me, his clarian call giving due and timely warning to all of my approach. As I further acquainted myself with this astonishing place, I came across a couple of workmen digging a hole at the side of the road into which they proposed to place a pole – likely for use in some telephone role or other.

I exchanged a few pleasantries with them – they had some English and told them where I came from etc . As I moved away from them, one of them called after me, "Ireland for the Cup!"

It just so happened that an international rugby tournament was taking place in either Australia or New Zealand, Ireland was playing in it, and these locals were up to speed with current sporting news in the Southern Hemisphere!

I took a number of photographs, and it is a good job that I did so then, because the weather deteriorated and a rapid recall to the ship was made as a heavy swell had developed. The actual entrance to the dock had been approached through a channel with some dangerous looking rocks in it, and indeed the actual withdrawal in the tender was made with some difficulty by the seaman crew.

Next morning, many were up early in anticipation of leaving the ship at eight o'clock for the full island tour, but it was not long before it was announced that departure of the tender was being delayed owing to the state of the weather, the captain feeling that the risk to life was

now with very much restricted accommodation wise due to the special requirements for storing 2,000 breadfruit shoots (or slips).

After leaving Tahiti on April 4th. 1789, Bligh sailed westward, and on the 28th. April 1789, was thirty nautical miles from the island of Tofua close toTonga. Here accounts reveal that the mutiny took place with Fletcher Christian and a number of the crew bursting into Bligh's cabin and restraining him.

In all, of the crew of forty two, eighteen men joined Christain, twenty two remained loyal to Bligh and two are listed as being "passive."

Bligh was cast adrift with eighteen men in the ship's launch (there not being enough room to safely embark any more. In the 23 foot open launch, Bligh navigated over what he calculated was 3,618 nautical miles – a voyage lasting an epic forty one days and making landfall at Timor.

The mutineers moved around the islands for about three months, but eventually they returned to Tahiti and put sixteen of the crew ashore while Christian, eight other crewmen, six Tahitian men and eleven women set sail to elude the Royal Navy (whom they knew might be in pursuit of them) and eventually landed on Pitcairn Island. When the island was found by the American sailing ship "Topaz" in 1808, only one mutineer, John Adams, nine women and some children were still alive.

The Americans were astonished to hear the children speaking in English – one of them had called out "Will you heave me a rope?" as they approached the "Topaz" in a small boat. Additionally, they were able to read and write having been taught as Sunday School children might be, in any part of the known world. This was due to the work of Adams (whose real name may have been Smith), and who in turn had been taught himself by fellow mutineer Ned Young using the only books available – the Bounty's Bible and the Book of Common Prayer. Services were therefore in accordance with the Church of England's book of Common Prayer. This bible is now on the island in the church which is now that of the Seventh Day Adventist denomination to which the islanders converted around 1890.

The mutineers and some not involved in the mutiny who had decided to live in Tahiti, were eventually rounded up by the Royal Navy. The ship bringing them back to England, H.M.S.

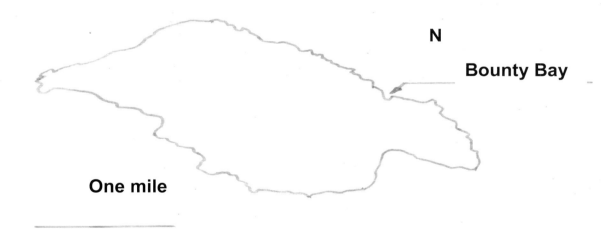

N

Bounty Bay

One mile

"Pandora" was lost on the Great Barrier Reef off Australia in 1791, four mutineers being drowned there – going down with the ship while still in irons. Eventually the remainder were brought back to England to be tried in September 1792 – three being eventually hanged. At Pitcairn, Alexander Smith, alias John Adams, was granted an amnesty in 1825, for his part in the mutiny, and Pitcairn's capital, Adamstown, is named after him.

We arrived off the island of Pitcairn in the early morning having been out on deck with many others for some time, waiting to catch a first glimpse of this place, so small, so isolated – yet with a history much embellished by numerous books, films and commentaries lavished upon it. This history seems entirely out of all proportion to the island's size, the number of people living there, and a landscape that to many, would appear wild and forbidden. Indeed it was the latter's uninviting characteristics that made it an ideal hideaway for the mutineers. It turned out a fortunate choice, because in spite of its apparent shortcomings, it had luxuriant evergreen forest slopes and soil that guaranteed a plenteous food supply all the year round. I would not be going ashore – no one would, because there are no docking facilities adequate for receiving a ship's tender which might carry perhaps fifty people, or, with other such vessels, perhaps one hundred people. Instead, the Pitcairn islanders would be coming out to us in their own launch which was accommodated in the little dock at Bounty Bay, and which dock also caters for the needs of their fishing business. Occasionally, one hears of visitors from cruise ships or other vessels being able, by using smaller launches to make it ashore - but only with the Islanders permission to do so. Anyone deemed hostile to the best interest of the Islanders would be refused permission to land.

Eventually, information came over the public address system that the islanders wishing to do business with us were on their way, and soon we saw a small speck among the waves that

> **Below: Pitcairn Islanders arrive by boat.**   Origin: Author

proved to be their launch. Upon reaching us they lay off a little to give us a chance for a photograph, and then they tied up alongside the gangway. After lunch they made their way to the Variety Show Lounge where they set about displaying the objects they had made and the Pitcairn honey for which they are famous. Another commodity of course was the rare Pitcairn postal stamps which are much sought after by those engaged in philately (stamp collecting), and indeed I suppose, by anyone who has had occasion to visit the Island. One of the first I had a chat with, was the Post Master, one Denis Christian. He had his franking machine with him, and those sending postcards presented Denis with their stamped cards, which he also franked in their presence. Some people were buying stamps only. Since Pitcairn is British (but administered by the British High Commissioner in New Zealand), postal arrangements are via New Zealand – and the good fortune of a passing ship going there! My cards posted there, reached Northern Ireland in six weeks. Another man I was speaking to was Jacques Leslie who described himself as a "Commissioner" – someone in authority.

Many of the wood carvings being sold represented things the islanders would be familiar with in their island home – walking sticks with penguin heads as handles, sharks or dolphins, tortoise (with one leg off the ground in walking mode), sea shell necklaces, Pitcairn T shirts and, lest one forgets – the grass skirts! The wood for carving is from the Mirav tree which grows on Henderson Island about miles away. On a yearly visit, the wood is cut int 6 ft. lengths – each about 12 ins. in diameter and brought to Pitcairn.

Just recently, a program appeared on U.K. television drawing awareness to a problem on Henderson Island. This concerned the tons of plastic waste that the ocean currents are depositing on the island's shores! So one can never get away from plastic waste!

Of the people who came aboard, the prominent names were Christian and Young - seventh generation descendants and certainly carrying names of the original mutineers.

Eventually, our new acquaintances packed their unsold items. Their spokesperson, Mayor Warren, later announced that they had had a "very good day," and attention now focused on the after deck where the islanders assembled as a choir.

They sang – part singing, three items. I was not surprised that one of them was "God be with you till we meet again." All three hymns were in a similar vein, the second one being "In the Sweet By and By."

I think for most of us it was a moving experience, with Pitcairn Island a backdrop to the scene on board. Here we were in such an isolated setting - being entertained by people with Polynesian features but singing in strains familiar to most of us. In fact, a feature of all "Voyages of Discovery" cruises has always been the well attended devine services that are held on Sunday afternoons. Just now, there was much use of cameras, and requests for autographs – is it not amazing that people living simple lives in such isolation can become the celebrities of the hour? One of those who came in for such attention was the island policeman – Warren Christian,

Pirate Paul Warren
7th. Gen. Mutineer
2007.

a truly giant of a man who, with a somewhat piratical style of clothing, rejoiced in the name of Pirate Warren Christian! Note his signature on the left , above.
I had got the impression that most of those I had met and spoken with, had been away from the Island at some time in their lives, working most likely, in New Zealand, and Tom Christian, who while on board had given a lecture on the history of Pitcairn, had spoken of having been in London. On one such occasion when there, he had asked the current holder for the return of certain artefacts which had earlier been removed from the island –but had not got them back yet.

The Island's economy.

As already referred to briefly, it will be a surprise to many, to know that one of the mainstays of the Pitcairn economy is its postal service. The primary link to the rest of the world is through the business of postage – letters, cards – see left, and parcels etc., and the sale of their famous stamps – especially to the world's stamp collectors. From 1830 until 1926 mail sent from Pitcairn was just marked "Posted in Pitcairn Island." New Zealand stamps were then used until 1940, after which Pitcairn stamps were issued, and this has continued since, with the stamps being delivered via the New Zealand Shipping Company as they are received from the crown agents in London.
As referred to,the stamps are mostly related to the island's people, the "Bounty," history, trees, birds, ships, or the things that live in the sea.
As is seen above, the stamps are colourful and of attractive design and indeed are much sought after in view of the island's remoteness.
There is a small Post Office on Pitcairn Island and a pigeon hole system is in operation for each family. Outgoing mail is given appropriate stamps and is then franked. It then awaits to be taken out by longboat and delivered to a waiting ship, but the service is subject to delays - especially due to the weather.
At one time everything arriving on the island had to be manhandled - usually by a wheelbarrow up the steep paths leading to Adamstown, or other places of residence. Nowadays, that burden is much lightened by using quads – similar to the ones farmers use here in European climes to tend their stock.

But the clock had moved forward and now, alas, it was nearly time for our visitors to return to their island home. After much waving, in the gathering evening dusk, we followed their progress - back to the little dock close to Bounty Bay,and their dark, island home and isolation.
There are no street lamps on Pitcairn.

Chapter 16

The South Pacific Islands of Raiatea, And Tahiti.

Raiatea.

One thousand, one hundred and seventy three miles later, lay the Society Islands, one of them being *Raiatea.* We passed Rangiroa Lagoon on the way.

We arrived at Raiatea early one morning, the ship being able to dock at the modern docks there. One thing was clear - that the infrastructure of a modern urban society was in place, with police station, power station, hospital, post office, and banks (the latter knowing how to charge for commission etc !) A conducted tour – virtually all around the island, revealed interesting features, history, culture and a glimpse of the islands botanical wonders. Our guide was an American, and a very interesting guy he proved to be. He told of how the early settlers on Raiatea had worshipped at a shrine constructed by themselves.Today, what remains of this consists of giant slabs of volcanic or even some of coral, dragged from the sea. These are in an upright position, and here was worshipped Oro, the god of war.

At the Botanical Gardens one could see the very rare Tiare Apetahi – the one sided flower (or half flower). It also grows naturally on Mount Temehani, having its three petals arranged around a semi-circle - see photograph.

There also was seen the No No fruit growing, a fruit that is said to possess health and healing powers and its juice is now sold commercially – even in Europe, as a health drink. However, its commercial name is now "Noni," which possibly sounds more agreeable if you are wanting to sell this product! Breadfruit was also growing close by, but was not ripe enough to eat.

 Just before the tour finished, an opportunity was afforded to sample some of these exotic fruits and juices at a reception centre. As noted, some of these fruits are, amazingly, finding their way into the supermarkets of Europe today. In the evening, it being the seventeenth of March and Patrick's Day, some energetic soul had arranged a little party to celebrate the occasion and the company was good !

Major General Sir Robert Corbett (whose family come from Co. Down in Northern Ireland) and his wife Lady Susan Corbett were there, adding to the rapport! Sir Robert was the last Military Governor of West Berlin before the unification of Germany.

The No No fruit (now the Noni fruit) – the juice of which now provides a health food, is widely available in Europe.
Origin: Author

Above: The Breadfruit Tree – but unfortunately we arrived before it was ripe enough to eat.   Origin: Author 2007.

Above: The rare Tiare Apetahi, the one sided flower with three petals around a semi circle that was seen at the island's Botanical Gardens (although it grows naturally on the slopes of nearby Mount Temehani). The only colour seen on this occasion was white.   Author 2007

Above: The Banyon tree – this one on Raiatea, but common on many of the South Pacific islands – and apparently in particular on Pitcairn. It is locally called the "Walking Tree," but takes a fair time to get anywhere!
Origin: Author 2007

Tahiti

Left:A Sunday morning welcome to Tahitia - a group of Tahitians are singing hymns to welcome the visitors. See next page.
Origin :Courtesy of a local well wisher.

With an area of just over four hundred sq. miles, the island of Tahiti was first visited by an Englishman when Capt. Wallis in H.M.S. "Dolphin" dropped anchor in Matavai Bay on the 24th. June, 1767.

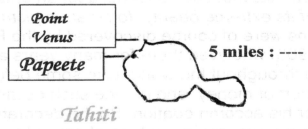

Tahiti is the largest island in French Polynesia, and typically, all kinds of fruits grow there, the breadfruit seasonally but others virtually all the year round. It was a cargo of breadfruit, of course, that was the indirect cause of the mutiny on the "Bounty."From the air Tahiti looks like a flat fish or a figure eight – with the lower half much smaller than the upper one. The main port was Papeete – our destination. Arrival was in early morning, and Papeete (pronounced Pah – pey – et – tey) and whose name in Tahitian means "water basket"), was already on the move. Tug boats were busy to and fro - after their manner, French warships were shifting berths, with cruise ships and container vessels and inter-island ferryboats all lying alongside the long piers of this modern port or on the move. Docksides had waiting containers, the latter having names well known in Europe, and one could not miss either, the streamlined yachts that were aplenty.

All this was against a backdrop of colonial buildings, modern shopping complexes, churches and the soaring volcanic mountains that might cause a passing cloud at any time to discharge its contents without warning.

Here and there, one could still see small conventional cargo ships of perhaps one thousand tons or less, suggesting that a need existed for shallow draught commercial vessels to do business around the many islands and lagoons, typical of this part of the South Pacific.

Strikingly when ashore, one found themselves in a modern city - one might say a French city, because the French built it. An interesting characteristic of local drivers was that if one was at a pedestrian cross, then upon seeing you the drivers slowed down when afar. If you showed hesitation to cross (as one is sometimes wise to do so in the U.K.), the drivers would then sound their horns and, with much waving of arms, invite one to cross.

There were also parking metres and traffic lights!

Tahiti is blessed with a luxuriantly beautiful landscape in every direction. Indeed it has been written that with such a landscape, an artist would *"only have to subtract some of its extreme beauty, to create a picture of tropical perfection."* These charms were of course discovered by the French artist Paul Gauguin (1891 – 1903) who lived there for many years and whose pictures

A local poses with Breadfruit
Origin: Author

today are found throughout the world. Like some before him, Gauguin was at times short of money, and on one such occasion had no money to pay the rent for his accommodation. So, he decorated three glass doors at the place where he was staying with paintings in lieu of rent!

When W. Somerset Maugham was staying there in 1916 - he was researching a book based on the life of Paul Gauguin ("The Moon and Sixpence"), he discovered the three decorated glass doors. He bought one of them which he kept in his French Riviera home until shortly before his death. Robert Louis Stevenson arrived there at the settlement of Tautira on the north coast of Tahiti in1885 where he wrote "The Master of Ballantrae."

Zane Gray, the American writer of cowboy books (sixty books in all), was in Tahiti from 1928 until 1930. He was a keen deep sea fisherman, and when there, caught a 1,000 pound Marlin, inside of which was a 200 pound shark!

Another famous person who was in Tahiti in 1914, was the aspiring English poet, Rupert Brooke. He fell in love with a beautiful Tahitian girl, Mamua, of whom he wrote his poem, "Tiani Tahiti." Brooke died of blood poisoning on a ship in the Mediterranean while serving in the First World War, and Mamua became a victim of a flu epidemic, in 1917.

Of course, Tahiti will always be associated with Captain William Bligh, master of H.M.A.S "Bounty" and the mutiny that took place on that ship. Bligh arrived in 1789, there to wait and collect breadfruit shoots, being there for several months in so doing.

It was quite amazing, after seeing the isolation of the South Pacific, to suddenly find this Papeete in Tahiti, this vibrant place of history, romance, culture - where, in one step as it were from isolation - why, a life like that possible in London, or Belfast or some French city, could indeed be lived here. This was because all the ingredients of which such places consist - were in place. It must have taken the French serious labour and expense to put it all together.

None of what I saw, of course, would have been there in 1789 when the "Bounty" first arrived, or a few years earlier when Captain Cook arrived to observe the transit of the planet Venus across the sun on June 3rd. 1769. He had the instruments to be used set up at the eastern most tip of Matavai Bay which hereafter was known as Point Venus.

I had booked on a tour to some of places of interest including Point Venus, and places connected with Gauguin, a tour to take place soon after arrival. But to my surprise, the tour was cancelled due to lack of interest - not surprising as we would have a busy time ahead - prior to departure later in the day.

The Faaa Airport at Papeete was at one time inadequate to receive incoming Trans – Pacific jets and in order to find enough flat ground for an airport expansion, part of a local lagoon and reef was filled in, and this was the location for our departure from Tahiti for the U.K.

Something special : The special warmth of Tahiti had not gone away. As we left our ship for the airport, we found ourselves passing a line of ladies – a kind of guard of honour, and each of us had a necklace of sea shells (some maybe of shark's teeth) placed around our necks. Responding to our astonished "Thank you(s)," they simply said, "It is our tradition."

*   *   *   *   *

Before us was the endurance test of landing at Los Angeles Airport at 4am, with hundreds of people – some in wheel chairs, all in an endless procession awaiting finger printing, eyes being photographed and our luggage being searched, some of those doing so assisted by a dog at times.

My dog indicated that he had smelled a rat (or so he thought) and informed his boss.

" Have you anything illegal in there?" the boss asked.

I said that I might have a ham sandwich, somewhere.

"Let's have a look anyway."

So the luggage was disassembled, and the boss – now joined by two assistants, myself and the dog – a spaniel, all tried their hand at tracking down an alien spirit.

We had no success, and the dog was – presumably, sent back to the drawing board and oh! An announcement:

"Would passengers travelling to London please be advised that your flight will be delayed by seven hours."

A reflection: *First note: Capt. James Cook was later murdered in Hawaii and eaten by the natives there - see reference in Chapter 2.*

When Captain James Cook returned from his attempt to observe and plot the transit of Venus to its intercept with that of the sun(unsuccessfully as it turned out), he wrote up his journals. But he was not alone in this.

There were many others willing to talk about such experiences and display the exhibits brought back from the South Seas. One group of course, included the "gentlemen" who had accompanied Cook.

But there were others – those of the ship's crew!

Included in the first group was Joseph Banks, a wealthy young man with a passionate interest in botany, Dr. Daniel Solander, another botanist, Alexander Buchan, an artist in portraits and landscapes(no throwaway cameras in those days), and others with connections with the Royal Society and the field of astronomy.

They, especially Banks, painted their experiences in lurid colours to willing listeners in the "jet set" classes of that period. Tahiti became the dominant discussion at societal functions in London and other places where the intellectual, the great and the good assembled.

However, in some other places, these things were also being downloaded to another type of willing listener, for the sailors also had their tales to tell. These tales were mostly told to the underprivileged and the slum dwellers, likely to be socialising where sailors of that era might be found. The sailors brought to the labourers of England their own accounts of the uninhibited lifestyle of the people of Tahiti, in a sunshine land of sufficiency. This encouraged discussion, and David Howarth put it well in his excellent book, **"Tahiti – A paradise lost."** Extract from Howarth below :

" One might say that Tahiti's Noble Savage was the first philosophical concept other than the teachings of the church to be eagerly discussed by labourers and the people of the slums."

This idyll was of a place devoid of poverty, lavished in sunshine, no class distinction and where all things were shared. No one owned anything outside the means of the provision of food and raiment – it was indeed a place that **those who had little of the world's goods** in England, might dream of escaping to.

One can see how such ideas – already propounded by Rousseau as early as 1750, fanned the wind of change desired by the poor and possibly culminated in the French revolution.

Both the French and the Spaniards had arrived in Tahiti as well as the English.

Thus, in the 18th. century, tales of the relaxed life style that existed on Tahiti became widely known. This style was apparently without any of the restraints on the behavioural traits of man or woman currently existing in European Society and it was hailed as enlightenment indeed.

The free thinkers of the romantic period in the nineteenth century – especially the French as represented by people like Rousseau, also hailed it as such. They held that there in the South Pacific, "the noble savage had broken the chains that binds us still here today, etc."

These tales caused much speculation on societal values.

The French artist Gauguin also had discovered that the "charms of Tahiti" and indeed those of other such islands, were very much to his liking. Yet over a century after Gauguin had "discovered" these charms, the "noble savage" is now likely to be wearing Levi Strauss jeans or a funny T- shirt – and maybe taking a Sunday School class on a Sunday morning!

Reputedly the rudder of the "Bounty." Painting shows Capt. Bligh asking for more provisions.
Photo taken in Suva Museum,Fiji by Dr. Chris Blair

An interesting E-Mail arrives in Antrim.

Sent :	15 August 2007 22 18
Attach :	Bouny's rudder in Suva Museum Fiji JPG
Subject:	Bounty's rudder pic

Bobby
Here's the snap I took in Suva Museum in Fiji in Sept 06.

Best regards
Chris.

The E-Mail which I received from Dr. Chris Blair in Australia shortly after I arrived home. I was very interested to receive this "snap" indeed ! Author 2017

Dr. Chris Blair, who comes from Antrim town ,was then involved in research at the Victor Chang Cardiac Research Institute in Darlington, Sydney, Australia.
The Rudder of the "Bounty": *To say I was pleased to receive his E-mail is a mild observation! A bonas is that the painting shows a level of technological advance in the use of composite structures ie the use of wood reinforced with wrought iron (presumably) clasps.*

Chapter 17

Canada : I revisit Montreal after 50 years
- and a thought for my lost Canadian cousins.

In 2010, a group of our family members travelled to Canada to visit our daughter, her husband and three grandchildren, where they then lived at Burlington, Ontario, which lies about a 45 minute drive from either Toronto in one direction, or in another, to Niagara Falls. Opportunity was taken to visit the Niagara Falls, and to some friends in the town of St. Catharines, as well as a

The "Maid of the Mist" boat approaching the U.S. Falls at Niagara.   Origin: Author 2010

visit to Niagara City, the latter being about a couple of miles distance from the "Falls." The "Falls" refers to the passage of the Niagara River as it tumbles about 170 feet (52 metres) over a precipice on the border between the USA and Canada, there in fact being two falls – the Canadian Falls and those of the U.S.A. and located about half a mile apart. This makes for one of the great spectacles in the world, and over time, a number of people have

ventured to plunge over into the abyss in such things as barrels etc. Some lost their lives in doing so, but others survived. This included the first person to do so, a woman in a wooden barrel - one Mrs. Annie Edison Taylor in Oct. 1901 on her 63rd birthday. See later photo of a " barrel," possibly used by William "Red" Bell, also one of the first to drop over the Falls - and survive. The "Maid of the Mists" incidentally, is a pleasure craft that plies its trade literally in the mists created by the Falls - see above.

The Niagara Falls are not the highest falls in the world – the Victoria Falls for example, on the Zambesi River and on the border between Zambia and Zimbabwe in Africa, is about 350 feet (108 metres) high. It is thought that there are about 500 waterfalls in the world deeper than

The ss "Rathlin Head."

the Niagara Falls, the deepest of all being the Angel Falls in Venezuela at just over 3,200 feet (980 metres) deep. However, by comparison with the Niagara Falls, most of these have only a small quantity of water flowing over them and few can match the Niagara Falls for actual volume of water flowing.

When in Canada, I felt that I had a nostalgic duty to perform - to visit the city and port of Montreal in Quebec province – my first visit there in over fifty years. I visited some former neighbours from Antrim who were now living in St. Catharines, not far from Niagara Falls, and it was from there I thus set off one morning on a seven hour journey of nostalgia by train for Montreal via Toronto.

Toronto also held a deep feeling of nostalgia for me because it was for Toronto that my Uncle John Cameron had set off from Kellswater railway halt near Ballymena in Co. Antrim in the early 1920's. My impression, when growing up, was that my father had but sporadic correspondence with him over the years but a firm contact with him took place in World war Two. It happened thus:

My cousin, Bert Cameron who was from Carnaughts, Ballymena (in the Kellswater area), had joined the RAF in World War Two and was selected for training as a navigator on the Mosquito De Havilland fighter bomber – the "wooden wonder" which contributed so much to the eventual defeat of the Nazi regime of Germany in that war.

Like hundreds – possibly thousands of others, Bert was posted for training near New York in the USA as a navigator and from there had made contact with John in Toronto, Canada, who was by now also in the services, and serving in the Canadian Army. He had then a family of two boys – Gary and John, and their younger sister, Audrey.

Above: St. James United Church of Canada, Montreal, Quebec, in 2010.

Origin: Author, 2010.

My train eventually pulled into the station at Montreal. I knew that the station was close to the docks, where I, as earlier revealed in Chapter 2, had first arrived as a crew member of a Belfast steamer, the ss "Rathlin Head," in1960. But here the first thing that I discovered, was that the place where that ship had docked all those years ago, was now known as the "old port. " Commercial shipping now used a new port - and not this place, where at one time, I had been able to buy and take home with me ten pounds of red MacIntosh apples in a wicker basket for one dollar and twenty five cents !

As we were due to leave Toronto the next day to return home, I was mindful of the time my return train would be leaving Montreal. I had choices to make and among the places I wanted to see again was the church, where at times, if the ship had been in port at Montreal over a weekend and I was not required for work , I would have attended worship there on the Sunday.

This was St. James Church, of the United Church of Canada.

It was situated on a street known as St. Catherin's Boulevard which was then fifteen miles long when I last walked upon it!

Recalling the scene of over fifty years ago, I remembered that from the docks where the SS "Rathlin Head" was tied up, one went up a street called St. Laurent or San Laurent until it crossed St. Catherine's Boulevard. Turning left here and proceeding along St. Catherin's, St. James United Church of Canada would be found along there. Now a doubt crept in. Was it a turn left – or, maybe a turn right?

But I turned left, and eventually found Montreal's St. James's United Church of Canada. I was amazed at its size and crossed over the street from it to view it more fully. I also beheld its three entrance doors and wondered which door I would have chosen to enter by in those days - and if anyone else might have accompanied me there? Indeed I actually recalled someone who would have accompanied me at times - he was one of my fellow engineers, and his name was Des Thompson. After I left the ss "Rathlin Head" to sail in warmer climes, I never saw him again but I heard later that he had gone to Australia. How swiftly one's life passes by. Fifty years had now indeed passed as an ever rolling stone and my late companions on the "Rathlin Head", alas, had almost become become "ships that pass in the night." But not quite.

Until a couple of weeks ago, I was in contact with only two of them. But on Friday the 17th. of November 2017, sadly, I attended the funeral of Jimmy Spiers, the Relief Second Engineer of the SS "Rathlin Head" on my first trip to sea. So now I am in touch with only one of them , namely Robert Aiken, Master Mariner , who was then Third Mate on the "Rathlin Head" and that is usually at one of the Head Line Reunions. I have no contacts at all now with crew members of English Company owned ships and there were five of those. See page 13 for Reunion photos. But now, I was once again in Montreal. I asked someone to take a photograph of me – see later photographs**, and I actually found the little souvenir shop (nearby the church) that I**

remembered shopping in! So I did as I had done fifty years before – I bought a few cards and a souvenir of Montreal – to place on the door of the fridge!

I was pleased indeed that I had managed to fit in this visit to St. James's, as it had always meant a great deal for me to join in the worship with the kind people I met there. I had travelled across the Gulf of the St. Lawrence and up the mighty St. Lawrence River itself to get there, having picked up river pilots at Escoumains, Quebec and Three Rivers - some 1,000 miles in total from the Atlantic. It was at Quebec in 1759, that Capt. James Cook had the responsibility to survey the river, in order that General Wolff and his troops could land safely and scale the "Heights of Abraham" on their way to the capture of Quebec. Later the two opposing generals, the French General Montcalm and the British General, General Wolff, would die in the battle - just before victory was won.

Cook would later also die a violent death – and was mostly eaten in Hawaii by the natives there. This had happened not far from Pearl Harbour. Now, however, it was soon time to depart Montreal again - no red apples this time!

Canada : A war time photograph : left: Cousin Bert in the RAF, and Uncle John, in the Canadian Army.

My lost Canadian cousins:

As mentioned, I grew up knowing that correspondence to my father from my Uncle John in Canada was rather sporadic. Long periods passed at times without Dad hearing from John. Wartime improved on this, with Bert Cameron meeting him in Toronto as recalled where they were photographed together – see that photograph. Another contact was through the circumstances of food shortages that existed in the UK and where early in the war, the essentials for survival were being brought across the Atlantic Ocean at such a frightful cost. Let us never forget that 30,000 men of the British Merchant Navy lost their lives in the struggle – and mostly in the North Atlantic Ocean.

However, as the pressure on shipping space eased somewhat, it became possible for the Americans and Canadians to send food parcels of commodities unobtainable in the UK to their kinsfolk there. I recall such goodies from John and his family arriving at our home outside Antrim. However, contact was lost again, and when my Uncle William (Bert's father) lost his life in a road accident in 1951, it was no longer possible to communicate this news to him. Sadly, the line was again dead to all our Canadian relations.

*　　　　　*　　　　　*　　　　　*　　　　　*

Ten years passed, and one day the police in Ballymena, Co. Antrim received a letter bearing a Canadian stamp. It was also directed to a "Mrs. Cameron" with a vague suggestion that she lived "outside Ballymena." To shorten the story, the police arrived one day to Mrs. Eliza Cameron, Carnaughts, Ballymena, the widow of my late uncle William. They handed her the letter and immediately, she saw that it was from Audrey, John's daughter, in Canada, a Mrs "Chuck" Whyte (or White.)

Some time later I established contact with Audrey, and also with her brother John. Photographs were exchanged, and I learned something of the life that John, her father, had experienced. In his early days in Canada, as someone with little money, he had crossed the country standing on the buffers of trains. He had been robbed, and was badly beaten up on one occasion the result of which was that he had required long periods in hospitals at times. It was poignant now hearing from Audrey, how her father had often spoken to her of her Granny "across the seas" at Kellswater (about four miles from Ballymena) in Co. Antrim, and something of the country he had left, to seek a better life in Canada.

In the course of our correspondence, I would pick up comments that one might hear in the UK, for example, that she would "have to fly now to get the dinner on" or that "I am just getting the children ready for Sunday School," or some comment about things we might have in common.We were now hoping for news of Uncle John.

But sadly,the news was not what we had hoped to hear for my Uncle John had died in 1960. Audrey sent me a photograph of his grave - apparently it is in Vancouver Island. The photograph puzzled me, because it appeared that there was a connection with the Services. The headstone bore an inscription, "Lest We Forget" and the letters RIR (normally taken locally to read here as, "Royal Irish Rifles") also appeared, as will be seen in the photo below. The Royal Irish Rifles title was changed after partition in Ireland in 1922 to the Royal Ulster Rifles. But John had served in the Canadian Army throughout World War Two.

*   *   *   *   *

In 1972, a friend of our family emigrated to Canada, working initially in Toronto. I arranged for this person to contact Audrey when she got set up there. Audrey had sent a phone number to me, although this was just before the days of cross Atlantic calls becoming common.

For some reason that I never found an explanation for, that contact never was made. I never received any more letters either from Audrey or her brother John, and unfortunately, I had not got around to establishing contact with Gary by that time. Once more the line was dead again.

Now in 2017,I still intend someday soon to pick up the trail.

How We grow older !

Left: Sitting on the roadside between Niagara City and the Niagara Falls is the "Barrel ," possibly the one used by William "Red " Bell to plunge over the Niagara Falls.

Origin: Author 2010.

In 1960: Author above, visiting Montreal last, when 4ᵗʰ· Engineer on the ss "Rathlin Head" as that ship traded in the St. Lawrence River ports. Origin: The ship's third Engineer.

Now in 2010 : Author above, now as a tourist outside St. James United Church of Canada in Montreal (contrast with the photograph left, which was taken in 1960!)
Origin : A kind passer by.

The art of hoarding: Extracts left, and below from the church service program at St. James' on September 25, 1960
How time flies indeed!

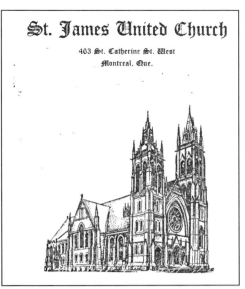

St. James United Church
463 St. Catherine St. West
Montreal, Que.

MINISTERS:

REV. NORMAN RAWSON OFFICE PHONE VI 9-123
HOME PHONE RE 7-221

REV. B.B. BROWN, D.D. HOME PHONE HU 6-809

ORGANIST & CHOIRMASTER -
GIFFORD MITCHELL, B.A., B.MUS. - RE 8-4633
MR. JAMES B. RATTRAY, BUILDING SUPERINTENDENT -VI4-1
CHURCH OFFICE 1435 CITY COUNCILLORS ST.
AV 8 - 9245.

I still intend someday soon to pick up the trail.

Cousin Audrey, photo sent in 1970. Note her father's Army photo on top of television set. Right: Her mother, Mrs. John Cameron.

Her father, my Uncle John Cameron - whose grave is in Vancouver Island. He died in 1960.

Audrey's children : From left. Janet, aged six years and in grade 1 at school; Charlie aged four years, and Danny aged two years old. This photo was probably taken in (1961 ?)

Mrs. John Cameron.

Janet, photo taken in 1968?

Cousin Gary's pre wedding photo.

Cousin Gary's wedding photo.

Note : During a period in my life when I worked for the Ministry of Defence at the Royal Naval Armament Depot in Antrim (the torpedo factory), one day, someone who was later to become a very good friend of mine, one Harry Lyttle, a fitter, came to see me – and he had a very interesting piece of information to impart. He had come from the Kellswater district where Uncle John grew up, and he told me that, as a child, he remembered the day, that with others, he had seen off John for Canada. Upon leaving, John's transport was a pony and trap which conveyed him and a wooden trunk to Kellswater Railway Station (where there was then a platform and a train stop) on the first leg of his journey to Canada. Considering the vast emigration that was common over the previous two centuries, it must have been a scene enacted hundreds of thousands of times outside the homes of those departing for, hopefully, a new life across the seas.

The Canadian Connection

Chapter 18

Travels in the East

To the Land of Punt.

To travel South from the Mediterranean Sea, via the Suez Canal and the mysteries beyond Port Said and Port Suez, was a burning ambition of mine that was earlier fired up following the cancellation of a hoped for trip to Borneo. It happened when the ship on which I was serving as an engineer was off the coast of Lebanon.

According to the Bridge, we now might have to call in Cyprus and pick up some urgently needed stores for the British army and then divert to Borneo where they were assisting in the struggle there against against insurgents from Indinesia. However, another Ellerman ship at Port Said in the Suez Canal was selected to do the job. Later, as the "Grecian" sailed from Tripoli in the Lebanon across to Alexandria in Egypt, I was to gaze in disappointment as we passed the entrance to the Suez Canal. For me, the Canal held the key – and the route to the mysterious lands that I had read about and would now lie just beyond.

I had read about a place called the Land of Punt about which my friends knew little although there were vague mentions of the Red Sea, Egypt – perhaps the Horn of Africa and beyond.That was all.

My imagined route therefore took me to the South East through the Suez Canal and the Red Sea to this mystical place – the Land of Punt. To improve on this it was going to need a lot of research indeed, to see where the ancient world had placed it. See the sketch of these Lands on two pages forward.

But alas, back in 1961, I could only say, "To morrow."

★   ★   ★   ★   ★

Arrival at Sharm el Sheikl :

Since those days, I had traversed the Suez Canal in both directions but only as far south as Sharm El Sheikl and Port Suez. However, in November, 2013, I took passage in a vessel, the MV "Voyager," a passage that matched my hopes of that day in 1961 when the old SS "Grecian," passed across the mouth of the Suez Canal on our way to Alexandria. I could actually recall then staring in the general direction of it as we did so.

After travelling by air to Sharm el Sheikl (which is the most southerly point on the Sinai Peninsula), I had joined the MV "Voyager" there. From there, the ship would spend a day at the Egyptian port of Safaga on mainland Egypt, which is also a holiday resort as well. Then, hopefully, we would press happily onwards to the mystical land (or lands) of Punt , over a thousand miles south, through the Red Sea.

At the time of the 1967 war, it could be said that Sharm el Sheikl was little more than a fishing village. But by 1973 the Israelis had turned it into a port, a thriving holiday centre, a major centre for water sports and additionally, having a busy airport.

The main holiday resorts - with other ports are now situated at the southern tip of Sinai at Sharm el Sheikl and along its East coast on the Gulf of Aqaba. South on the Arabian coast is Jidda (the port for Mecca). Then on the African coast, are the commercial port / towns of Safaga in Egypt, and Port Sudan in the Sudan. Sinai was restored to Egypt, following the peace agreement with Israel.

Where are The Lands of Punt?

Above: A large Maersk container ship going north - in the Red Sea. Origin: Author 2013.

The name "Red Sea" originates from the reddish algae that is a phenomena at certain times of the year. The Red Sea (with the Suez Canal) is the water way connecting the Mediterranean Sea to the Indian Ocean and is virtually tide-less. It has a sub ropical climate virtually all the year round with temperatures around 20°C plus in the winter and up to 26°C plus in the summer.

The Red Sea itself is about 100 miles wide and over 1,000 miles long, and for a ship travelling at fourteen and a half knots, it would take about three days to travel its length.

Now in November, it was indeed pleasant , and steady at 24°C. As noted, the only ports of consequence on it are, Jidda in the East on the Arabian coast (the port for Mecca), and

Left: A column of "modern" rams seen on a road outside Safaga – but not unlike those to be seen at Karnak. Origin: Author 2013

on the African coast, the port / towns of Safaga in Egypt, and Port Sudan, in the Sudan. Note however, the little port of El Quseir on the Egyptian coast at the Northern end of the Red Sea, for it was from there that the fleets of Hatshepsut, Egypt's female Pharaoh (and said to be the world's first great woman,) sailed to do trade with the **"Land of Punt"** (shaded), in the 15th. century BC.

But where was the "Land of Punt?"

For some ideas, see the shaded parts on sketch on next page. Today, majority opinion is based on a study of the inscriptions to be seen on the MortuaryTemple of Hatshepsut situated below the cliffs at Deri el Bahari near Luxor. This can be seen on the west bank of the Nile near Luxor, and this opinion regards what they seem to mean, as of the utmost significance as to where Punt really was.

These inscriptions show the products that Egypt obtained through trade with Punt in the past, and are **identified as coming from territory on both the Arabian and Horn of Africa coasts.**

These products thus illustrated in the MortuaryTemple of Hatshepsut, are divided, with one selection showing gold, myrrh and aromatic resins that one associates with Arabia. Then another selection shows inscriptions which depict gold, ivory and wild animals suggesting an African source – presumably animal skins would have been a product in high demand. This suggests that business was being done in Africa and also across the Red Sea in Arabia. (Another school of thought claims that Punt was solely in Africa, incorporating Eastern Ethiopia, Somalia and all of Eritrea.) But how would these latter explain the gold, myrrh, and aromatic resins?

I had been very impressed with the people who had researched the subject of Punt, and had come up with such a lot of intelligence about it.

Some pointers to the road for the land of Punt

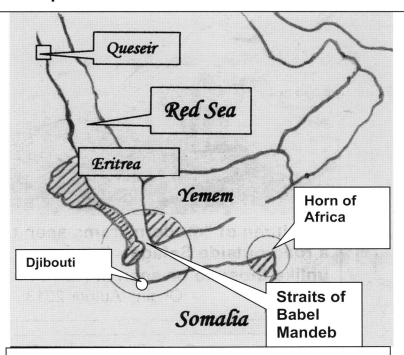

Queseir

Red Sea

Eritrea

Yemem

Horn of Africa

Djibouti

Straits of Babel Mandeb

Somalia

The Land of Punt – Diagonal Shaded Areas

Arrival at Punt ?
After three days "steaming" * at fourteen and a half knots, the Red Sea narrowed in to about thirty miles from shore to shore. Now, according to the shaded parts of the sketch above and constructed on the information there, we undoubtedly had the legendary Punt on both the Arabian and Horn of Africa coasts.
This equates with present day Eritrea in Africa and Yemen and South Yemen in Arabia of yesteryear.

Below: A lady of Djibouti.
Origin: Author

A Lady stall holder, in Djiboutie City.
Origin: Author 2013

Right:An advertisement.
We *had definitely arrived at Djiboutie City !* Author 2013.

PRODUITS FABRIQUES A DJIBOUTI

Our Arrival at Djibouti

Shortly we were passing through the Straits of Babel Mandeb and soon we arrived at the port of Djibouti City in the little country of Djibouti, formerly French Somaliland in East Africa. See the sketch map on previous page..

Note: An article by the famous seafarer in sail, Alan Villiers, and entitled "Ships through the ages: A Saga of the sea,"appeared in the National Geographic, April edition, in 1963. Here voyages to Punt from Quseir (see sketch) are described, and Punt is referred to as Somaliland. Also mentioned, is the finding of a rock inscription made about 2,000 B.C. which tells of an expedition to the "Land of Punt" (again meaning to Somaliland). The same article recalls a voyage made by the famous Egyptian Queen Hatshepsut around 1500 B.C. and thus about 200 years before the Exodus.

Arrival at Sharm el Sheikl. Origin. Author

Sorry chaps- there's no room in the Inn.
Origin: Author 2013.

Due to the ongoing presence of pirates who were to be found all the way from Djibouti and due East – indeed as far as Hong Kong, Indonesia and the East China Sea, our movements would now be subject to local scrutiny. This would be led by the co-ordinating authority which comprises twenty five countries who are each contributing fully operational armed vessels – mostly frigates in security surveillance of shipping in the area. Instructions to our ship would be that it should sail along a channel designated by them, and also at a given speed precisely, for example, at fourteen and a half knots. Hereafter, if, during the radar watch by one of these vessels, our ship were to be observed behaving in an otherwise irrational course and speed ie moving out of the designated channel, or been shown to be having to change speed without an explanation by radio, then the duty patrolling vessel would investigate quickly.

Our ship was fitted with razor wire (see later photograph on p196) around the stern of the ship, and water cannons, see top of page, were mounted off the weather deck on the ship's sides. Guards were also in evidence at times. On leaving Djibouti, we would be proceeding in a

travelling eastwards to the Persian Gulf, our final area of travel. Read about this later, but just now, the revelations

The area generally known as the Middle East. See also in Fourth Coloured Selection. Origin: Author 2013

of Djiboutie awaited us. When leaving Djibouti, we would pass the tip of the Horn of Africa on our starboard side - effectively (as per sketch) the final area in the ancient world known as the land of Punt but in today's world, Somalia. But first a look at the country of Djibouti: Djibouti is a country of small area and population, and it lies where the Red Sea meets part of the Indian Ocean - namely in the Gulf of Aden.

It is also where Africa encounters the Arab world. (See **sketch maps** later on). However its commercial importance is out of all proportion to that small size and population. Its importance as a natural harbour was recognised by the French around 1842 and they lost little time in doing deal with the local war lords in Northern Somalia to purchase this port area of such potential and later some of the hinterland bordering Ethiopia. It was a shrewd move because they soon began to negotiate other deals with the then Emperor of Ethiopia, Menelik II. This was to build, in 1888, the structures necessary to create from this working port, a railway line between his capital, Addis Ababa and the port of Djibouti. Ethiopia had no coast line, and the railway line, completed in 1915, would enable the outgoing goods of Ethiopia to pass that way to the port of Djibouti and their markets abroad. Imports would travel on the same railway line - but in a different direction. It is still doing so today.

Today, the port of Djibouti is a major container centre for onward transit goods and is also an important bunkering port where its proximity to oil producing nations, gives it considerable strategic status.

Upon arrival, we found the port of Djibouti to be in semi darkness. Our berth was right along side a type of covered accommodation and mostly constructed of high wire mesh.

But who would live in a house like that? As our eyes got accustomed to the dimming light as the sun was going down, we began to discern those who were living there – hundreds of them. They were camels, and this was their transit holding.

A ship, green in colour, was waiting for them on the other side of the quay. Even though it was quite dusk, people crammed the ship's rails and began taking photographs. Some people might have said, "You will have plenty of time tomorrow." But seasoned research travellers know full well the benefit of the opportunist photograph. These hundreds of camels might be loaded during the night onto that ship now waiting for them - and be gone by morning.

Notwithstanding the fading light, half a loaf would be better than no loaf!

So, this was the port city of Djibouti, the capital of a place originally known as French Somaliland. This was what the area was known as after 1862 when the French signed a series of treaties with the chiefs of the Afar and Issa tribes to buy this piece of Somaliland. It covers 8,960 sq. sq. miles (23,200 square Km).

During the next few days one would gather a surprising amount of information about this place. This would be through travelling around the city port and hinterland, and also through listening to the excellent lectures on board our ship. The French proclaimed the city port of Djibouti the capital of this French colony in 1892. However, after a colonial period of 114 years, it became a republic in 1977.

Djibouti is very much built largely in the French style and the population of 850,000 is a diverse one. It is made up of local tribes (dignified finely featured Afar and Issa people), Indian women in saris and glittering nose-rings, Pakistanis, Chinese, Malagasy and turbaned Arabs.

As one would expect, there is of course, a considerable French community - after all, they had run this place for 114 years! They account for perhaps the upwards of 30 % of the population and now share the city with those mentioned above. One assumes also, that they still have a dominant position in the operational management of the port - and the railway to Ethiopia!

Djibouti City : The city is laid out along French lines, with streets crossing each other at right angles and, of course, similar in form to other former French Colonial creations already met with in this book eg Montreal in Canada and Papete in Tahiti. It is a large city, and almost without exception, the streets are named after French people and places, and the principal thoroughfare is named after the First World War French Field Marshal

Clemenceau – thus Avenue Georges Clemenceau! The Presidential Palace – formerly the Governor's Palace is a handsome white building set in a leafy sea of green foliage. Close by there are banks, a Tourist Office, and fruit, vegetable and camel markets.

The mosques, however have more Afro/Arab sounding names like Hamoudie Mosque, Nouriye Mosquaée, Mosquée Al Sada etc.

Sadly, there are many thousands of refugees to be found in areas outside the city, the aftermath of the Ethiopia / Eritrean wars, the Central African conflicts and the current dreadful situation at present in 2017 in the Sudan.

As stated above, it is a city laid out along European lines, The entire population of Djiboutie is about 850,000 with about 500,000 living in Djibouti City. It is bustling with traffic with quite a few shops all selling the same goods and reasonably priced; T-shirts, souvenirs made in brass or wood, with many of the latter featuring animals, and of very good quality. A colourful scene, with many shop owners, of Arab/African origins, being quite capable of sorting things out when faced with customers with different languages and with different currencies! One was shortly to see this in practice at first hand.

Author with Sir Peter Brenton

Author with Sir Peter Brenton one of the Lecturers and who also accompanied us on our trip to the hinterland of Djibouti. He was formerly Ambassador to Russia and to Japan in his diplomatic service.

It had been thought best to travel out into the hinterland in organised parties, and in one of these, I made acquaintance of the stony desert that one finds outside the city of Djibouti (and which probably makes up the rest of the Republic of Somalia next door!)

The Hinterland. The transport that I was in, was a most decrepid vehicle, a small bus with a single seat on one side of the aisle, two on the other, filthy, and falling in pieces.
(It was indeed, hardly owned by a French Concern !)

The coastal region is lined with white sandy beaches, but, alas, they see few tourists. This fascinating country has not yet developed the facilities capable of coping with a modern tourist industry - not to mention the unsettled politics of the bordering countries.

In fact, after my return to the UK, a certain terrorist organisation announced that it had placed Djibouti on a list - for its attention.

However, there are some interesting physical features that tourists can visit, and one is the remarkable salt lake of Lake Assal, the lowest point in Africa at 512 feet below Red Sea level, and which is deeper than Death Valley in the United States.

The people seen in these more desolate places are generally of the poorer classes, living in shanty towns of wood and scrap materials. A little over 10° north of the Equator, Djibouti is one of the hottest places on the Earth - especially during the months of June to August. The events in Djibouti currently being described took place in November and even then, the day temperature was in the mid twenties. There is a lack of water near the surface in most places, so agriculture is rare. The traditional way of sustaining life for these people is a nomadic one, raising small herds of sheep and goats. Also on a dusty occasion, one would come across a camel - often with young, being milked on the hoof into an aluminium bowl, with the owner offering a drink to anyone wanting to sample the fare. A small fee might be charged here.

Sir Peter Brenton - seen on the previous page, was a former Ambassador to Russia and also to Japan during his diplomatic career. He was one of a number of our travel wise guest lecturers who accompanied our group during our experiences in the hinterland of Djibouti City, their presence being somewhat reassuring at times. But most of us realised that we were adjacent to possibly the most destabilised group of what some might call **failed countries in the world.**

One night after our return to the UK, and in fact when working on this very page, I retired to watch the 10 o'clock TV news. It was not all good. A Malaysian Boing 777 air liner had been lost over the Ukraine and guess who was on television giving his opinion in the aftermath of the loss of the air liner? Sir Peter Brenton!

Is this a camel's choir practice or – are they just glad to see me safely returned from the hinterland ?

Origin: A friendly passer by.

But there was a worse kind of living to be had than here in these open desolate spaces– the living of the numerous people who had no camel, or sheep or goats, perhaps not even an aluminium bowl. That was the living of the mass of people living here with nothing of this world's goods.

These were the refuges fleeing the wars in their own countries, wars that had caused them to come here. These were the thousands of refuges here in this desolate place.

Their plight was so painfully evident, that one felt caught in a moral dilemma about even taking a photograph of such in their pitiful plight. We usually take photos to entertain, for self gratification,for the entertainment of friends looking at these photographs back home, or in the club after morning coffee.

"Here is an announcement: " The green ship "Shebelle " presently tied up alongside, is waiting for you. Please have your Passports ready for Passport Control." Author 2015.

Upon returning home, I found that in fact I had not taken any still photographs of them - only a few feet of video through a bus window at a distance.

The immediate problem for them upon arrival in that barren waste was firstly to seek shelter from the hot sun beating down. A priority here was being able to find four uprights – poles if available, and then some cover on top, typically some leafy branches, an old carpet or some other discarded material. The indigenous people wandering with their flocks, had, by tradition evolved a method of building round shelters using curved sticks. A straight part up, and then, the curving part over the top to secure with an opposite from the other side. Then a covering of leafy branches, leaves – some kind of matting etc. This type of shelter provision was in competition with the need to find firewood for cooking! A few days later I would contrast their condition with what I thought of as obscenity, when I saw the marble pavements of Dubai. (I flew home from there).

Is it any wonder that so many seek to try and get to the UK or other European country in order to find respite from such a condition into which they have been driven by the hostility of their neighbours?

Surprisingly, there were other areas outside the city where it was actually possible to see an area flourishing with wild olive groves, acacias and other trees amid a wildlife which included gazelles, jackals, hyenas, antelope – even pink flamingos. How these birds and animals survived extinction without being eaten in such conditions prevailing, is puzzling.

Presently we returned to the dockside in Djiboutie to see what the fate of the hundreds of camels one saw there was going to be. We had been watching their progress each day, but neither food or water was seen being given to them - unless it was done at night.

Progress took the form of numbers being added to them, and this was a pantomime at times. Firstly, the gate of a pen - already packed full with roaring camels would be opened, with new camels approaching this opening in a not very willing manner since the pen appeared already to be filled to capacity. They further demonstrated disdain when an attempt was made by the herdsmen to force them into the said pen. One problem was that the resident camels were equally unwilling to move over in order to facilitate the new camels with a stand for the night. As stated, there was already standing room only. Stalemate - but not quite!

These herdsmen had a way of dealing with such a problem and the resident boys holding their ground would soon know what it was: First, enter a long bamboo pole about 2 to 3 inches in diameter with a pointed end directed by a herdsman towards the resident camels. Thus armed, he advanced boldly, holding the pole in a horizontal attitude not unlike that favoured by medieval foot lancers or jousting knights on horseback. Launching himself forward - his aiming point being the back end of the first dissenting camel he could see, battle was commenced. Very soon this roaring and protesting dissenter had thought twice about further resistance, and made himself scarce leaving other dissenters in turn to find themselves on the receiving end of the pole. Soon the herdsman with the bamboo pole emerged a clear winner, the dissenters were induced to move over and behold, suddenly found room in the pen they never thought had existed!

A semi "wild" parkland Frankincense Tree.
Origin: Author 2013.

The bamboo pole was an effective persuader! However, the resident boys were still not in a friendly mood to receive visitors, but the newcomers, having seen what was on the menu, choose not to face the pole wielding herdsman's wrath, and decided to enter the resident camels' den where, bookings made as described, they got their stand for the night.

We tried to find out where these camels were going and were told fairy tales, like, that some were going to Saudi Arabia to be trained as racing camels and again, that others were going to Egypt for breeding purposes. Three days later, from standing room only and apparently without food or water during that time, they departed. We later found out that they were indeed going provide "cheap food" for the Egyptians and that was the last we heard as to their fate. We ourselves were now leaving for the Omani port of Salala.

The firm, with whom I had booked passage, was aptly known as "Voyages of Discovery," and the ship was the MV "Voyager" which one assumed was owned by the firm, but it could have been on charter. Their previous cruise vessel in use was the mv "Discovery," a very comfortable but larger vessel than the MV "Voyager." The company specialised in going to interesting or unusual places, and I had used their services before. Most of the itineraries available will attract a clientele whose personal calling in life perhaps has promoted an interest in people and places, and whose thirst for such knowledge still grows.

Indeed, it may be reflected in every thing they themselves will be seen doing while on board. So it is certain that there will be few requests for bingo sessions, no room full of one armed bandits and no mediocre cabaret where anything goes in order to draw applause. Instead, there will be lectures on the places being visited, and given by those who are highly experienced in and appropriately qualified to speak on their specialist areas. Instead of the bingo in the after dinner hours there may be ballroom dancing and if you cannot dance, well, you will be taught ballroom dancing in morning sessions, mostly when the ship is at sea. In place of mediocre cabaret, you may want to attend, for example, an art class - even though the only brush you have ever handled has been a yard brush ! And you will have opportunities to meet with and have chats with intresting people including the guest lecturers as well.

As mentioned earlier, " Voyages of Discovery" Divine services are always held on Sunday afternoons and since part of the cruise would extend into December, the last service now on board took the form of a Christmas Carol presentation with a very good and balanced choir, comprised wholly of passengers who had practised diligently under a guest conductor to bring to us all an early Christmas fare. It was well received.

A "tame" Frankincense tree

*Leaving East Africa.*Leaving Djiboutie we headed for the port of Salalah in Oman, from where we would later proceed to other Arabian ports. Oman could conjure up visions of desert forts and white robed guards, ancient rifles and curved bejewelled daggers. Other thoughts might focus on the myth and legends of Ali Baba and the Forty Thieves, magic carpets, and the home port of Sinbad the sailor.

But Salalah had in fact something more tangible than these mysterious beings and things of magical promise. Because it is in Salalah that one finds the Frankincense tree whose resin is tapped – in much the same way as rubber is extracted from the rubber tree. A cut is made with a knife across the trunk – not too deep and with each cut several days apart to allow recovery of the tree to take place.

The white resin is collected during each cut and eventually emerges as a quantity of crystals. When these are heated, aromatic incense is produced. Frankincense is celebrated as one of the gifts brought by the Wise Men from the East, to Bethlehem at the birth of Jesus.

The trees may be up to twenty feet tall, quite bushy and with multi trunks, each from three to five inches maximum in diameter. It is amazing that such a sap producing tree can exist at all in such a hot region with little surface water available, but it has been doing just that for thousands of years.

Oman has indeed a shortage of surface water but it has a unique system for the distribution of water upon which the irrigation of crops depends. Water is found by tapping underground water supplies often in conditions of difficulty and danger and often at a depth of over one hundred and fifty feet. In the country, open stone water channels snake across the land, but covered as the channels approach villages in order to prevent pollution and to ensure that bans on watering animals are observed. The frankincense trees still grow wild about five miles inland, but the tree is often to be seen in local parks and around State buildings - a symbol of pride.

Anti pirate coils of razor wire on ship.
Origin: Author 2013.

As well, the resins of several other local types of tree are used to provide incense.

The question is asked at times as to how frankincense in a resin form, found itself 1,000 – 1,200 miles to the north in Bethlehem for the birth of Jesus. Consensus holds that both frankincense and myrrh came north through the Red Sea or, through the mountains running

on the north east coast of the Red Sea. As mentioned earlier, demonstrations were available by local guides showing a Frankincense tree being shallow cut with
a pen knife, and the white showing sap being collected before being allowed to reform in crystal form.
In a further demonstration, charcoal was ignited in a little Frankincense burner and
some frankincense crystals laid on top of the charcoal where, as the frankincense melted, it gave off its characteristic incense smell. As mentioned above, the resins of several types of trees – such as the Sandlewood tree all produce incense and were also on sale in the market.
Back in the centre of the town, the sale of souvenirs was in full swing and first on my list was some frankincense. This I bought along with the tools of the trade - a frankincense burner and some packets of charcoal - deed accomplished. I then made my way to a kiosk selling postcards and to my surprise, it was "manned" by two females – complete with head dresses as was the normal custom but with faces fully exposed. But what surprised me most was that I was left unattended while the two shop keepers ignored me completely as they laughingly chatted up two of my fellow travellers! I had never seen Arab females in a selling role, nor any engaging in humour of any kind before. But our guide book had stated that in Oman, there was a cautious opening up to tourism and "giving visitors the chance to discover a friendly, fascinating corner of Arabia." Maybe the guide book was right !

Muscat:

The capital of Oman, the land of Sinbad the Sailor.

Due to the threat of piracy we were now also in the monitored channel as prescribed by the monitoring authorities. Shortly after joining the ship, **life boat drill** had been observed by all on board. During this time we were advised by the ship's captain that another similar exercise would be observed shortly and this would also be compulsory for all again – and even more so because this would be known as "**Pirate Alert.**"
During this exercise, we were instructed as to what to do by way of preparation in the event of an attack by pirates on the ship!
 Upon entrance into the prescribed channel - which was parallel with the southern coast of the Arabian Peninsula, the first security action that took place was the securing and fastening down of our cabin steel dead lights. These are fitted over all the port holes in every cabin but usually only used in conditions of heavy weather at sea.
 Lighting in open deck spaces was reduced to a minimum and passengers were asked to avoid using these dark spaces at night. The atmosphere in these dark areas was decidedly eerie if one choose to pass through them. Note the razor wire coils showing up faintly below the crane on the stern of the ship and above the square openings, as seen in the photo two pages back. However, if my fellow passengers were apprehensive about the next few days, it didn't show on their faces – and they were very busy at times taking photographs of the razor wire around the after end of the ship and the water cannon ranged along its flanks. As well, using their binoculars they outwardly showed little concern and seemed to be taking part in the game – "Who can spot the pirates first." However, I think we all were serious "watch keepers" who realised that this was actually a dangerous area and probably seen ourselves as making a valuable contribution to the ship's safety. See photo of the ship's water cannon on later page.
But a speeding hostile inflatable, a mile or so off the bow, would have been a difficult enough object to spot - even to a trained eye.
One of our guest lecturers was Brigadier Philip Sanders CBE. He had served for thirty years in the British Army, retiring after commanding the 4th. Royal Tank Regiment. He was director of operations at Joint Force Headquarters during the First Iraqi War and as a young Lieutenant, he had served in the Dohfar Rebellion (which was supported by the USSR, China and South Yemen) against the Sultinate of Muscat and Oman. It lasted from 1962

until 1976, the rebels being defeated with British help, but the state of Oman had to be radically reformed in order to cope with the campaign and its social aftermath. The present Sultan (who at one time had served with the Cameronians after his time in Sandhurst) had come to power at this time.

The Brigadier was a considerable authority on matters concerning Arab traditions. I sensed that he would be well informed regarding the current state of play concerning the pirates.

I was therefore interested in hearing his opinion about things when quite often I shared an early buffet breakfast fare with him on a veranda over the stern of the MV "Voyager."

With Brigadier Philip Saunders CBE, former Commander 4[th.] **Royal Tank Regiment.** Orig. Mrs. P. Saunders

One morning I asked him if he thought that things were quiet in terms of pirate activity.

"Well, actually there was an incident last night," he replied. "Pirates were detected approaching the ship and were then investigated by local security. They made off quickly when the duty frigate in turn approached them.

The Chinese were on duty here last night. They took up position here recently and they are beginning to make their presence felt."

Needless to say, the Brigadier had an interesting turn of conversation when the subject of tanks came up!

Muscat was similar in layout to Salalah, but with more bustling streets thronged with movement, better pavements and more traffic lights. There were more colourful displays of merchandise, but with similar shops selling similar souvenirs –T-shirts, wooden camels, bags of every size and purpose, head scarfs, carpets and cushion covers etc. But the

Before leaving Muscat, it was possible to fit in a two hour cruise on a traditional wooden dhow, newly made and fitted with a diesel engine. We also managed to visit a fort, Mutrah Fort – built by the Portuguese in the 1580's.

Upon leaving Muscat, the final leg of my travels on the "Voyager" took me into the Persian Gulf and to those small countries and kingdoms which combine to make up the federated country known as the **United Arab Emirates** – the UAE.

The United Arab Emirates is a federation of seven emirates; **Abu Dhabi, Dubai, Sharjah, Ajman, Umn al-Qaiwain, Ras al-Khaimah and Fujairah**. The Federation was established on the 2[nd.] December, 1971.

United Arab Emirates (UAE)

Four- fifths of the UAE is desert but in spite of that, it is claimed that the UAE is one the worlds fastest growing tourist destinations. It claims to have all the right ingredients for the perfect holiday – sun, sand, sea, sport, unbeatable shopping, top class hotels and restaurants etc. But it was not always so.

Until 1962 the area was one of the poorest regions on earth with Abu Dhabi the poorest of all the sheikhdoms of the Trucial Coast. Now it is the wealthiest.

Oil brought the change from rags to riches although Abu Dhabi is the only real oil state and appears to bale out the others when they get into financial difficulties.

A few hours after leaving Muscat in Oman, we arrived in **Fujairah,** a small emirate, in all about the size of a medium sized town.

Lying entirely on the East coast, it is the only emirate without a presence in the Persian (or Arabian) Gulf. This is fortunate indeed because it differed in a significant way from the other emirates – an oil pipe line termination had arrived from **Abu Dhabi** and was up and running. – read on.

Left: Typical of the water cannons fitted to the MV "Voyager" to deter pirate boarders. Passengers were often seen scanning the horizon with binoculars in the chance of spotting a pirate inflatable approaching! PS: We did not need to deploy the water cannon!   Origin: Author 2013

An Omani gentleman in a outfit that many Omanis feel comfortable in. They are a race of people quite dignified in their dealings with others.
        Origin: Author, 2013

Left: Author on an Arab dhow in Muscat, constructed of wood in a traditional way and fitted with a diesel engine.
        Photo taken in 2013

Oil Pipeline By pass.
The pipe was designed to bypass the Straits of Hormuz which are overlooked by Iran - see sketch map. As above, Fujarirah is the only emirate which does not have an outlet to the waters of the Arabian Gulf, being entirely on the East coast. It means that the Emerites is

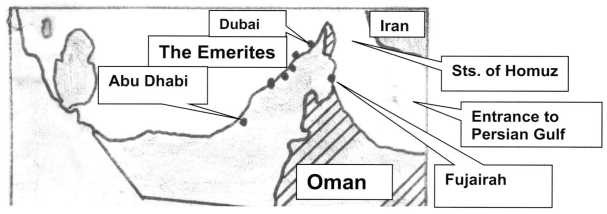

likely to have a safe outlet for its oil - free from the attentions of Iran - should Iran develop hostile relations with them!

After a few hours of stopover here, our ship left at 5 pm for Dubai where we arrived the following morning at 9 am.

Dubai.

Second largest of the emirates after Abu Dhabi, it is the Emirate's Commercial and communication hub and has an area of about 1,500 square miles. Its faith in putting infrastructure development as the driving force in commercial expansion (it has the busiest airport in the region, and arguably the best airline – Etihid Air), is testimony to a glittering manifestation of Arab enterprise, although sometimes appearing reckless. Facing bankruptcy in 2010, Dubai was baled out by Abu Dhabi and while Dubai has some oil, oil based products account for less than 10% of this emirate's wealth.

Who lives in Dubai?

Dubai has a population of under 2 million and of this, about 80% are expatriate workers – from Europe, South East Asia and the Middle East etc.

It is largely they who carry out the construction work, like the building of the Burg Khalifa (towering 830 metres into the air), the leisure centres, the Burj al-Arab hotel (built to resemble a dhow's billowing sail), the Palm Islands, built in the shape of palm trees, high rise apartment and office blocks and the streets and marble like pavements there of remarkable hue and design. For mile after mile literally, the new building display seems endless. **Note:** Dubai has now a Dry Dock. In fact the travelling crane seen in the photographs on next page and in the following "Fourth Coloured Selection," resembles closely (although smaller), the two cranes, known as David and Goliath, built by Krupps of Germany and which now tower over the shipyard of Harland and Wolff in Belfast, Northern Ireland. All this is what one now sees in Dubai – a cosmopolitan city whose pattern of development is constantly set to change. And Dubai has here set the bar so abnormally high for things normally considered mundane, that even what one walks upon here, is indeed of remarkable hue and design – and expence!. Yet, only a few days previous, I had seen a people whose concerns were focused on a reality - light years away from this lot.

This "people" was collectively the refugees whose earthly condition pointed one's conscience to exercise constraint in the taking of their photographs for social occasions.

So who lives in Dubai ?

Well, something interesting and educational turned up. I was on a bus tour when we had a brief stop in down town Dubai to stretch the legs, when I came across - it.

There, beside a wall, stood an ancient bicycle complete with its own stand. "Now," I wondered, "who might the proud owner of this bicycle be?" (see photograph, next page and in the following coloured selection.)

This was one bicycle that surely did not fit into the scene before my eyes! This scene was the one of Dubai with its expensive footpath tiles, multi lane highways, designed indeed for drivers of powerful expensive cars and who drove past with such nonchalant ease. But this antique cycle just did not fit the scene at all. As I had a good look at it, of a certainty it was not of British or European design. It was a piece of technology dating back to the First World War or before. It was an ancient steed indeed with that extra top bar, and an incomplete oil bath for a chain that one could see was now red with rust – (but surely not with so much oil about ?)

It also had a stand that would have supported a modern Honda Four motorcycle!

Well, it just had to be one of the millions of such, once made in China to enable its peasant workers of a not too long past, to get to their work in time.

I decided to hang around a bit and was soon rewarded by the appearance of two gentlemen who just might have come from China. As well, they had another similar bicycle with them, and shortly both made off - but wheeling their steeds along these streets "paved with gold."

I had just seen two of those expatriates who make up the 80% of those who live in Dubai today!

The "haves" and the "have nots."

Considering the recent past, a magical transformation has taken place with the advent of these high rise cities, and, yet amazingly, only over the past fifty to sixty years. The major oil producer here, Abu Dhabi, is the richest and largest of the Emirates and as referred to, they have been economically, able to bank roll Dubai out of economic disaster upon the approach of an eminent collapse of that economy in 2010.

Yet when Wilfred Thesiger, the British explorer arrived in this area in 1848, he could only, **at low tide**, reach the island on which the present Abu Dhabi now stands - and on horseback! He is reported as having said that Abu Dhabi was "a small dilapidated town dominated by a large castle." So the history of this present Arabian metropolis, only goes back little more than the middle of the nineteenth century when it was " a small dilapidated town dominated by a large castle." The castle is still there – now of course in the shade of the city and its sky-scrapers. So, what can the average tourist see that is of historical interest in the Emirates?

Now when a westerner goes on holiday in a foreign country, a significant number will book a tour in order to find tangible things ie things visible and above the ground e.g. a historic building, or a building associated with, in the past, a famous person, or perhaps a natural phenomenon - like a waterfall, a St. Paul's Cathedral (as in London, built in AD 1666), a St. Sophia Church (Istanbul, built AD 537 and now a museum), a St. Basil's Cathedral (Moscow, built AD 1555 – 1561), a Louvre, (Paris), or excavations that have **produced something tangible** - like the Roman Baths at Bath, England - and so forth.

There is however, no such apparent legacy in the Emirates.

Left: The 830 m. Burg Khalifa in Dubai. The top spike seems like a final comment, that there is a limit for frail man, as here he reaches his limitation to achieve. Origin: Author, 2013.

It looks like a scene from Harland and Wolff's shipyard in Belfast, were it not for the palms !

Now who in Dubai, would own a bicycle like this? Origin: Author 2013

To see these in colour, turn to P 202.

Can any history be found available to see - and touch?

Well it is fair to say that there are no really historical buildings as such to see, although the odd old fort – most likely built by some former occupying European power - can be trundled out, and with suitable restoration, give some semblance of a past.

But in several of the Emerites and in other Arab countries, shadows of the Louvre are beginning to fill out, with visible art collections etc. becoming popular presentations in places.

I was moderately pleased that I had fulfilled my early ambition of fifty years before - to proceed through the Red Sea and visit part of the ancient Land of Punt.

My abiding memory of my visit to that part of East Africa (formerly known as French Somalia) and now Djibouti, must surely be seeing the plight of those pitiful refuges encamped there, a people with no material possessions save what they had stood up in. I had not taken any photographs of them, not wishing to reduce further their dignity. Not making them figures of comment and remark in the comfort of our living rooms or indeed our lecture forums, is the better option.

The photograph of that bicycle with the rusty chain has been placed in somewhat ironic taste close to the photograph of the 840 foot tall Burj Khalifa! I think it says it all, the "haves" and the "have nots."

I had again seen the "haves" and the "have nots" of this world, the latter now represented by those refugees who have found shelter in Djiboutie. I had even found a word, obscenity, to describe how a seemingly endless supply of money is available to build the modern Towers of Babel. Yet, a relatively short distance away, starving people, driven from their homes and country through conflict, struggle to find enough cover to shade them from the sun. Children are starving as well - and with little prospects of learning to read or write.

*   *   *   *

I left the MV "Voyager" at Dubai, and that vessel then proceeded Eastwards, towards India – to yet another land of "haves" and "have nots" and yet India is said to be set to become one of the world's largest economies in the near future!

Our fore fathers put it simply - "It is an ill divided world."

*   *   *   *   *

Presenting another view point on life:

Above: The MV "Logos," which in 1970, commenced service with " Operation Mobilisation," a Christian organisation, distributing its message world wide and with practical help to those in need. Then, its library was said to be the largest floating library in the world. In 1988, the ship grounded on rocks in the Beagle Channel off Tierra del Fuego, Chile while under direction of the local pilot. No one was lost or injured, but the ship is still there! See right.

Above: The skeletal remains of "Logos" is still on those rocks in the Beagle Channel, and is now a tourist attraction in the area. Grounding took place in weaher described as atrocious. Note: All those serving on board OM ships, are in voluntary service. Their present ship – in 2017, is called the "Logos Hope."
Origin: Courtesy of Operation Mobilisation.

202

H.M.S."Hampshire" mined off Marwick Head – below.

Marwick Head

Mainland Orkney

Stromness

Kirkwall

Old Man of Hoy

SCAPA FLOW

St. Mary's

U-47 Entry

Hoy

U47 Exit

South Ronaldsay

Italian Chapel on Lamb Holm Island

Pentland Firth

Burwick

Kirk Sound

H.M.S. "Royal Oak"

Scrabster and Thurso

John o'Groats

Caithness

Churchill Barriers

Areas where the German Fleet Scuttled in 1919

North East Scotland and Orkney

The Great Harbour of Scapa Flow. Sketch Origin: Author : 2012.
(From "Antrim and Beyond" Part Two –They served in time of war.)

Author at the Newfoundland Memorial (which takes the form of a Caribou) and trenches near Thiepval. Orig: S. McMurray
Origin: Sam McMurray

Above centre:The German Memorial on "Robinson Crusoe Island" to those lost when their cruiser "Dresden" was sunk in 1915. * See Ch. 15

Thiepval Wood on right; Connaught Cemetery, distance right, and faintly, the Thiepval Memorial, far distant left. It was here the 36th. Ulster Division was virtually lost on 1. 07.1916. See Chapter 20
Origin: Sam McMurray

"Pirate Alert"- water cannon on the MV "Voyager."
Origin: Author 2013

Above: Author with Michael Molchof, son of the White Russian, General Molchof, who escaped from Russia in 1917 to eventually arrive in San Francisco, USA. and work on a chicken farm there! Orig: Michael's friend, Boris 2007

Above : **This is a rare and unique flower, the Tiare Apetahi. It is a one sided flower – actually it is a half flower, having only three petals inside its semi circular parameter. It was seen on the island of Raiatea, about 300 miles from Tahita (in a sub tropical climate.)**
Author 2007

Above : Who in Dubai would own a bicycle like this?
Origin: Author 2015.

Below: Atlantis submariners await their "dive" certificates.
Origin: Author 2006

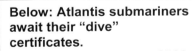

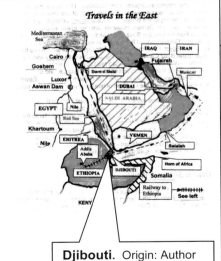

Djibouti. Origin: Author

It looks like a scene from Harland and Wolff's shipyard in Belfast, were it not for the palms ! Author, 2013.

Below: Note the statue of the Virgin, once referred to as the swinging Virgin, now restored aloft the rebuilt tower. Compare above with the photo on the right of the swinging"Virgin" in 1916.
Orig: Sam McMurray, 1995.

Below: 1916: Here the "Hanging Virgin"statue is in a precarious state, still attached to the tower but later lo st when British Artillery finally destroyed the remains of the tower in 1918.
Note: This photo is thought to have been taken by an Australian officer – one Captain Frank Hurley. This or similar photos of the tower also appeared on postcards sent home.

The "Bengore Head" of Belfast's Head Line, was torpedoed south of Iceland on 9. 05. 1941 by the U-110. British destroyers were quick to react, and the U-Boat was forced to surface. Georg Högel, a Radio Operator was told to leave the secret current Inigma Codes plus an Enigma M-3, set up for use and - " get out."
The British boarded, captured the U-Boat, and recovered a hoard of secret codes in particular the "Officer Code" and an Enigma set up in the current code in use ie for the month of May and possibly the codes for June and July. These were rushed to the cryptanalysts in Bletchely Park in Buckinghamshire, the British Code and Cipher School. Improvements in reading the German signals were soon evident in the sinking of nine out of the ten German supply ships in the North Atlantic by the RN. Some commentators claim that it marked a turning point in the battle of the Atlantic as well as shortening the length of the war. Sub Lieut. Balme who led the boarding party, was decorated with the DSO - at the age of nineteen years.
The late Georg Högel from Munich and late of the U- 110, and the late John Kerr, late of Whitehead and the "Bengore Head," gave much information to author on the battle for Convoy OB308 on 9. 05. 1941 which King VI described as "the most important single action so far in the war at sea." This info' was invaluable and indispensible in obtaining quite literally, an inside view of the action.

Above: Georg Högel, photo taken just before he was captured with the U-110 in1941. Photo below, taken in 1988.
Origin: Georg Högel, Munich.

A rare and unique photo – the 1922 built SS "Bengore Head," torpedoed 9. 05. 1941, by U- 110, when in convoy OB 308 off Iceland.
Origin: By an unknown hand- photo found in a house clearing .

Above: The late John Kerr, Whitehead, Co. Antrim, the Chief Engineer on the ss "Bengore Head, " when sunk by U-110 on 9. 05. 1941. Family archives.

The late Georg Högel, Munich, Radio /Op., U-110, in 1988.Portsmouth Ch.

Left: This photograph was taken in 1988 in Portsmouth, when Georg met Captain Guy Griffiths, the man who saw the U-Boat attaching the SS "Fanad Head." He dived his Skua, had bomb pre detonation, blew up and was taken prisoner by Georg's U-Boat, then the U30, off Rochall. Courtesy: Portmouth Chronicle

Post W W One, the British submarine E11 was scrapped at Malta, but her bell went to Canada. It was returned to HMS "Dolphin," Portsmouth, in 1967. Three surviving crew veterans attended the ceremony, George second from right. Origin: George Plowman (collection).See further photographs on next page.

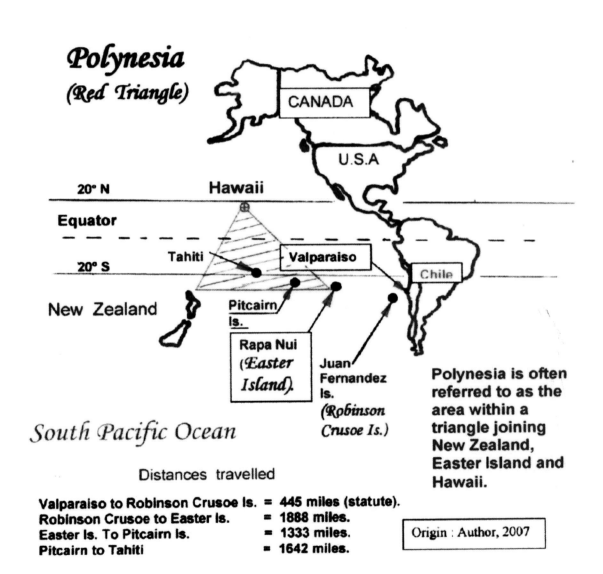

Polynesia
(Red Triangle)

CANADA

U.S.A

20° N   Hawaii

Equator

20° S   Tahiti   Valparaiso

Chile

New Zealand   Pitcairn Is.

Rapa Nui (*Easter Island*).

Juan Fernandez Is. (*Robinson Crusoe Is.*)

South Pacific Ocean

Polynesia is often referred to as the area within a triangle joining New Zealand, Easter Island and Hawaii.

Distances travelled

Valparaiso to Robinson Crusoe Is. = 445 miles (statute).
Robinson Crusoe to Easter Is. = 1888 miles.
Easter Is. To Pitcairn Is. = 1333 miles.
Pitcairn to Tahiti = 1642 miles.

Origin : Author, 2007

206

George Plowman DSM, and author at his Wellingborough home in 1978. He was Leading Signalman in E 11 at the Dardanelles in1915. Origin: Mrs Lily Plowman.

Post W W One, the E11 was scrapped at Malta, but her bell went to Canada. It returned to HMS "Dolphin," Portsmouth, in 1967. Three surviving crew veterans attended the ceremony, George second from right. Origin: George Plowman (collection).

The amazing Turkish shell that went through the E11 periscope when fired from a sinking gun boat in the Sea of Marmora in 1915. It is now in the VC's Room in the British War Museum in Lambeth, London. Origin: George Plowman DSM

Left: Memorials in a Norwegian Church Yard to the crews of the Royal Navy midget submarines lost in the attack on the"Tirpitz" in Kaa Fjord, Norway in 1943. Origin: A passing Missionary , travelling to Russia.

Above: The British semi diesel Mark 8 torpedo, once overhauled in quantity, where author worked at R.N.A.D., Antrim, Co. Antrim, N.Ireland. Origin: Author, at Birkenhead Historic warships Museum

"Operation Deadlight"This Memorial is placed on the spot where the first glider landed in the early minutes of D-Day, 6. 6. 1944, and followed shortly by two others to capture the Bridge over the Caen Canal which they did within fifteen minutes of their arrival.The Memorial carries a bust of Major John Howard, their commanding officer.
Origin: Author 2015.

Above: Lord Lovat and his piper Bill Millen landed on Sword beach on D-Day, about 6 miles from the Caen Canal Bridge and arrived piping in support of Major Howard's Glider troops. One can see Bill's pipes in the local "Pegasus" Museum. Origin: Author 2015

Author at the "Seven Pillars" mountain range rises from a dried up river bed in Jordan called "Wadi Rum." Well known to "Lawrence of Arabia" in 1917. See Chapter 9.
Origin: Author 2002.

Heavy German bunker,Cher,g.
Author 2015

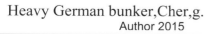

Left: The twin locks at Mirroflores, Panama. The MV "Regal Princess" awaits to enter second locks and enter the Pacific Ocean. Origin: Author, 2006.

The Churchill Barrier, Scapo Flow: The plaque where the author's bicycle is resting, recalls that the main constructors were Balfour Beatty.

Origin: Author 2009.

The Churchill Barrier, Scapo Flow: It is seen running from left upwards to right across this inlet of water.
This is where the German U-Boat, the U-47, Cmdr. Gunther Prien, penetrated the defences of Scapa Flow on 14th. Oct. 1939 and sank HMS "Royal Oak." Origin: Author 2009.

With , from left: Johnny Cooper DSO and right, Lord Jellico DSO. Both served with Blair Mayne in North Africa campaign - at the unveiling of the Blair Mayne Memorial in Newtownards in May 1997.

Captain Derek Kemp seen manouevring the main engines of the MV "Discovery" remotely from the bridge. Binnicle to right. Origin: Author

A large group of Moai now upright again and installed on a piece of sacred square set forecourt on Easter Island, South Pacific.
Courtesy of "Voyages of Discovery."

Small Maoi (borrows author's flask and yellow/blue bag) on Easter Island. Origon: Author

The SS "Mona's Isle," later to become the SS "Onward" of the South Eastern and Chatham Railway. As such, it carried part of the 36th. (Ulster) Division to France in 1915. Possibly an old railway source

The former headquarters of the White Star Line, now a fantastic Maritime Museum but still known as the "Titanic, Building," Cherbourg. Origin: Author, 2015.

A Horsa glider preserved in the "Pegasus" Museum close to Pegasus Bridge. Author 2015.

Sam McMurray at the Thiepval Memorial to 73, 000 Allied soldiers who have no known grave. His uncle served in the 36th. (Ulster) Division.
This is indeed a special photograph: Sam's uncle George McMurray's name is on this Memorial - near the top of the photograph. He was seventeen years old when he was lost on the First of July, 1016.   Origin: Bobby Cameron

The Newfoundland Memorial near Thiepval, to over 800 hundred troops from Newfoundland lost in the Somme Sector of Operations on 1. 07. 1917. Sam McMurray is lower right, in the frame. Origin: Bobby Cameron.

Left: Charles Warwick Clark from Rathmore, Antrim, enlisted in the North Irish Horse at the start of the 1914-18 war. He was later seconded to the 54th. (Anglian) Division, and again later to the Royal Irish Fusiliers. He died in 1983.

The DangerTree : Not far from Thiepval, it no longer blooms, but it is still there. In 1916, it was considered an extremely dangerous place to operate from.
                Origin: Sam McMurray.

When with the 54th.(Anglian) Division, Charles Warwick Clark took part in the Suvla Bay landings on the Galipoli Peninsula, Turkey, in August 1915 and was evacuated with frostbite two days before the general withdrawal there at the end of that year. He recovered in time to take part the Battle of the Somme, became an officer with the Royal Irish Fusiliers and finished out the war at Arras in France.
                Origin: Family archive

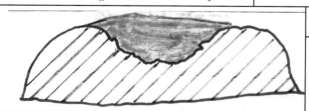

No full volcano action.

Here coastal erosion has taken out the front half of a once active volcano leaving the exposed crater in section. See Chapter 14

But here volcano eruption has only managed to penetrate surface crust. See Chapter 14

Panama Canal Profile, *Elevation and Plan.*

Origin: Author 2006.

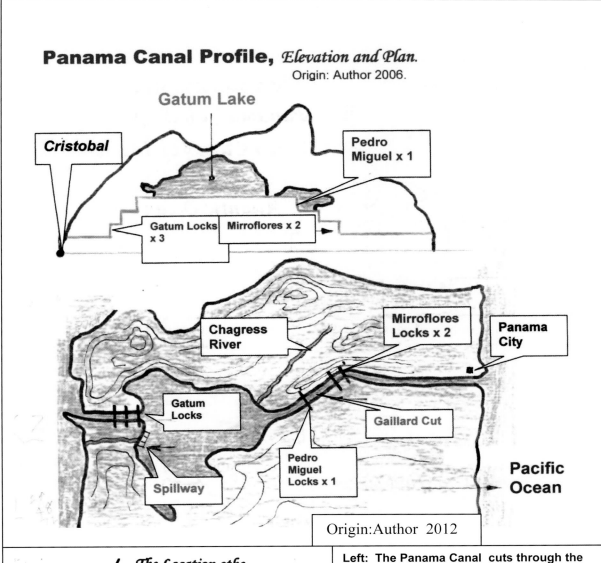

Gatum Lake

Cristobal

Pedro Miguel x 1

Gatum Locks x 3

Mirroflores x 2

Chagress River

Mirroflores Locks x 2

Panama City

Gatum Locks

Gaillard Cut

Spillway

Pedro Miguel Locks x 1

Pacific Ocean

Origin:Author 2012

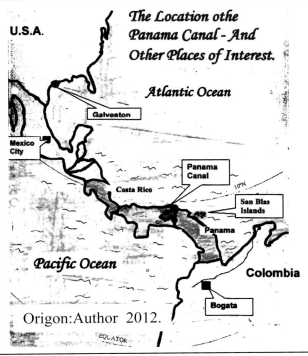

The Location othe Panama Canal - And Other Places of Interest.

U.S.A.

Atlantic Ocean

Galveston

Mexico City

Panama Canal

Costa Rico

San Blas Islands

Panama

Pacific Ocean

Colombia

Bogata

Origon:Author 2012.

EQUATOR

The Location of the Panama Canal

Left: The Panama Canal cuts through the small country of Panama, a country which was virtually a province of Colombia until around the turn of the century. One would have thought that travelling from the Atlantic Ocean to the Pacific Ocean you would be further west than when travelling commenced . But actually the Canal - by a few degrees travels East.
it cut the distance from New York to San Franscisco by 5,000 miles.

Below: Author at top of Waterloo Memorial Belguim, overlooking the battlefield of Waterloo.   Orig: author 1973

Chapter 19

Travel by cycling :

(1) *To the Great Harbour of Scapa Flow – Orkney Main Island.*

In this chapter my object is to describe a bicycle journey that took me to the Great

Harbour of Scapa Flow – in Orkney Main Island.
I have found myself compelled to find space to include a mention of this – the use of humbler means of seeing the world. It is simply by using a common push bicycle, a means that also has given me many days - indeed years of enjoyment and also modest achievement by accessing places where other means would have been less suitable.
 I here think of times in France when one could cycle along narrow paths through French cornfields in order to reach small, isolated Great War Cemeteries.

*   *   *   *   *

I should mention, *that a time when I was in the Outer Hebrides*, the Scottish Youth Hostel Association had not established any of their hostels in the Outer Hebrides.
But I had met a man by pure chance on the ferry from Oban, from whom I discovered that an organisation known as the Cunliffe Trust had in fact set up what was referred to as a "primitive" hostel in at least one of the Islands - namely in South Uist. The object was to assist European Youth in finding somewhere to stay in order to visit these, the most Westerly inhabited parts of Europe and I was to find that this very economic Hostel in South Uist had all the basic needs travellers as I might require. This man was of further interest to me when he revealed that on one memorable occasion, he had been given a dram of whiskey salvaged from the wreck of the 8,000 ton SS "Politician" of the Harrison Line. This vessel was said to be carrying thousands of bottles of Scotch whiskey to the USA and Jamaica and went aground in 1941 on the rocks on the small island of Eriskay between Barra and South Uist. Some of this valuable cargo was "liberated" firstly by locals and soon by others in vessels - some from as far away as Stornaway in the northern part of the Hebrides, and all helping in the "liberation !" Eventually the Customs people arrived and the "liberation" came to an end. Some "liberaters" actually spent some time in jail!
I regret I had no camera with me on the occasion of this cycling tour, which took me up through most of the Outer Hebrides.

*   *   *   *

At this point I will digress again for a short period of time and depart briefly from my present journey to the Orkneys. This is in order to mention some of the interestion people I have typically met up with on my travels. Such meetings have often happened by pure chance, and consequently, some of those people find themselves the subject of my humble writings and reminiscence - perhaps thirty years later!
It so happens that this example relates to a short stay on the Island of Arran when I was on my way to the aforesaid Hebrides!

*   *   *   *

I had arrived on the Isle of Arran one Saturday afternoon in 1985 after cycling up from Stranraer to catch the ferry from Ardrossan to the little port of Brodick on the island. I had then made my way by cycle to Lochranza in the north of the Island and up that rather nasty climb over the 900 foot Goat Fell mountain. There, I had booked into the Youth Hostel there which is run by the Scottish Youth Hostel Association.

Later on that evening, I had made my way down to see the jetty from where next morning it would be from where I would be leaving to cross Kilbrennan Sound to Tarbet on the Kintyre Peninsula and onto my way to Oban. This "jetty" took the form of a sloping ramp on which a ferry would ground itself while embarking / disembarking passengers etc., its position being stabilized no doubt by running the engine(s) slow ahead.

And it was at this little jetty, that this story begins. It opened up a chapter in my life that lives on - over thirty odd years later.

Because I would here meet one "Spud" Taylor, and his wife Jessie.

A ferry was just leaving the ramp at Lochranza and my attention was drawn to a man who was departing on the vessel. He was a well built man, wearing a blazer and sporting a noble moustache. I noticed a motif of some sort on the blazer.

He had obviously been accompanied to the ferry by a man and woman who were now waving to him, and he in turn was waving back to them.

I was fascinated to watch this little pantomime which continued right until the ferry was almost out of sight.

It was a pleasant evening, the sort that encourages strangers to stop and share a chat with those whom they might meet, or spare another thought for. And so it was, as the couple withdrew from the ramp and came to where I had been watching their "performance."

As I responded to their inevitable opening bat - that it was a "nice evening," this was, apparently, enough to tell the world where I came from, because the man immediately asked a question:

"I noticed your accent. Have you ever heard of Blair Mayne?"

I said that I had - very much so.

Reg Harmer, "the man departing on the ferry." Orig: Author 1985

So this was how I came, in 1985, to meet "Spud" and Jessie Taylor from Lamlash on the south eastern coast of Arran, and now in 2017, they have been my close friends for 32 years. I had that day, stumbled upon the second reunion of the 11th (Scottish) Commando, a unit formed in the dark days of 1941. This Commando had trained with other commando units, there in the Isle of Arran.

The man departing on the ferry, and who wore the blazer with the motif, was one of those who had trained there. His name was Reg Harmer MM, his decoration having been won during the invasion of Sicily later in the war. "Spud" Taylor, now in 2017 in his ninetees, had served in the Royal Navy throughout the Second World War, and had met Jessie when his ship called in at Lamlash. They had married after the war.

Jessie was sixteen when the 11th Commando had sailed from Arran to fight their first battle at the Litani River in Syria, against the Vichy French in 1941. There they sustained heavy losses and Lieut. Blair Mayne from Newtownards, Co. Down in Northern Ireland, got a "mention in dispatches" after the battle - his first honour. This was followed by four DSO's, a recommendation for the Victoria Cross and foreign decorations.

This made him, arguably, the most highly decorated serviceman of the Second World War.

The next question "Spud" asked me was if I knew how they might come by a photograph of Blair Mayne. As I had some contacts with Dougie Mayne, his brother, I said I would see what could done. I visited them a year later when again cycling through Arran, and I was there to see a photograph of Lieut. Col. Blair Mayne DSO, resplendent with his medals. (That photograph is also in a permanent presentation display featuring Lieut. Col. Robert Blair Mayne DSO, in the Masonic Hall, Newtownards, Co. Down. He had became a member of the Order there in September ,1945.

Later, following these meetings with "Spud" and Jessie, there were other veterans late of the 11th (Scottish) Commando whom I would meet at times in the future. They would return for reunions etc. and among these returning, were some of those who had survived the Litani River battle.

But all my connections with these veterans and others, had their origins in that chance meeting with "Spud" and Jessie at the Lochranza Jetty. I will now recall a few of these brave men and one was the late Sir Tommy MacPherson MC (and two bars) and another was the man whom I had first seen departing at the jetty at Lochranza and whose name was Reg Harmer MM – see below. But the one whom I knew the longest, was the one I had made the detour in order to visit, one Jimmy Storie, late of the 11th.
(Scottish) Commando, and later I attended his funeral when he died in 2012. He was the last surviving member, of "L" Detachment (an "Original") , which was the forerunner of the SAS.

On the morning they left Arran, Blair Mayne, a six foot four inch giant and a rugby international, asked Jessie to run and purchase an item for him. She often recalls the occasion!

Someone else had a memory of Lieut. Blair Mayne in Arran! He was their piper, Jimmy Lawson, still hale, hearty and a former local acquaintance of Jimmy Shand, of accordion fame. Now in 2017, Jimmy is 96 years of age, a veteran of the Second World War, the battle of the Litani River, and the Korean War. He still attends his local Masonic Lodge, lives at Kirkaldy in Scotland, and I am in communication with him from time to time. Jimmy Lawson was seconded to the 11th. (Scottish) Commando from the Gordon Highlanders, first having qualified as a Pipe Major at the Army School of Piping. See left.

Pipe Major Jimmy Lawson, late of the Gordon Highlanders, and 11th. (Scottish Commando), the Royal Corps of Signals - the latter service in Korea, 1951-53. He was also a veteran of the Litani River battle in Syria, and had strong connections with the Territorial Army after full time service in the Army.
Origin: Courtesy of Jimmy Lawson.

Back row: Jimmy Storie ; Sir Tommy MacPherson MC; author. Front; Reg Harmar MM, the man on the ferry at Lochranza - still with his moustache and the motif on his blazer!) Jimmy, Tommy and Reg were at the Litani River battle with the then Lieut. Blair Mayne, 1941. The latter got his first " mentioned in dispatches,"there.
Isle of Arran in 2005.

Jimmy arrived at the little port of Brodick in Arran one Saturday afternoon to join the 11th. (Scottish) Commando from the Gordon Highlanders - as their piper. He paused to watch as a platoon of solders marched into the port area. He further watched – now in some amazement as they kept marching on to the water's edge and then into the water its self. "I began to wonder what sort of a bunch of idiots I was joining – and who really were these folk. I soon found out that I had been been watching Lieut. Blair Mayne's platoon undergoing their training!" See Jimmy's photograph on the previous page.

Above from left: "Spud," author and Jessie. Origin: Some kind passer by.

Above left: At the unveiling of the Blair Mayne Memorial in Newtownards, Co. Down in May, 1997: From left, Johnny Cooper DSO, author, and Lord Jellico DSO. These photos are also in the Fourth Colour Selection. Origin:The same kind passer by!

Jimmy Storie had first met Blair Mayne - who had come from the Royal Ulster Rifles, when both had joined the 11th. (Scottish) Commando.

Both had trained together in the Isle of Arran, had both fought at the Battle of the Litani River in Syria in 1941 – as had Jimmy Lawson, and both were foundation members of "L" Detachment of the Special Air Service, when it was formed at Kabrit in Egypt in 1941. It was later to be known as the S.A.S. **Apart from the author, all the people in the photographs on these three pages, all knew Blair Mayne very well indeed, either through serving in the 11th. (Scottish) Commando in Syria with him, or with him in the SAS - in Jimmy Storie's case, in both.** *

Lieut. Blair Mayne DSO (and three bars)

And Jessie had ran that message for him on the morning the 11th. (Scottish) Commando left Arran for the journey around South Africa to do battle with the Vichy French in Syria. Jimmy Storie was later captured when in the SAS in North Africa when behind the German Lines in1943. Hitler's edict was "shoot those Commandos – even if *surrendering*. But Jimmy was probably lucky to have been captured by a Luftwaffe Patrol and not by members of a Gestapo unit or the regular German Army.

As a POW he convinced the Germans that he had been in the RAF. Even so, he was flown to Germany where his interrogation continued there. After twenty seven days in solitary confinement, " when I counted the nails in the door of my cell to preserve my sanity," he narrowly escaped execution, and spent the rest of the war in Stalag Luft 8B POW Camp in Poland. The RAF cover story had held.

* Over 70 years after these events took place, I was writing up these very lines in July 2017 when I received a call one evening from Jessie and her husband. They had a telephone number for me to ring.
Later that evening I lifted the telephone and dialled that number. It was answered by a man speaking with a very distinct English accent and I was astonished to find that I

was speaking to yet another survivor of the battle of the Litani River in what was then Syria, but now is in Lebanon. He was Captain Bryans and he had survived – but only just. Now ninety three, he told me how, beginning with Lieut.Col. Peddar, all the senior officers were killed – and then he too fell under sustained enemy machine gun fire. He was severly wounded and became a casualty Prisoner of War during which time one of his legs was amputated. After six weeks, the local conflict ended and he was returned into British care. He spoke of his days training in Arran where he was attached to an engineering unit, of knowing Jimmy Storie, George Dove (who also survived after being shot at the Litani River), and of course Jessie, from meeting her at one of the reunions on Arran after the war. Captain Bryans is presently in nursing care but is in good spirits and capable of invigorating conversation. A veteran indeed of the Battle of the Litani River in 1941 - of which, sadly, little has ever been spoken written.

Returning now to Jimmy Storie, who, in the winter of 1945, was to take part in the 500 mile forced "march of death" westwards – but hardly as a volunteer. This was when the Germans were retreating before the advancing Russian Army. Many of Jimmie's comrades perished in the severe winter weather during that forced march, since they were provided with little suitable clothing – especially footwear. Their memory was so etched in his memory that Jimmy never wore his medals in public, and on one occasion he told me that "those medals were for the boys who did not make it home."

As above, Blair Mayne was decorated with the DSO on four occasions and was recommended for the Victoria Cross, a claim that is still being pursued today. He is also reported as having explained to General Montgomery the reasons why Monty's plans for the capture of the Bridge at Arnhem would fail. (One understands that Montgomery did not like being told things like that!)

Blair Mayne died in a car accident in Newtownards, Co. Down in 1955.

In an earlier book, "Antrim and Beyond" Part Two, (They Served in Time of War), Chapter 5 is devoted to Jimmy Storie.There, is a description of the unveiling of the Memorial by Lord Jellicoe to Blair Mayne DSO (and three Bars) in Newtownards, Co. Down in 1997.

I was very privileged to receive an invitation from the Blair Mayne Research Group in Newtownards with whom I had some fellowship to attend this and the proceedings later. Briefly, that night I met many of Blair Mayne's former comrades - those of the North African Desert Campaign behind the lines in 1941 – 43, and in addition, those others who were with him behind the lines in France in 1944- 45.These were men about whom I had hitherto only read about in books. Reg Seekings, Dougie Arnold, Jim Almond , "Hamish" Lappin, Johnny Cooper, Lord Jellico and a good few others. Sadly, one who was not there, was Billy Young from Randalstown, a town in Co. Antrim five miles from where I live. I knew his brother.

Billy was captured behind the lines in France in 1944 when his group was betrayed by a local French man. That group were shot by way of execution - in fact by the the German Gestapo, but two or three, in either feigning death or in making a break for it, survived and escaped. I also met their Padre, the Rev. Dr. Frazer McLuskey MC, their Padre who dropped behind the lines in France with Blair Mayne and his group. I got many autographs that night, which have now appeared in "Antrim and Beyond," Part Two, Chapter 5. One rather humorous incident I must now recall. It was on this wise:

After leaving the statue of Blair Mayne - now unveiled outside the Town Hall in Newtownards, those remaining for the later proceedings that evening were asked to proceed to the Queen's Hall in Newtownards - about five minutes walk away. Shortly to my astonishment , I was approached by two much bemedalled men who professed themselves well and truly lost! "Do you know where this place is that we are supposed to be going to?" These two were Johnny Cooper and Lord Jellico , men, who at one time could navigate in the North African desert - hundreds of miles from base with maybe only a sun compass to assist them, had found the geography of Newtownards a step too far! For me, of course, it was a fine opportunity for a photograph too good to miss! I didn't miss and presently conducted these two gallant gentlemen to the Queen's Hall! See previous page for the photograph! Same photo in the "Fourth Coloured Selection."

*   *   *   *   *

As mentioned, on the night I arrived at Muchalls, the chat was good and indeed again during most of the next day as well. I then prepared to continue my journey to the Orkney Isles. Thus the "horse" was led out and saddled up and it was time for our good bye's as I took my leave of these dear people, who, like so many others, had stood on the thin line between Hitler and the free world in 1940, and gave over the best years of their lives to appalling deprivation and danger of the utmost reality. Morag herself had served throughout the war in the Royal Artillery, being involved in the prediction – using an early form of radar, of enemy aircraft over Britain in so doing. Like many others, their deeds were mostly unrecognised and I wondered if many at home ever had said "Thank you folks, for allowing me to sleep in my own bed at night when you stand out on that line for me." (Actually about five million people wore British uniforms of some sort in World War Two out of a population of just under fifty million.)

But now, however, like a scene from "Kidnapped " by Robert Louis Stevenson, Jimmy and Morag walked with me up to the top of the Muchalls road to where it joins the Stonehaven /Aberdeen main road.

At their invitation, however, I would join with them again - in Perth in 2009 where Jimmy would be attending a Special Forces day. (As it turned out, Jimmy, in 2009 was the only veteran of World War Two Special Forces able to be present on that day,and he was now beginning to feel the heat of the day. See photo on P 216).

Perth would be the last place I would see Jimmy, an unsung hero of the Second World War who never wore his medals ("always, they are for the lads who didn't make it back"). As referred to previously, I always understood that he was here thinking of his POW pals in the winter of 1945 on that cruel "March of death." They had to be left behind in the snow, sometimes with a bullet in the head fired by some sadistic German guard. I was to be, however, in frequent contact by telephone with Morag and Jimmy. One New Year Jimmy taught me over the phone his New Year Greeting :

" A guid New Year to yine and all,
  and mony may ye see.
  And al through oot the coming year,
  a happy guid New Year."

(He passed away in 2012, aged ninety three years, and I attended his funeral in Aberdeen. I speak with his wife Morag on the phone quite often – she herself is now in her nineties.)

But now I took my leave of them. It was our parting of the ways, but not before Morag had

thrust a packet of Aberdeen "butties" * into my rucksack.)

        *   *   *   *   *

I arrived in Aberdeen an hour before my ferry left for Kirkwall in Mainland Orkney – and a crossing of the Pentland Firth.

It was thus into Kirkwall on that Saturday evening near midnight, that I had cycled into, after a pleasant little cruise from Aberdeen. I had pre booked a B / B for the night in Kirkwall and my main object now was to visit the great harbour of Scapa Flow, the home of the Royal Navy in two World Wars.

There I would, hopefully, see where the remains of the former British battleship HMS "Royal Oak" lies and also to visit the Churchill Barriers now built across the entrance. This was where the German U-boat, the U-47, had slipped through to torpedo the battleship - two weeks into WW2.

                                        *   A type of Aberdeen pancake.

Extract : " *The Orkneys consist of a group of islands lying to the north of Scotland, the nearest being about ten miles from mainland Caithness and its famous landmark, "John o'*

Groats." Between those two landfalls however, lies a stretch of water connecting the Atlantic Ocean to the North Sea, which has a claim, indeed, to be one of the wildest stretches of water in the world.

It is known as the Pentland Firth, and through it, the elements engage in battle with themselves and anything else that may stand in their way.

About a dozen of the most southerly islands of the Orkneys are formed approximately in the shape of a horseshoe, open to the south and forming a natural deep harbour. This is a large expanse of water - perhaps upwards of one hundred square miles in area, with a number of entrances in the south. It is known as Scapa Flow.

West of Scapa Flow on the coast of Mainland Orkney, is Marwick Head, close to the town of Marwick. It was here in July 1916, that the cruiser H.M.S "Hampshire," en route Russia and carrying on board the British Minister of War, Lord Kitchener, struck a mine in heavy seas and sank – see map. Only twelve men survived, and Kitchener was not among them.

Scapa Flow was a major base for the Royal Navy in two world wars, the scene in 1919 for the spectacular mass scuttling by the Germans of their fleet (over 70 ships - interned in Scapa Flow since the previous year), and later the place, where on the 14th Oct., 1939, the British battleship H.M.S. "Royal Oak" was torpedoed by the German submarine U-47.

Sinking in less than 15 minutes with the loss of over 800 young Royal Navy personnel (with only about 300 crew members surviving in the cold waters of the Flow), it was indeed a disaster there- and only two weeks into the war. **From "Before That Generation Passes," Author, published 2001.**

After breakfast the next morning, I again saddled the horse, checked his tyre pressures and set off heading south for the "great harbour," the harbour of Scapa Flow as described above, the home of the fleets of the Royal Navy in two World Wars.

Scapa Flow In The Orkneys

On leaving Kirkwall, I stopped at the magnificent red sandstone * Cathedral of St. Magnus, upon which building work was commenced by one Earl Rognvald in the spring of 1136 or at least that is what the history books on Orkney tell us. (The "Earl" part of the name was his title, and not a Christian name.)

Unfotunately I could hardly see the cathedral for the trees, but I took a photograph- seeing I was there! It is a steep climb up past St. Magnus until one reaches, as it were, the Orkney "plateau." After this it is a series of steep hills – up and down, but eventually, in the distance, the southern entrances to the "Flow" lay before me, and the "Churchill Barriers" came into view from perhaps four miles away. I had arrived. ***See in "Fourth Coloured Selection"** the sketch map of Scapa Flow on page 202.*

I had arrived at the little village of St. Mary's, and from here, the most northerly end of the Churchill Barriers, the Barriers stretched across the former entrance into the Flow until it reached the Island of Lamb Holm. Attempts had been made to seal off this entrance against German U-Boats from the days of the First World War using block ships but the raging storms at Scapa Flow constantly moved them. Thus, the current position of these block ships in this former entrance to the Flow was noticed in aerial photos taken by German aircraft in 1939.

Extract:
"*Upon examination of the photographs, German intelligence, led Donitz the Flag Officer of the German U-boats, estimated that on a high tide, and with probably thirty minutes of slack water, a U-boat could manoeuvre successfully between Mainland Orkney at St. Mary's, and the nearest block ship of the group sunk across the opening to the island of Lamb Holm. Accordingly, shortly after midnight on the morning of the 14th October 1939, Lieut. Cmdr. Günther Prien in the German submarine U 47, stealthily crept past Mainland Orkney at St. Mary's and the nearest block ship – catching briefly on an obstacle at one point. He got*

217

through, though, and although only a few major units were in the anchorage, he successfully torpedoed the battleship, H.M.S. "Royal Oak," albeit at the third attempt.

From "Antrim and Beyond " Part Two
- They Served in Time of War. Author.

I spent some time there, as fascinated I looked across waters where, in the early morning mists of that fateful day, a German U-Boat made its stealthy way into the Flow to take the lives of over 800 young men. **See photographs in " Fourth Selection in Colour,"starting on P 202.** Gunther Prien and the crew of the U-47 got safely back to Germany and were decorated personally by Hitler. However, they had not long to live.

Extract: " *But Nemesis, that goddess of vengeance was planning a banquet to overtake the evil-doer!*

In March 1941, Prien,* still in U47, attacked a North Atlantic convoy. He sank the Head Line steamer, the S.S. "Dunaff Head," of 5,000 tons, one of the ships of the Head Line, Belfast, which had sailed from Glasgow to join the convoy. He was spotted on the surface however, and subsequently depth charged to destruction by escorts under Commander Rolands. Interestingly, the reports of the demise of Prien recall a spectacular under water detonation, an under water illumination "as if someone had switched on a powerful torch." They also refer to blue or orange lights appearing on the water afterwards. Speculation suggested that this mayhave had to do with lights on U-boat life jackets – but that was all. Prien and the U 47 were gone. There were no survivors."

From: "Antrim and Beyond " Part Two
-They Served in Time of War. Author 2012.

*A survivor of the " Dunaff Head" sinking was Mark McAughtry, fireman, father of Sam McAughtry , who after wartime service in the RAF, became a well known Belfast journalist and writer. Sam's brother Mark was lost at sea in the SS "Kenbane Head."

HMS "Royal Oak."

Above: The magnificent red sandstone cathedral of St. Magnus, Kirkwall, Orkney (but hidden by the tree), dates from the 11th. Century. Orig: Author

A Churchill Barrier from St. Mary's village across to Lamb Holm Island. This was where the U-47 passed to enter the Flow and sink the "Royal Oak."

Beside author's bicycle is the plaque telling of the construction of the Barriers by Balfour Beattie and Co.

Left: With Jimmie Storie at Perth where he was the only WW Two Veteran to attend Special Forces Day.

Visiting the wreck site of HMS "Royal Oak" in Scapa Flow.

Later on my way back to Kirkwall, I made inquiries as to the site of the wreck of the "Royal Oak." I met a local farmer who lived there, and he told me that for seventy years there has always been a sheen on the waters of the Flow there, due to leaking boiler fuel from the "Royal Oak" and that "the wreck is marked by a large green buoy."
I had met this farmer having just passed close to a place known as the Gaitnip Banks (or cliffs) where the "Royal Oak" had been lying at anchor when torpedoed - close under these cliffs of Gaitnip, and not far from Scapa Pier. Scapa Pier could be seen a few miles out of Kirkwall town, and although the green buoy attached to the "Royal Oak" was but a short distance away, here it was "around the corner" below those cliffs and out of sight. I inquired of the farmer – seated in his Land Rover, if it was possible to see the wreck site from anywhere near where I was.
"No," he replied. "It's not possible, because she is in below the cliffs and you would need to go to the other side of Scapa Bay to look across and sight the buoy."
Upon hearing this, I withdrew to consider this difficulty and to photograph Scapa Pier, a place in two World Wars very well known to ships of the Royal Navy. When I was thus engaged, the farmer had reversed his Land Rover back down to where I was.
"Do you think that you could get yourself away down into yon field?" he asked. "I had forgotten – one can see the buoy from there. She is still leaking oil – it is now diesel you know, and that's why the Navy people were up here last week. They were probably trying to remove some of it from the ship's diesel generator tanks."
I clambered down the hillside and, accompanied by the farmer, got to the desired field. From there, I saw from about a couple of hundred yards, the green buoy that is attached to the wreck of the former battleship which seemed to have been anchored surprisingly close to the shore. The buoy, which I photographed from a distance , marks the spot where once a terrible disaster had taken place – over 800 young lives lost in an event still within living memory.
It was now time to complete my journey back to Kirkwall from the Barriers. This done,I was having a meal in the local British Legion when at the table where I was seated, I noticed a newspaper lying. Casually glancing at it, I was amazed to see on its front page, a full account of the sinking of the "Royal Oak!" It was,of course,a reprint from a paper of 1939 and it had been procured from the local Tourist Office! It belonged to a group of my fellow diners - from the Channel Isles actually, and they had been on a pilgrimage to visit the wreck site of the "Royal Oak!" One of them had actually lost his uncle on the ship. This was an unexpected bonus – meeting people with such a personal interest in HMS "Royal Oak."

Presently I set off on my return to mainland Scotland, first to Stromness, where hopefully, I would take passage on a local ferry to Scrabster on the mainland. During a very wet ride to Stromness, I stopped briefly close to where the Germans had scuttled their fleet in1919. I identified a number of features that one reads about in books written about Scapo Flow and the scuttling of the German fleet. One such, was the island known as "The Barrel of Butter." From Stromness on mainland Orkney, the ferry run brought me past the "Old Man of Hoy" – a stack of rock lying off the Isle of Hoy and whose challenge is well known to mountaineering enthusiasts.
A short time after passing Hoy, the ferry arrived at Scrabster on mainland Scotland, a port well known to thousands of Service people in two World wars. Then a short cycle run of about three miles brought me to Thurso. After spending the night there in a local private hostel, I was up early the next morning and to get a start made, I and my bicycle presented ourselves at the Railway Station for the early train south – at about 6.30 am.
I was here approached by a man, a railway employee – (one hoped), and who inquired if I was going to Inverness.
His further message was that there were few ranks available on the train to accommodate bicycles and kit bags and if I would not mind if he took my bicycle and gear by van to Inverness to free up another rank for some other cyclist on this first section of track. Well, I

am sure I asked for some proof of identity but at Inverness, to my great relief, my bicycle was waiting for me. If I recall aright, bad weather induced me to use the train again before Glasgow. But at Glasgow things improved a little, and I rode from there to Cairnryan in about seven hours, eventually getting a ferry to Larne in Co. Antrim. A further twenty miles in the saddle brought me to the door of my home in Antrim. It had been a good little trip.

Chapter 20) contd.
(Part 2)
Travel by cycling :

(2) *A cycle tour of the Somme Battlefields at Thiepval.*

This was a nostalgic one. Because it was that of visiting, when accompanied by a cycling colleague, Sam McMurray, some of the British and Commonwealth cemeteries of the First World War and in particular, the area around Thiepval Wood where the 36th Ulster Division gallantly took part in an ultimately futile battle which later became known as **"The Battle of the Somme."** It is also described in some histories as the **"First Battle of Albert,"** the name of the front line town of Albert. Albert also acquired some fame as " the town of the Swinging Virgin," the statue of which had been placed aloft the tower of the local cathedral, **the *Basilica of Notre Dame de Brebières.*** The British became aware that the tower was being used by the Germans for artillery spotting and they shelled it, leaving the Virgin statue swinging out from the tower rubble – see later photograph.
When about halfway through our tour, we came to Albert, once a front line place in the First World War.
We happened to stop at a café/ store for provisions and there, right in front of us, was the restored cathedral with a new statue of the Virgin aloft. That original statue which enabled the town of Albert to acquire its title as **"The town of the Swinging Virgin,"** was never salvaged following the eventual total destruction of the tower later in the war.
(Shortly I will recall how our own venture would prove an example of when "victory was narrowly snatched from the jaws of defeat," following the breakdown of a component on my cycle - as is presently revealed!)

Thiepval Wood:
Here, Sam and I had a lot in common on which to contemplate.
Because there, at the ground in front of Thiepval Wood –(see photograph on the next page), his uncle,17 years old George McMurray from Kells, Co. Antrim, and in the 11th Battalion, the 36th Ulster Division, and my Great Uncle William Stewart from Curran, Magherafelt, who was with the Tyrone boys in the 36th Ulster Division, crossed that ground at around 7am on the 1.07.1916 in the advance of the Division.
Sadly, they did not return.
Their remains were somewhere out there, and they are remembered today on the Thiepval Memorial to the Missing, not far away.

Thiepval Wood far right, with the Thiepval Memorial on the distant horizon. Here, emerging from Thiepval Wood, the Battalions of the 36[th.] Ulster Division which were on the South side of the River Ancre (a tributary of the River Somme), advanced on 1. 07. 1916. The Connaught Cemetery is seen in the centre distance, with author on the road and Sam McMurray's cycle on the grass.
A poignant place in the hearts of Ulster folk.
Origin: Sam McMurray 1995.

Note: The "Somme" here means the "Somme Sector of Military Operations in France, July 1916." During the "Battle of the Somme," the 36[th.] Ulster Division was actually astride the River Ancre, a tributary of the Somme and some miles from it.

How to get there:

We flew from Belfast International Airport to Charles De Gaulle Airport in Paris. A bicycle travels in a similar manner to the way a suitcase travels. The only request from the powers that be was that we turn the handle bars around so that they were in line with the frame to reduce overall width.

To do so, it was necessary to slacken that long, hexagon headed screw that extends down through the headstock to engage - as in all cycles, with a tapered nut – see later sketch. This allows the handle bars to be turned through 90 degrees in order to present the minimum width of the cycle - as requested. So the handle bars were turned as requested, the cycles moved off onto the conveyor belt to the aircraft hold, and soon we set off for Paris where we arrived in a little over an hour or so.

In view of what was to happen after we landed in Paris, a description of this long hexagon headed screw and its conical nut etc might now be wise, in order to understand how its failure, likely caused by poor thread quality, was to play a central role in causing despair, frustration and uncertainty (to me in particular), until that moment, upon my return, that I reached the sanctuary of my home back in Antrim!

To steer a bicycle:

For steering to function, the headstock - with handle bars attached, and the forks, must move as one - see sketch two pages forward.

The headstock is pushed down into the fork tube – as in sketch, the long hexagon headed screw passes down through the headstock - the lower extremity of which has an internal taper.

This lower end of the headstock is also split vertically over an inch or more of its length at this lower end. This is to allow the headstock end to be expanded inside the fork tube when the conical nut is pulled into the taper in the headstock. Thus, when the long hexagon headed screw is screwed into the conical nut below it, the nut is drawn up into the taper just mentioned, thus expanding the split end of the headstock inside the fork tube.

When sufficiently engaged, the headstock and forks move as one, in order that the handle bars (attached through the clamp in headstock) can be turned through any angle as required. So good, so far.

Albert in 1993: *Basilica of Notre Dame de Brebières restored.*

Albert in 1916: *Basilica of Notre Dame de Brebières.*

Above: Albert, where we parked our cycles on the right – just out of camera sight and purchased some cakes. Note the statue of the Virgin, now restored aloft the rebuilt tower. Compare above with the photo on the right of the "Hanging Virgin" in 1916.

.Sam McMurray took the above photograph of a place which made news in WW1- the tower of the basilica of Notre Dame de Brebières (Mother and Child) shown now above restored. Early in the war and thought to be a look out spot for German snipers, it was shelled by the British. However as seen in the photo on right, the statue hung out for a time thus gaining its title but it was finally demolished by British shelling in 1918 and the statue of Dame de Brebières was lost in the rubble. Orig: Sam McMurray, 1995

Here the "Hanging Virgin" statue is in a precarious state, still attached to the Tower but later lost when British Artillery finally destroyed the remains of the Tower in 1918. Note: This photo is thought to have been taken by an Australian officer – one Captain Frank Hurley. This or similar photos of the Tower also appeared on postcards sent home by troops stationed around there.

Arras

Dismal ditches in Arras where Resistance leaders were executed by the German Gestapo.

So upon arrival at the General de Gaulle airport, with our cycles and kit bags retrieved, the first job was to turn the handle bars of the cycles into the cycling position. I turned the bars around accordingly and started to tighten up the long screw. Alas, trouble was awaiting.
The long screw turned alright, but the handle handle bars remained slack. I quickly realised what was wrong. The threads at the end of the long screw had stripped, and the conical nut had thus failed to engage into the internal taper in the headstock itself!

Below: Headstock Assembly of a bicycle.
Origin: Author 2013

Handle bar clamp

Long threaded screw

New conical recess required- by filing out!

Conical nut

Stripped threads on long screw

Fork tube and forks

Origin: Author 2013

We decided that our immediate task was to get out of the airport, head north, and for me, to try and steer the bicycle as best I could until we found help. But it was a useless exercise with the handle bars swinging helplessly, and after my good self had fallen off a few times, we had to now decide as to how a repair might be affected.

Presently Sam suggested it would involve cutting off the tapered part of the headstock and making a new taper there (by filing) and then cutting off the stripped threads of the long set screw so that the new threads of the long set screw might now engage with threads in the conical nut - and pull the nut into the new taper if reforming the same was a success. It would be a difficult enough little job – if we could get the tools we needed.

This account may appear as containing an extravagance of explanation, technical or otherwise, *but it is the only way to fully explain the nature of the predicament that we were about to find ourselves in. We were about to require either a repair, or, a replacement component for my cycle - indispensible for the furtherance of our journey. Either way, we were far from help - and while Sam had some navigational skills in the use of the French language, alas, I had little.*
Afterwards we were able to reflect on Murphy's Law :
"If it is possible for something to happen – it will happen.
So, bear up!"
After much difficulty in explaining our plight to numerous people and drawing little sketches of a hacksaw and a rat tail in vain, we finally met two ladies who took us to a workshop and tools of ancient lineage, and there set us loose to cut off the stripped threads - thus leaving the screw much shortened. As a consequence of shortening the screw, the internal taper in the headstock had to be shortened and reformed to something normal by filing. Eventually, we reassembled the bits and pieces and gingerly engaged the long headstock screw with the tapered nut and hoped for the best!

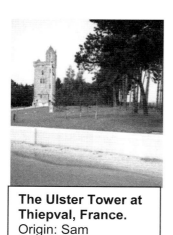

The Ulster Tower at Thiepval, France.
Origin: Sam McMurray 1995

The "Danger Tree" near Thiepval, and recalled as a dangerous spot to be caught out near!
S. McMurray 1995

We thus set off north, stopping over the night at Roye, and by the evening of the next day getting as far as Vimy Ridge. This is where the Canadians defeated the Germans to capture the Ridge and we were able to see the unique Canadian Memorial to the Canadian lost. We stayed that night at Arras and at noon the following we reversed direction and headed south. After staying one evening in Amiens, we headed for Albert the next morning where we passed rather unexpectedly, a building which we knew could only have been Amiens Jail. This was the Amiens Jail which the RAF, using Mosquito aircraft , had bombed in 1944 in an effort to assist condemned resistance prisoners to escape. Unfortunately, we omitted to photograph the prison.

By the evening, we had another overnight stop, and the next day we arrived at Grandcourt near Thiepval, and finding a nice B / B, we stayed there for a couple of days. In Thiepval Wood, we saw the trenches of the 36th. Ulster Division, picking up some souvenir shrapnel while there. Strictly in those days – 1995, the Thiepval Wood was out of bounds on two counts namely it was private property and also there was a possibility of live
 shells and other armaments, unknown in quantity and condition, being not far from where one might tread.

 We saw one huge crater which we could not see the bottom of. Then, among the pieces of metal which one would see, would be some pieces still retaining the unmistakable trace of threads – possibly like where a fuze had been screwed into a shell. Of course we visited the Ulster Memorial Tower and then the Thiepval Memorial where the names of 73,000 plus missing British, Irish and other Commonwealth soldiers are inscribed and remembered.There, with information obtained before he left home, Sam McMurray quickly found his uncle's name and was photographed close to it and the other names beside it - a unique photo indeed. Upon his return, he was then able to present it to his father, then over ninety years age (and the brother of George) - see this photograph on the Fourth Coloured Selection page.

We eventually left Thiepval and visited other sites and cemeteries of World War One – places like Pozières, full of memories of the Australians, and while heading for Paris, cycled over the River Somme, a relatively small river before again stopping overnight at Roye.

 The next day's cycling brought us close to the Eiffel Tower in Paris. There we stopped in a nice accommodation for the night, and the next day made our way to Charles de Gaulle airport - about fifteen miles out of that part of Paris where we had stayed over night.

Then, with the handle bars turned through ninety degrees to lie parallel with the frame, we passed our cycles and kit bags through to the luggage conveyer belt at check out, and after an incident free flight, we arrived back at Belfast International Airport.The cycles were retrieved and the handle bars returned their normal position – mine to their normal still precarious position! Home sweet home and the conclusion to a very interesting, educational and sombre experience.

 No further tightening of the headstock nut had been risked since the temporary repair was affected (which I think was an engineering triumph). Although the headstock (with the handle bars) had worked round inside the fork tube – at thirty degrees to the frame at times, they always allowed themselves to be put back to bed again!

Sufficient grip was always maintained between the headstock and fork tube to enable me to juggle my way on the right hand side of French roads and make an evening landfall at the Eiffel Tower in Paris as recalled ! There we could say that "we had hacked it!"

Sam McMurray at the Thiepval Memorial to
73, 000 Allied soldiers who have no known grave.
His uncle served in the 36th. (Ulster) Division.
This is indeed a special photograph: Sam's uncle
George McMurray's name is on this Memorial - near
the top of the photograph. He was seventeen years
old when he was lost on the First of July, 1016.
Origin: Bobby Cameron

Sam McMurray at the
Newfoundland Memorial,
Beamont Hamil. Of the
Newfoundland Battalion, over
700 became casualties. Note
their trenches. Known also as
the Caribou Memorial.
Origin: Bobby Cameron 1995.

Author at the Carabou Memorial
overlooking the Newfoundland
trenches.   Origin: Sam McMurray

Left: The
Highlander, the
Scottish
Memorial at
Beamont
Hamil, France.
Origin: Sam
McMurray 1995.

Above: The SS "Onward" on which
part of the 36th. Ulster Division,
including the 11th. Battalion (South
Antrim) sailed to France in October
1915.

Some of these photographs are also
in the "Fourth Coloured Selection."

Chapter 20

A visit to "Pegasus Bridge," Normandy, France.

I arrived in Cherbourg, France, in October 2015 after a seventeen hour overnight ferry journey from Rosslare in Eire. The port of Cherbourg had been badly damaged by retreating German forces in 1944 and I later learned that twenty five German heavy Artillery Bunkers were spread across the port area. After spending the night there, I then travelled by rail the next day from Cherbourg to the city of Caen, a place flattened - mostly by the RAF in World War Two, following the invasion of Europe by Allied forces in1944. A local taxi then brought me a few miles to the "Pegasus Bridge" over the Caen Canal.

Leaving the taxi, I had only a few yards to walk until I was on Major John Howard Avenue (- *Avenue du Major Howard*). Here I found a slightly tapered, square base Memorial to him – see photo below left, and compare size with my small yellow and blue rucksack.

Major John Howard Avenue – note the faithful bag!
Origin: Author 2015

Then, only a few yards away, one comes within sight of the bridge itself. This was the bridge over the Caen Canal in the Normandy area of France, that I had come to see. It was late October, 2015

Here, the Canal passes northwards, after flowing through the World War Two front line French city of Caen to enter the sea near Ouistreham on the English Channel coast. This bridge lay about 6 miles north of Caen, and close to the small town of Bènouville, itself about 4 miles inland from the coast. That part of the coast would soon be designated as "Sword Beach,"and soon to be be landed upon by British forces on June 6, 1944, for the purposes of the Allied invasion of France. It then was occupied by German forces since 1940.

As explained later, the bridge is now known as **"Pegasus" Bridge.**

There are actually two bridges of significant interest, being about half a mile apart. As stated, one was over the CAEN CANAL – and soon to be known as the "Pegasus" bridge.

The other bridge was over the RIVER ORNE which lay about half a mile further East (see sketches.) It would also be renamed, and would be known as "Horsa" Bridge, named after the glider of that name, which in turn was named after an Anglo-Saxon warrior in the 5th.century AD.

The waters in both flowed northwards to enter the English channel at Ouistreham and with the latter formed the eastern flank of the overall Allied invasion front of approximately fifty miles, in June 1944.

When I passed the Major John Howard Avenue, the bridge that I had come to see came into view. But as well,uniquely, so did almost everything else that I had ever read or heard about in this whole operational area. To my left, I could see the Caen Canal. I could also see that narrow green strip of sloping ground between the Canal and a pond in swampy ground that was to be the landing ground for a small British glider borne assault force. It was onto that narrow, uneven ground, that each of three gliders had crash landed a few minutes into the morning of the 6th June, 1944. The first to do so, was the one which carried the force commander, Major John Howard, it coming to rest with its nose having broken through the German wire security fence at 00.16 hours on 06. 06. 1944. Here also the force suffered their first casualty when, it was said, a paratrooper was thrown from his crashed glider and drowned *as his glider landed partially in that pond in the swamp. Other sources claim that he was trapped beneath glider wreckage and drowned.

Thus was the start of a serious mission, on which depended what degree of success which might be obtained for the Allied Invasion of France. That mission was the successful capture by these British forces in the gliders, of the bridges over the Caen Canal and the River Orne.

* He was Lance Corporal Fred Greenhalgh in the glider which landed at the pond. Note: Each man carried about 70 pounds of ammunition, personal weapons, hand grenades etc (see "Landing ground sketch," later.)

*   *   *   *   *

The Allied Invasion of France, June 1944.

The Overall Invasion Plan: It was vital that these bridges should be in Allied hands. One reason was so as to prevent German armour stationed nearby, from gaining road access to attack the British bridgehead on "Sword Beach" – six miles away. A second reason was to allow, hopefully, ease of access for a future British armoured and infantry breakout into the French hinterland ie command of suitable roads and bridges etc.leading from the beaches- inland.

Thus on the night of the 5th of June 1944, three **AIRBORNE DIVISIONS** prepared to parachute in to secure both flanks of the entire seaborne attack on the Nazi occupied Atlantic coast in France. The **Eastern** flank was to be secured by the British 6th **AIRBORNE DIVISION**. This was commanded by Major General Richard Gale, and the small glider force commanded by John Howard was part of it.

Therefore, with reference to above, a pre invasion spearhead role of breathtaking daring had been planned to secure two bridges, and was to be entrusted to Major John Howard's force of six gliders – these being part of part of the British 6th **AIRBORNE DIVISION,** and carrying a total force of 180 men. The attack on each bridge was to be carried out with troops carried in Horsa gliders, three to each bridge. The Horsa was constructed by using wood in the main, had a wing span of 88 feet and an overall length of 67 feet. Those contesting the **CAEN CANAL BRIDGE** were mainly of the Oxfordshire and Buckinghamshire Light Infantry, and they would be would be accompanied by Major John Howard of the Oxfordshire and Buckinghamshire Light Infantry.

In civilian life, he had been a policeman, and was to be decorated later with the DSO. As previously noted, a road was named after him and near what was then the **CAEN CANAL BRIDGE**. The latter is now known as the "Pegasus" Bridge – see later photograph. Once secured, they were to defend these positions until relieved, hopefully, by British troops advancing from seaward ie from "Sword Beach" (including Lord Lovat's Scouts), and other units of the 6th **AIRBORNE DIVISION.** Lord Lovat himself would be accompanied by his piper, Bill Millen! See later, the photo of Bill's pipes, which are now in the Pegasus Museum which is close to the Pegasus Bridge.

Like the bridge over the Caen Canal, the bridge over the River Orne doubtless featured heavily in the minds of those tasked with a battle plan for the successful invasion of France by way of the Normandy coast. In particular it hinged on a crucial operation: It depended heavily, as just stated, on a precision spearhead role of breath taking daring, namely the capture of these bridges from the air - and to capture them intact. The operation would be known as **"Operation Deadstick"**and its timing in operation was of crucial importance.

The Bridge name.
How was a name like "Pegasus" chosen ?

Pegasus was one of the best known creatures in Greek mythology and was depicted as a Winged Horse – usually a stallion. He is often shown as being ridden by another who figures in Greek mythology – Bellerophon. Thus Pegasus, the Winged Horse, became the emblem of the Parachute Regiment, and the insignia of a Winged Horse with Bellerophon riding on its back, was worn as a shoulder patch on the sleeves of all the men of the **AIRBORNE DIVISION.** It was in deference to this creature, that it was from the air that the bridge was to be captured. The insignia was, one understands,

General Sir Frederick (Boy) Browning DSO.

chosen by Daphne Du Maurier, the author. She was also the wife of a war time commander of Airborne Forces, General Sir Frederick (Boy) Browning, see below. Browning had fought in the First World War where he acquired the nickname "Boy" and was decorated with the DSO in 1917 at the battle of Cambria where British tanks were used for the first time in significant numbers. He was now commander of the FIRST AIRBORNE DIVISION in the Second World War, and which he also led during "Operation Market Garden," flying into the assault himself in one of the gliders.

Late on the evening of June 5, 1944, six Horsa gliders carrying 180 men – mostly of the Second Battalion, Oxfordshire and Buckinghamshire Light Infantry - plus a detachment in each of Royal Engineers, took off from the airfield at Tarrant Rushton in Dorset.

They were, as mentioned, under the command of Major John Howard of the Ox and Bucks Light Infantry and were towed by Halifax bombers as part of the British 6th. **AIRBORNE DIVISION**. Troops in three gliders were to seize the **CAEN CANAL BRIDGE,** and troops in the other three gliders were to do likewise at the **RIVER ORNE BRIDGE**. This spearhead known as **Operation Deadstick,** was underway.

        *   *   *   *   *

Also about this time, twelve hundred warships and thousands of other merchant ships of all descriptions in support of the sea landings, had assembled off the Southern English coast and other places – including Belfast Lough. In all, over 100,000 troops were about to sail for the Normandy coasts. The three **AIRBORNE DIVISIONS,** part of which of course was Major Howard's glider troops, would soon also be heading for France. In Major Howard's glider, one of those tasked with the capture of the **CAEN CANAL BRIDGE,** most of those with him were about twenty two years old and most had not seen action before.
Some however had – as in North Africa and in Sicily.

The gliders in "Operation Deadstick" leave England:

The tugs - the Halifax towing bombers with engines warmed up, presently took the strain of the tow – and they were off.
The atmosphere has been recalled as at first being nervous, but presently they started to sing while others smoked, and tenseness lessened.

They were soon approaching the coast of France and here Howard called for silence and shortly the pilot shouted that he was casting off. After this the sound of the Halifax's engines began to recede. They were on their own but not for long as they levelled out at one thousand feet. Now the pilot manoeuvred to align with what was a narrow strip of bramble and bushy undergrowth. This covered the ground between the Caen Canal to their left and a swamp or pond to their right, and each of these features is still there. Howard could see the Caen Canal Bridge clearly and they began to open the doors - one at the back and one at the front. All fastened their seat belts, and with their feet off the floor and with arms linked, they prepared themselves for what was literally a crash landing. It was later estimated some time afterwards as being undertaken at over one hundred miles per hour instead of the usual speed of perhaps eighty miles per hour. The precision of landing was however, amazing.

In darkness, and with only a stop watch, a compass and a map to assist in navigation, Howard's glider, piloted by Jim Wallwork – there was also a second pilot, John Ainsworth, had cast off from the towing Halifax bomber about three miles from the bridge. It now appears that this glider passed by to the left of the bridge ie to the East of it, travelled on towards Caen and then after a complete circle of right turns and again in the direction of Caen, landed with the glider's nose punched through the Germans' security wire fence, fifty yards from the bridge! They had arrived!

It seems that virtually everyone was knocked out, temporarily, due to the violent impact of the crash landing, but presently, after a few moments, all in the first glider regained full consciousness.

But their doctor, in another glider however, was out for half an hour!

With the German fence wire flattened, they therefore did not need to use the Bangalore torpedoes which they had brought along for the purpose of destroying this security fence, and their silent approach had achieved complete surprise. A Bangolore torpedo was basically a steel tube filled with explosive – for destroying wire defences.

Howard's Memorial (his bust) and to left, the Memorial to the first glider to land –Howard's.
Origin: Author 2015.

Bust of John Howard on the spot where the first – Howard's glider landed. This is the Memorial to John Howard.   Orig. Author 2015

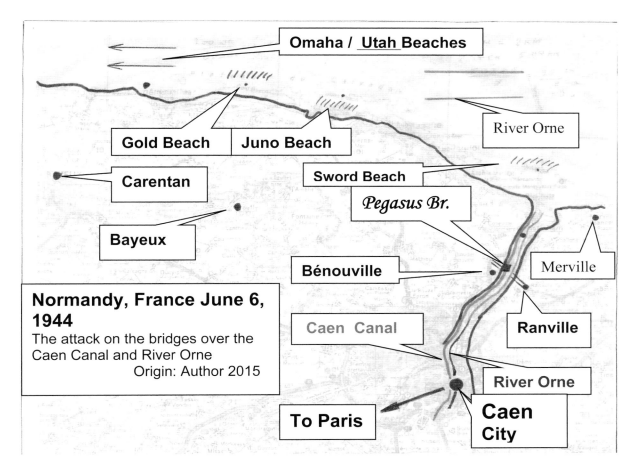

Omaha / Utah Beaches

Gold Beach   Juno Beach

River Orne

Carentan

Sword Beach

Pegasus Br.

Bayeux

Bénouville

Merville

Normandy, France June 6, 1944
The attack on the bridges over the Caen Canal and River Orne
Origin: Author 2015

Caen Canal

Ranville

River Orne

To Paris

Caen City

Lieutenant Den Brotheridge, Howard's leading platoon commander was in Howard's glider. This glider was the first to land, and its platoon was the first to approach the bridge. Actually each of the two other platoons knew exactly the parts they had to play if they were first to reach the bridge: First a German pillbox had to be put out of action and it was just across the road from the anti tank gun referred to as Rommel's anti tank gun. The latter was situated right on the corner to the entrance onto the road leading to the bridge and in front of the large Canal Operatives' Control Tower. See the photograph of the anti tank gun's location in front of the Control Tower, and also later when photographed post landing, with Howard's crashed glider etc. This gun seems to have been photographed many times, sometimes with an overhead protection. In most of the photographs of it which appear here, it is shown as it is seen today, low, with rails around it in an open gun pit. This latter facilitates visitors' viewing of the gun. When thus seen by the author in October 2015, it appeared as a rather small gun of possibly 5cm. calibre,appearing to a layman as a rather small weapon o stop a tank. It was weather beaten and showing its age! Regretfully, through an oversight, no still photograph of it was taken then. Returning now to the attack, it was close to the anti tank gun that the first British glider troops turned left off the path from their glider, and onto the road which passed along the bridge. They really had arrived!

The Bridge Structure: A unique design from 1934.

The structure of the "Pegasus" bridge is of a type known as a single leaf Bascule bridge, and is the choice of many designers. It is a not a hinged, cantilever type of bridge but may be correctly referred to as a moveable or rolling bridge – it lifts and also moves backwards when lifting, thus giving more clearance for the bridge from passing ships, etc. To achieve this combination, the principle of the rack and pinion is incorporated in its working. However, its "gear teeth" could hardly be described as gear sprockets as understood in involute spur gearing! See sketches.

The old girl herself is now at the Pegasus Outside Museum, a short walk from where she toiled as the bridge across the Caen Canal. Just above the name "Pegasus Bridge" can be seen the Quadrant, above which is the massive water counter weight. For those actually visiting the Bridge, half way along on the far side may be seen her battle scars - holes through some side lattice members, brought about by an RAF fighter. Also, a miner deformity happened here when the bridge was struck by a single 1,000 bomb from a German plane after the bridge was captured. The bomb hit the side lattice railing, but did not explode!   Origin: Author: 2015.

Script contd:

In lifting, the bridge lift arms swing upwards with the bridge platform ie the roadway attached, aided by a huge counterweight understood to be a tank filled with water. The effect is partially a see-saw mechanism - possibly from the French word bacuaction.

At the same time, the complete bridge structure rolls backwards on two slowly rotating quadrants (and a quadrant is defined as a sector of a circle enclosed by two of its radii and the arc of 90 degrees cut off by them.) These two quadrants are very large, highly visible and easily seen from afar.

They comprise sectors of two wheels which require limited rotation and represent the pinion referred to above. Their rims have precisely positioned concave indentations around their outer surfaces on which it rolls carrying the complete bridge. These indentations in the surface of the outer rims mesh with corresponding projecting "studs" (representing the equivalent of gear teeth) on two special treaded horizontal runners – (the racks), one laid along each side of bridge structure – see sketches.

Some information about the mechanism of the "Pegasus" Bridge.

To initiate rotation of their machinery, early bascule bridges - around 1850' s, used hydraulic means, typically with steam engines providing pressures to such means of up to 700 lb/sq. inch. As suggested, the name Bascule probably comes from the French word bacule, meaning see saw. Today, probably only electric power is used.

On this visit, from what one could see of the working of the "Pegasus Bridge," use is also made of a simple gear arrangement which has some claim of relationship to epicyclic gearing. *

The rotation of the Quadrants

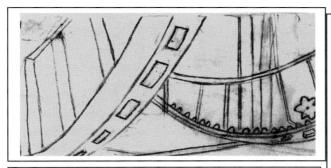

Above: The L.H. side of sketch shows how the Bridge moves backwards ie as the Quadrant to the left meshes with the track (or rack) as shown. The R.H. side of sketch shows how the Quadrant is turned (here represented by a small gear (or pinion) and shown turning clockwise as does the Quadrant. Note that the gear teeth are cut on the inside of the rims on both Quadrants, with corresponding small driving pinions in mesh with them. For simplicity and clarity, this arrangement is only shown on one side, ie on only the right hand quadrant. The input drive to give movement to the Quadrants therefore is by way of these small pinions – which today are likely driven by electric motors . Thus, the small input pinions (or small gear wheels) drive the larger gear which here is represented by the teeth cut on the inside of the Quadrant rims. Shown therefore is a driving pinion with a small number of teeth meshing internally with the larger number of teeth cut on the inside of the driven one ie the Quadrant. The Bridge roadway (attached to the Quadrant) lifts as the Quadrants turn, and the Bridge body moves horizontally backwards as the indents on Quadrants engage with "teeth" on horizontal racks. The Bridge was built in 1934.

Above: Sketch showing the uniquely strong "teeth"of the horizontal "rack," in mesh with the sockets in quadrant (the pinion). There is a very heavy load on these "teeth"- thus their robust appearance.

Sketches are based on photographs, visual and on site video recording.
Origin: Author 2015

Author, with Bridge mechanism to the left (note the steps), the road approaching the bridge centre, and the waters of the Caen Canal in distance. Rommel's anti tank gun is just off camera, left.
Origin:2015.

Script contd.
This is where a small gear wheel (a pinion) imparts motion to a large gear wheel through gear teeth cut on the **inside** of the circumference rim or part of such. This is so, as, in the case of the Pegasus machinery, where a sector of the rim - actually of 90 ° enclosure, is sufficient and is referred to as a quadrant as seen in sketches on previous pages. Considering the large difference in the respective number of gear teeth on the pinion compared to that on the inside of the quadrant rim, it is in this case therefore, a speed reduction device as well - again see sketch, showing a very simplified principle of operation. In the case of the quadrants of the bridge, a very low pinion speed is required, the pinion itself being supplied with power at low R.P.M. and already probably reduced through a reduction gearbox. The small pinion itself is likely rotated through electric or hydraulic means. See previous page.

Technically, simple epicyclic gearing may be defined as two gears where the centre of one revolves around the centre of the other and in most cases is used to increase the speed of output. "Pegasus" has some relationship! As in the earlier sketch , speed of output rotation ie that of the Quadrants, is therefore reduced.

The Caen Canal

Rommel's anti tank gun.

The Caen Canal Bridge in "lift" operation: The Café Gondrée is on extreme left, the surround of Rommel's anti tank gun is in position as arrowed, and this important photo taken between Rommel's inspection and D- Day. A German photo? Origin unknown but probably German.

The German defence Measures:

The Germans knew that sooner or later the Allies would invade Occupied Europe, somewhere. But where? Hitler was obsessed that it might be in Norway. A successful Allied landing there would threaten his ore trade with Sweden so he stationed a number of divisions there. Most Nazi leaders, however, favoured France, with Calais as the most likely place since it was the shortest distance to travel to - for the Allies. So General Rommel was appointed to build an Atlantic wall along a significant length of coastline, a wall of metal, concrete obstacles and mines. Now on one of his frequent inspections of these defences he looked in on the bridges over the Caen Canal and over the River Orne. There he found no anti tank provisions at either, but he saw that a road of extreme importance passed over both. He gave urgent instructions that an anti tank gun was to be installed beside the bridge over the Caen Canal, the work to start immediately. **See photograph above.** The latter always seems to have been an open pit type – as it may be seen today. It was built right beside the bridge where the control tower was situated to permit the operation to lift or lower the Caen Canal Bridge.

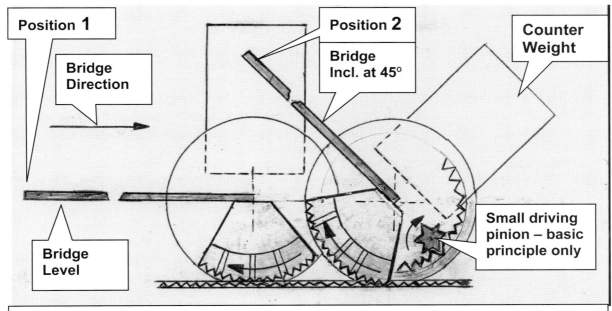

Position **1**

Bridge Direction

Position **2**

Bridge Incl. at 45°

Counter Weight

Bridge Level

Small driving pinion – basic principle only

A sketch impression of a very simplified version of the bridge mechanism, showing the principle of a bascule bridge in the (1) horizontal position, and (2) when elevated to 45°. The backward movement to right, gives additional clearance for shipping ie between the elevated bridge platform and, for example, a passing ship.

Sketch origin: Author 2015

The Germans were, happily, never permitted to ever use that anti tank gun in anger.

The Café Gondrée was run by Georges and Thérèse Gondrée. Both were passionately pro British. Thérèse spoke German (something she did not disclose to many) and was thus able to eves drop on German conversations. Géorges was fluent in English having worked in an English bank in Paris for years previously. Since the Café Gondrée was but the length of the bridge away from the anti tank gun mentioned, it was therefore not long before London knew how work was progressing on the pill box which was meant to defend the anti tank gun .

As related presently, one highlight of my time at "Pegasus" Bridge, was in spending some time over coffee in the Café Gondrée which is currently run by Arlett Gondrée, one of the three daughters of Georges and Thérèse Gondrée. As a child she grew up and indeed lived in the prevailing, historic atmosphere of the Café Gondrée then. Arlett has many memories of that atmosphere. It was where one could be picked up at any hour for questioning by the German authorities. As recalled later, she was not, unfortunately, present on the morning that I called! However, her staff were most helpful to me.

Now, relating to the gun itself , if the one saw by author was the original weapon as installed by Rommel, it looked very small indeed to be taking on a tank, and unlike some other close up photographs taken of "Rommel's anti tank gun" after its installation there. Sitting in that cafe, I tried to think of what it must have been like in this house when, on that historic early morning of June 6th. 1944, Georges and Thérèse Gondrée answered a knock on their door.

Two heavily armed men stood outside, who, speaking in a language they were not used hearing, demanded to know if any Germans were in the house. However, they soon realised that these were two Allied soldiers and welcomed these liberators, who had arrived from the air. In the years after the war, no former member of the platoons in the gliders that landed that night, were ever asked to pay for a drink in the Café Gondrée.

See "More on the Café Gondrée," later on.

The attack goes in: recollections by John Howard.

Returning now to the attack by John Howards's men, Howard recalled afterwards, that initially a smoke bomb was thrown first, and through the smoke, grenades were then thrown through the gun slits of the pillbox by Corporal Bailey with Private Wally Parr being active in achieving this end, plus a couple of dugouts cleared in due course.

While this was taking place, others rushed to capture the other end of the bridge – which was about fifty yards in length. Included in this group was William Gray, a Bren gunner, who was, with Den Brotheridge, notably active in overcoming German resistance along the bridge. Sadly, about three quarters of the way across the bridge, Den Brotheridge took a bullet in the neck and died a short time later. Reports say that he was throwing a hand grenade when shot.

The Café Gondrée   Origin: Author 2015

Two others of the rushing troops had by now reached the door of the Café Gondrée at the East end of the bridge. These were the two heavily armed men who, as described earlier, had knocked on that door in order to ascertain whether there were any Germans hiding there. By now the bridge was in British hands, and Georges proceeded into his garden to dig up the 100 bottles of champagne which he had hidden there against such a day of freedom!

Howard's men had captured the bridge over the Caen Canal in less than fifteen minutes, and shortly news came to him that the bridge over the River Orne had been captured as well – and intact.

Thus ninety minutes after leaving Tarrant Rushton in Dorset, Howard's signaller, Corporal Edward Tappenden sent out the famous signal, **"Ham and Jam, Ham and Jam, Ham and Jam,"** indicating that both bridges were in Allied hands. As above, the actual capture of the "Pegasus" Bridge, took less than fifteen minutes!

On June 26th. 1944, the **CAEN CANAL BRIDGE** was renamed as the "Pegasus Bridge," and Major John Howard was later decorated with the DSO. The **RIVER ORNE BRIDGE** was renamed "Horsa Bridge."

Den Brotheridge is buried in the graveyard of Ranville Church nearby and a memorial was placed at his grave by the Gondrée family after the war.

The daring role of **Operation Deadstick** had been entrusted to just a force of six gliders and 180 men!

This small but important photograph, shows clearly the landing spots of Howard's three gliders at the Caen Canal bridge, the centre one being close to the swamp – which seems to have less water in it, now.   Origin: An internet source.

The Landing Strip.

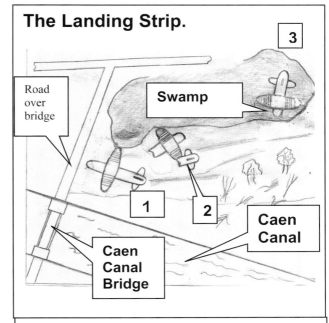

The Landing Strip.

Road over bridge

Swamp

3

1

2

Caen Canal

Caen Canal Bridge

Above: Sketch plan view of where the three gliders came to rest.Orig: Author 2015

"More on the Café Gondrée,"contd.

Georges Gondrée died in 1969, but Thérèse, supported by Major John Howard on one side and her cane on the other, attended the proceedings held at Ranville Church Cemetery in 1984 on the 40th. Anniversary of D-Day (which of course included Operation Deadstick). Later that day, she was confined to her bed and died six weeks after the 40th. Anniversary of Operation Deadstick. One of their daughters now runs the Café Gondrée.

"Sword Beach" was the most easterly of the Normandy beaches to be invaded, and would be attacked by British forces on D-Day.

In 1984, on the 40th. Anniversary of D-day 1944, many of those who had participated in the Bridge's capture were once again present on "Pegasus" Bridge, and a BBC television documentary had interviews etc in situ with several of them.

Now a friend of mine, by an amazing stroke "of inward guidance," had recently given me a copy of Roderick Bailey's excellent book, "Forgotten Voices of D-Day – a new history of the Normandy Landings,"   where many such recordings of what the veterans said have been set down in print for posterity.

Typical of such recordings is the account of Private Wally Parr which I once had seen on my video tape!

Wally Parr: (slightly abridged) *" I dashed to the first dugout, whipped out a 36 grenade.* * *Charlie was there with a Bren gun. I opened the door, pulled out the pin, slung it in, shut the door and waited. Terrific explosion. I shouted to Charlie, 'Get in.' He went to the doorway with his machine gun and sprayed it."*

Wally went on to say that a second dugout was given the same treatment, and recalled that he also had used a 77 phosphorus grenade. As he moved across the bridge in the direction of the Café Gondrée at the other end, he came across Den Brotheridge lying on the bridge about three quarter way across - he had been struck on the neck. My video, I remembered, had recorded Wally drawing heavily on a cigarette. He then recalled Den's final moments:

"He lasted about four minutes. What a waste."

* Standard hand grenade and also known as a Mill's bomb.

The capture of the bridges was at a cost of two lives. As recorded one was Den Brotheridge, and the other was Lance Corporal Fred Greenhalgh, who was drowned after his glider, the third leave to Tarrant Rushton and piloted by Staff Sergt. Barkway, crash landed on the edge of the pond (see the recent photograph and sketch three pages back.). Note: All these landings were "crash landings."

*   *   *   *   *   *

It is interesting to learn of some others, distinguished in their own ways, who were shortly to be not far away from these bridges at this time. One such was Lieutenant Richard Todd, 7th. Battalion, Parachute Regiment , later to become well known as an actor. His Battalion was there initially to reinforce Howard's Ox and Bucks people. Part of his early upbringing took place on the River Lower Bann about ten miles from the town of Antrim, Co. Antrim in Northern Ireland. Twenty years later he would act the part of Major John Howard in the film, "The Longest Day."
Another nearby was Alastair Pearson, commanding officer of the 8th. Battalion, Parachute Regiment . He was destined to become, with Blair Mayne of the SAS, (who was from Newtownards, Co. Down, in Northern Ireland), one of the two most highly decorated members of the Armed Forces in World War Two. Both men received four DSO's, Blair Mayne being recommended for the VC. A campaign is still fighting to have this recommendation implemented. (Captain John F. Walker RN, the U-Boat killer, was also decorated with four DSO's.)

The 40th. Anniversary of D-Day

On the video of the 40th. Anniversary of D-Day, the documentary had also recorded veterans gathering at midnight on the spot where the first glider (Howard's) had landed, and where John Howard proposed the toast to missing comrades. The champagne was poured out by two of the daughters of the late Georgés Gondrée. Thérèse, his wife, while having been able to attend a ceremony earlier in the day, had taken ill and was unable to attend this nocturnal ceremony.
It was then the veterans had that walk over the "Pegasus" Bridge with John Howard, by now using a walking stick – as just recorded. What memories must have been recalled by those who had crossed it there, forty years before. Now they made their way to a get together in the Café Gondrée, which is still, as earlier described, situated at the Eastern end of the "Pegasus" Bridge over the Caen Canal. The Café Gondrée is still in the ownership of the Gondrée family and on this occasion John Howard, in the midst of all that was going on, requested Edward Tappenden, his former signaller, to announce to all once again, his famous signal.
This Edward was pleased to comply with thus: "Ham and Jam, Ham and Jam, Ham and (Bleep) Jam." And so the signal which confirmed that the **CAEN CANAL BRIDGE** and the **RIVER ORNE BRIDGE** ie ("Ham") and ("Jam,") were in British hands rang out again! John also had a say here as when Tappenden finished the signal (with a certain adjective before the final jam) John was heard to call out, "Good old Tappers!" John died in 1999.
The Café Gondrée has a claim therefore, to have been the first house in France to have been liberated on D-Day, but this has been challenged by the claim that the nearby home of a French man by the name of Picot, had been liberated an hour or so before the Gondrée family were. But who were his liberators ?

237

Below: Icons of a past age in Cherbourg, France.

Above: The old Atlantic Terminal Building of the White Star Line at Cherbourg. This photo shows less than half of the actual size of the building, now a Maritime Museum of huge proportions –it has several full size replicas of certain areas of the "Titanic," including the Wireless Room(s) or Shack (with period communication equipment on display.) The building is still known as the "Titanic"Building.   Origin: Author 2015.

Above: A German Heavy Artillery Bunker at Cherbourg, one of nineteen sited around the city by 1944.This one is close to the old Atlantic Terminal of the White Star Line – see left.
Note the author's yellow and blue bag in the middle of the " lawn."
                    Origin: Author 2015.

So on 6th. June 1944, Jim Wallwork, the pilot, had fulfilled Howard's request of the previous day to **" land preferably through the German wire. "** He fulfilled it (with his co pilot Ainsworth) - to the letter!

It is where today indeed, that memorials to each of the gliders and their paratroopers now stand - on those very same three landing spots, Wallwork's landing being about fifty yards of track from the bridge.

Today, those fifty yards of track have been extended down to the site of the crash landing of the **Number 3** glider. This is a somewhat poignant place among the tall reed beds, and furthest away from the Pegasus Bridge. The tall reeds that now grow around the pond, provide a background of almost sacred seclusion. For here, the pond claimed the life of Corporal Fred Greenhalgh, drowned, as recalled, when, weighed down with 70 pounds of equipment, he was trapped in the water following the crash landing of his glider, the third to land.

A conclusion on my visit to the "Pegasus Bridge."

As already mentioned, the success or otherwise in the invasion of Europe by the Allies depended to a large degree on the capture by British forces of the bridges over the Caen Canal and the River Orne – certainly in the short run. On the morning that I had arrived, my taxi had set me down outside the Pegasus Museum and I soon had the bridge that I had come to see right in front of me, as well as the landing strip and the Café Gondrée.

Further progress took me up the road past the Canal's Control Tower, and then, onto the tread plate of the bridge itself.

Close by on the left side, and on the west front of the Control Tower, was a sunken gun pit, complete with what looked like a large version of a Bren gun (it looked small for an anti tank gun.) Could the gun which I saw be the one which Wally Parr and others took over for the day, and actually fired at suspect German snipers thought to be operating from a nearby water tower. I believe it was not.

My time at "Pegasus" Bridge, so filled with the experience of walking with history, seeing interesting physical features and talking to the interesting people whom I met by the way, was time spent in an experience, unique out of all proportion to its duration.

The road over the bridge and past the Café Gondrée leads to the **RIVER ORNE BRIDGE** (now known as the "Horsa" Bridge), about half a mile away. This bridge, close to the small town of Ranville, also had to be captured on 6th. June 1944 to help forestall any German opposition to the beach landings. Three gliders were assigned to this task, one unfortunately landing eight miles away. The troops in the other two gliders however, landed close to the bridge and overcome the German opposition to capture the **RIVER ORNE BRIDGE -** intact for Allied usage.

*　　　　　*　　　　　*　　　　　*　　　　　*

The Café Gondrée: Returning just once again to experience sitting in the Café Gondrée, I had a strange yet relaxed feeling as I sat surrounded with memorabilia relating to the events that had taken place here in this very abode. Indeed, stirring events took place out on the old bridge - not much more than fifty yards from where I was sitting. Had not Den Brotheridge received his fatal wounds there? This was also where, in the early minutes of D-day, the Gondrée family had answered the knock on the door and were confronted by the two heavily armed men who inquired if they had any Germans in the house. Their liberaters from the air had arrived !

As I continued to savour the atmosphere there, I had the experience of feeling that I had been there before. Of course I had not been there before, yet my prior knowledge of the events that had taken place there on 6th. June 1944 did indeed give me a glowing feeling of considerable familiarity with those events.

Unfortunately, lack of time and space does not allow for further description to be included here, of all that one may see in this historic cafe – or in the magnificent "Pegasus" Museum to which I would soon make a fleeting visit.

*　　　　　*　　　　　*　　　　　*　　　　　*

Leaving the Café Gondrée I stood again at the entrance to the Pegasus Bridge, East side, over which I would now return. This of course was exactly the place where the structure of the old Bridge had stood on June 6th. 1944. Looking along the Bridge now, I could see, just a few yards along from this end, the location where Den Brotheridge was fatally wounded on the Old Bridge which stood right here. It was an icon which I would shortly see.

As recalled, two of the daughters of Georges and Thérèse Gondrée were there at the spot where Howard's glider had crash landed minutes into D-day. They were there to pour the champagne, as, in darkness at around midnight on the Anniversaryn of 1984 of Operation Deadstick, they joined John as he proposed the toast to "Absent friends."

There are two Memorials at this spot: One, to the men of the first glider to land, and another, topped by a bust of John, to John Howard himself. There is also additionally, a Memorial at each of the other two landing sites. Then, as earlier referred to,the documentary moved to the bridge where John Howard, aided by a walking stick, was seen leading the veterans across the bridge from the west to the get together in the Café Gondrée.

Here as the veterans entered into the spirit of the occasion (or should one perhaps say that the spirit(s) entered into the veterans ?), the party appeared in the documentary to be going well. What reminisce would have taken place. Perhaps Oliver Goldsmith in his **"Deserted Village,"** had suggested some of the ways in which conversations might have gone – like the **typical welcome for all** to the Headmaster's house with the following verse:

The broken soldier, kindly bade to stay,

Sate by his fire, and talked the night away;

Wept o'er his wounds, or, tales of sorrow done,

Shouldered his crutch, and shewed how fields were won.

From "The Deserted Village," by Oliver Goldsmith 1728 – 1774

(Spelling as in original script)

A most interesting photograph taken sometime after the Bridge was captured. It was taken close to the Bridge as Howard's glider – the first to land, is clearly seen to the right and the distance those glider borne troops were from the Bridge is normally quoted as being fifty yards. Rommel's anti tank gun is shown on extreme left - note barrel. It appears to have an outside diameter similar to the average trees, uprights around there - say about three inches(75 mm). A very interesting photograph but the gun is much larger than the one in the pit as seen by author in 2015. Is there a dusting of snow on the ground?

Bill Millin's pipes .Origin: Author 2015

Some years after the war, the original "Pegasus Bridge" was lengthened when the Caen Canal was widened, and in 1994 it was completely replaced by a new bridge. The new bridge was, as will be seen shortly, identical in appearance and mechanism of operation with the original "Pegasus," but, with a small increase in mechanical strength.

* Hand held anti tank weapon

The Museum

I had spent more time around the Bridge than I had intended. I had earlier hoped to have done this visit to Normandy by cycle. It would have been but a short distance from Pegasus Bridge to the Horsa Bridge over the **RIVER ORNE** near Ranville – about half a mile. Indeed it would have been but another six miles to the Merville Battery near the Normandy coast and less than that to Ouistreham - virtually on Sword Beach. Perhaps that will keep for another day. Just now, however, I had to visit the **Pegasus Museum.**

Thus I presently made my way back, westwards over the bridge, where I paid another visit to that narrow sloping ground where the landings took place. Here I stood once more beside each of the sites marking the places where these remarkable gliders came to rest. I tried to picture their wrecked remains (see recent photograph), tumbled up as they appear in photographs of the time. Once again, in many ways through seeing what was asked of those pilots, one's feelings was for regarding them as the real heroes in the Bridge's capture. Without their skills, competence and courage, Operation Deadstick could not have taken place.

Now I headed for the Museum where my path back to the Pegasus Bridge was along that same one, taken by the men that stormed the bridge early on D-Day. It led past the 5 cm German anti tank gun which I have earlier described as "appearing the worse for wear." But was this the original calibre of anti tank gun that Rommel had installed. It looked an insignificant weapon to take out a tank with.

This was the gun which Gen. Rommel had ordered to be set up as he inspected the defences in the area. As also recalled, Wally Parr had enjoyed firing it until,
 according to the 40th. Anniversary Documentary, John Howard ordered him to stop as he, Howard, "couldn't hear his ears."

And do you know what? I forgot to photo Rommel's anti tank gun - if that is the one in the pit today!

*   *   *   *

The Museum – Outside: This is a magnificent purpose built creation, both inside the building and the outside presentation – possibly the latter more so, because out there lives

the original Bridge over the Caen Canal, the real "Pegasus Bridge," verily the jewel in the crown! It is looking well, and it wears its Purple Heart, its wounds being the result of an attack by a single German bomber on the day after its capture by British forces. A 1,000 lb bomb, which did not explode, struck one side lattice member, causing a small distortion which is clearly visible.

However, there are also holes punched through the steel side lattice work in the same area, this steel being about half an inch thick. This is said to have been the work of a Spitfire on a strafing run, some days previous to D-Day. If so, it shows the potential of an armour piercing bullet - even of Second World War vintage.

To walk across this historic structure is quite a sobering experience. One can stand on the East end of the original bridge, and with a little imagination, point out the approximate spot where Den Brotheridge, the man who led the assault on this bridge, was mortally wounded and now lies but a short distance away in a local churchyard at Ranville.

One can view a number of heavy anti tank guns, both 17 pound and 25 pound calibres. Towards the end of the war German armour was almost impervious to a standard 75 mm tank gun as fitted to an American Sherman tank.

The Shermans were then refitted with 17 pound and possibly 25 pound guns and renamed "Fireflies." A "Firefly" is on display here, and
these heavy weapons penetrated German armour eg the German Tiger tanks to a much greater extent than the previous 75 mm guns as fitted on the Shermans did.

Inside the Pegasus Museum:
Inside the Pegasus Museum is an Aladdin's Cave of very interesting exhibits. The pipes of Bill Millin, Lord Lovat's piper are on display – the very ones that Bill played along the Caen Canal banks as Lovat's troops arrived to relieve John Howard and his weary Ox and Bucks troops- see previous page.

Previous page; "If those pipes could only talk." These pipes, now in the Pegasus Museum, were played by Bill Millin (Lord Lovat's piper) as Lord Lovat's troops marched from "Sword" beach to reinforce the Ox and Buck's on D-Day at the Caen Canal – later, Pegasus Bridge. One of Lord Lovat's favourite tunes was the 6/8 march, "Blue bonnets over the Border." Note: Above the pipes is Bill's bonnet. It looks like a "Balmoral," with a "Toorie" on the top.

241

.Apart from a huge variety of small arms (but including a Bren gun or two) that were on display, there were some exhibits of novel interest. One was a machine which, when a Euro coin of small value was placed into it, produced a small medallion, elongated to twice the diameter of the original coin and on which was inscribed a precise outline of the "Pegasus Bridge," complete with the name – a quite unique souvenir. There was also a working model of the "Pegasus Bridge," but of how much was based on the original technology one was uncertain. There were many rare photos and donated medals in the "Pegasus" Museum, and also a selection of weapons – to numerous to mention here except to record a Bren gun, which apparently was in the action to secure the capture of the original bridge over the Caen Canal,

I then had a last look around this old bridge, the original "Pegasus" Bridge, now at rest in the outside Museum. This old lady puts on a brave face, and I may even see her again one day. I stood once again, looking at the holes in her fabric (caused by a Spitfire with armour pierceing bullets, I belive, and the approximate place where Den Brotheridge received the wound that led to his death. Just like Nelson, he died at the moment when the victory, to which he had contributed so mightily, was in sight.

It was now time for me to depart for Cherbourg.

*   *   *   *   *   *

Above: The old war time " Pegasus Bridge" during her "working days" in situation over the Caen Canal. This photograph must have been taken pre 1994 – when it was replaced, and judging from the car, it has probably been taken in the 1980's. The Café Gondrée is to the right just behind the car and just out of camera. Origin: Thanks to Wikipedia, the Free Encylopedia.

But now, I was about to get a taxi to Caen Railway Station - and there board a train to Cherbourg. Hopefully a day later, a ferry run of seventeen hours would take me to Roslare in Eire. Train journeys to Belfast and then to Antrim, would complete my journey. I had travelled from my home town of Antrim in Northern Ireland to see a special Bridge. But one incident, recalled there, exercised my mind:

" But what if ------------"

On D-Day,1944, Major John Howard's Ox and Bucks Light Infantry were fully stretched in holding the captured Caen Canal Bridge as German light armour approached. One of his men – Sergeant Thornton, confronted the leading German tank, and armed with their only available PIAT anti tank weapon, succeeded in destroying it, causing it to block the road. This enabled Howard's men to hold on until they heard Bill Millin's pipes coming along the Canal with Lord Lovat's Special Service Brigade on foot - straight from the Sword beachhead, about six miles away.

And now this thing that exercised my mind:
"But what, if that PIAT had missed - with the road across the bridge now open to German
armour?"   **Note:** PIAT stands for Projector, Infantry, Anti-Tank.
                              *   *   *   *   *

I had also visited a Museum – where there I saw Bill Millin's pipes. It was a Museum
dedicated to the battles that had evolved around the Bridge. With the clock ticking, it
was time to say farewell.

And so, my almost complete recollection of my wanderings across part of the surface of the
earth is at an end - I'm sure. These wanderings began with an incursion into a country new
to me, but one which hardly could be called "foreign." In 1922 indeed, had not my Uncle
John left Kellswater near Ballymena in Co. Antrim, to cross Canada - sometimes I am told
travelling on the buffers of trains etc. when funds were low?

As will be seen in the photographs in Ch 2, this was Canada. It was there that I took my first
two photographs abroad, which happened as recalled, when sailing as a crew member on a
Belfast registered steamer, the ss **"Rathlin Head,"** nine days out of Belfast, and sailing to
the Canadian city of Montreal. I had arranged for another engineer to take over my watch
in the engine room for a short time, as we sailed up the mighty St. Lawrence River when
approaching the "Heights of Abraham" (where surely history was made - see Ch. Two),
and the Château Frontenac - now a hotel complex.

 Being now acquainted with the history of the old Caen Canal Bridge – the "Old
Lady," I was reminded of a well known piece of choral music and verse, often
performed by the late and lamented Glasgow Orpheus Choir under the baton of Sir
Hugh Roberton. It was called "The Old Woman," origin at present uncertain.

Let a verse of it become our **Epiloque :**

As a white candle in a holy place,
So is the beauty of an aged face.
Her brood gone from her and her thoughts are still,
A-as the waters - under a ruined mill.

Bibleography

Blue Nile	Alan Moorhead
Business in Great waters	John Terraine
Canadian Naval Chronicle	Frazer McKee, and Robert Darlington
Chile and Easter Island	Carl Hubbard
	Brigette Barla and
	Jeff Davis
Chile and Easter Island	Wayne Bernhardson
Captain James Cook	Bill Finnis
Daughter of the Desert - Gertrude Bell	Georgina Howell
Queen of the Desert - Gertrude Bell	Georgina Howell
Disaster at Scapa Flow	H.G. Weaver
Easter Island	Anne Van Tilborg
Florence Nightingale	W. J.Winton and F. Witts
Forgotten Voices of D-Day.	Roderick Bailey
(In association with Imperial War Museum.)	
Head Line (Ulster Steamship Co.)	W.J. Harvey
I Remember, I Remember	Martin Armour MBE BSc FIET
Island at the end of the world	Stephen R. Fischer
Journey to Pitcairn	Frank Clune
Mini Guides to Djiboutie, Oman	
and the Emirates	Courtesy of "Voyages of Discovery"
Khartoum	Michael Asher
Orkney's Italian Chapel	Chapel Preservation Committee
Pegasus Bridge	Stephen E. Ambrose
Ramesses II	Joyce Tyldesley
The Seven Pillars of Wisdom	T. E. Lawrence
Tahiti – A paradise lost	David Howarth
Submarine	Capt. John Coote
Scapa Flow - This Great Harbour	W.S. Hewison
The 11th. Battalion, Royal Irish Rifles, the	Capt. A.P.Samuels
36th. Ulster Division, 1915 – 1916	
(A Brief History)	
The Tea Time Islands	Ben Fogle
The Path Between the Seas	David McCullough
(The Building of the Panama Canal)	
The Sinking of the ss "Kenbane Head"	Sam McAughtry
The Wonder Encyclopedia for Children.	J. Crossland /J.Parrish
St. Lawrence Seaway.	Clara Ingram Judson

Old Testament References. (mostly Relating to the Journeys of the Children of Israel following their Exodus from Egypt).

New Testament References (mostly matters relating to the Apostle Paul).

"Antrim and Beyond" Part Three
(Tales From Distant Lands)
By Bobby Cameron

The author grew up in the district of Crosskennon, a quiet rural and pastoral setting three miles north of the town of Antrim in Northern Ireland.

In such a setting as a child, early memories might have been the sounds of curlews calling during long summer evenings, or the sound of the snipe, whose call sometimes sounded like the bleating of a goat; or that of the corncrake whose wakeup call often started at three

o'clock in the morning – and onwards. Or one might occasionally hear the bark of a fox.

There, farming operations generally moved at the speed of a horse, and few indeed would ever have failed to hear the sound of a distant horse drawn reaper, although gradually, here and there, tractors were making an appearance.

And frequently one would encounter a flock of sheep along the road – a pastoral scene indeed.

But unexpectedly, things were about to change.

With schooldays over, it was from this quiet rural setting that the author would travel each day to Belfast while serving a mechanical engineering apprenticeship in the aircraft and missile firm of Messrs Short Bros. and Harland Ltd., in centres at Queens Island, Aldergrove and Castlereagh, Belfast.

After some time there, he had periods of employment in the armament industry, at sea as an engineer, and the Northern Ireland Civil Service before becoming a Lecturer in Mechanical Engineering in Lisburn Technical College in Co. Antrim.

But in the earlier part of his life mentioned, change indeed was under way. One was soon to be at full stretch in the exigencies of the Second World war and memories there would soon include those of our troops – perhaps of them sleeping in local barn buildings or in hay sheds at night. Presently the Americans arrived, soon to be followed by the Belguims. Strangers indeed had arrived on the very doorsteps of Crosskennon. Then a reminder that the war was closer than anyone thought: A twin engined Hudson bomber of 202 Squadron, Aldergrove, Co. Antrim, setting out on anti U-boat duties over the Atlantic, crashed into the forest on nearby Carnearney hill. The resulting visible carnage and deaths brought the consequences of war into every local home. For the author as a child, the imminent arrival of hundreds – indeed thousands of men, was an advent indeed.

Some were from England, Scotland, Wales and Eire, all speaking English with mildly different accents, but later the Americans arrived - with an even more distinctive accent to master. Finally the Belguims arrived. Thus, they all arrived for training from fields afar.

Undoubtedly, such sights planted the seeds of curiosity in many local minds about them and the places they had come from - and not least among the local children. This included the author who witnessed the first arrivals of the American Army in all its mechanised array. What a scene changer for children to witness – seeing for the first time tracked vehicles, jeeps and large covered lorries etc. These men were to become part of the local scene over a period of up to two years or more, during the author's childhood. They would be seen daily on their manoeuvres on local roads and fields.

That early image of those "faraway places with their strange sounding names" was undoubtedly a latent incentive in the author to see some of these places.

This book sets out something of what was seen during some of the author's travels in some distant places and also of places not too distant. But without a doubt, the recurring predominant feature is the meeting with so many interesting men and women – some eccentric, some regal, some destitute of this world's goods, some very ordinary yet whose bravery had helped on land, at sea and in the air to save us from the tyranny of evil men.